Applied Population Health

Delivering Value-Based Care
with Actionable Registries

Applied Population Health

Delivering Value-Based Care with Actionable Registries

Barbara Berkovich, PhD, MA • Amy M. Sitapati, MD

CRC Press
Taylor & Francis Group
Boca Raton   London   New York

CRC Press is an imprint of the
Taylor & Francis Group, an **informa** business

A PRODUCTIVITY PRESS BOOK

First edition published in 2020
by Routledge/Productivity Press
52 Vanderbilt Avenue, 11th Floor New York, NY 10017
2 Park Square, Milton Park, Abingdon, Oxon OX14 4RN, UK

Library of Congress Cataloging-in-Publication Data

Names: Berkovich, Barbara, author. | Sitapati, Amy, author.
Title: Applied population health : delivering value-based care with actionable
registries / Barbara Berkovich, Amy Sitapati.
Description: Boca Raton : CRC Press, [2020] | Series: HIMSS book series |
Includes bibliographical references and index.
Identifiers: LCCN 2019037299 (print) | LCCN 2019037300 (ebook) |
ISBN 9780367196677 (paperback) | ISBN 9780367404567 (hardback) |
ISBN 9780367196714 (ebook)
Subjects: MESH: Population Health | Electronic Health Records | Registries |
Epidemiologic Methods
Classification: LCC RA418 (print) | LCC RA418 (ebook) | NLM WA 300.1 |
DDC 362.10285—dc23
LC record available at https://lccn.loc.gov/2019037299
LC ebook record available at https://lccn.loc.gov/2019037300

Visit the Taylor & Francis Web site at www.taylorandfrancis.com

Disclaimer

Every effort has been made to make this book as accurate as possible, but no warranty is implied. The information provided is on an "as is" basis. The authors and the publishers shall have neither liability nor responsibility to any person or entity with respect to any loss or damages arising from the information contained in this book. The views expressed in this book are those of the authors and do not necessarily reflect the official policy or position of the publisher.

Additional Resources

Visit the textbook companion website at www.appliedpopulationhealth.com

Contents

Tables

Figures

Acknowledgements

With deepest gratitude for the unfailing support of our families, without which this book would not have been possible.

Reviewers

The authors would like to extend a sincere thanks to our reviewers who offered significant time and thoughtful insights that further refined our book. We are forever grateful for their contributions.

Jennifer Holland
Adam Royce
Angela Scioscia, MD, MBA

Contributors

Erik Geissal, MD, FACP
Chief Medical Information Officer,
OCHIN (Oregon Community Health Information Network), Inc.
Portland, Oregon

Ryan Peck, MHA, CPHIMS
Senior Manager, Epic Population Health & Government Programs,
University of California Davis Health,
Davis, California

Lucy A. Savitz, PhD, MBA
Director of Kaiser Permanente Center for Health Research,
Northwest, Portland, Oregon

Adam Stone
Manager of Clinical Analytics
Oregon Health & Science University
Portland, Oregon

Scott Thompson, RN, MBA
Quality Program Manager, University of California Irvine Health
Irvine, California

Special Thanks!

This book was inspired by

Michael Hogarth, MD

Population Health Team

Jamie Anand (UC Irvine)
Jeannine Kameeta
Michael Klade
Tracy Magee
Carlos Ramirez
Liz Traubenkraut
Jason Votaw

PRIME Steering Committee

Heather Erwin
Larry Friedman, MD
Jennifer Holland
Dustin Lillie, MD
Angela Scioscia, MD
Chad VanDenBerg, MPH

Operational and Clinical Leadership

Duncan Campbell
Brian Clay, MD
Tyson Ikeda, MD
Eugene Lee
Christopher Longhurst, MD, MS
Marlene Millen, MD
Thomas Moore, MD
Jeffrey Pan
Dean Pham

Graphic Design

Paola Luzardo

About the Authors

Barbara Berkovich founded the consulting and professional education company, *Applied Population Health,* in 2019. She is developing courses in applied health data analytics and population health for the academic year 2019–2020. Her goal is to assist health providers with implementation of their population health goals and to train the next generation of health informatics professionals in a standardized practice of applied population health.

She accrued 10 years of work experience at the University of California San Diego Health (UCSDH), where she designed and built tools in the electronic health record (EHR) to drive quality, safety, and outcomes to enhance patient care and meet state and national performance targets. As the lead population health architect, she became an expert in sustainable, timely operational registries in the EHR and managed an extensive portfolio of registries to track active patients, payor groups, affiliate members, medications, wellness, and chronic diseases. In 2018, her local work on the UCSDH Get to Green quality campaign helped claim nearly $5 million of at-risk Public Hospital Redesign and Incentives in Medi-Cal (PRIME) incentive payments that were in jeopardy.

Her PhD research focused on the automated selection of disease cohorts for the delivery of evidence-based care. She has lectured nationally on population health methods, registries, and medical terminologies and has taught graduate-level courses at the University of California San Diego. In addition to a PhD in biomedical informatics from the University of Texas Health Science Center at Houston, she holds a Master of Education degree from San Diego State University and a Bachelor of Science in industrial and systems engineering from the University of Southern California.

Amy M. Sitapati is the Chief Medical Information Officer of Population Health for UC San Diego Health (UCSDH), providing leadership, strategic vision and oversight to the organization. Using enterprise solutions that improve quality, safety, and outcomes, she leads the design of population-level systems that support workflows for organizational goals. Dr. Sitapati is the executive lead at UCSDH for two Centers for Medicare and Medicaid Services (CMS) programs. Together, the Public Hospital Redesign and Incentives in Medi-Cal (PRIME) and Quality performance Incentive program (QIP) are worth more than $25 million annually in eligible performance incentive payments. In this role, she directs more than 20 projects containing more than 80 quality measures supported by more than 150 active team members. Across the health system, Dr. Sitapati synchronizes the strategic vision, mapping, prioritization, and expertise-related quality infrastructure supporting pay for performance (P4P), the Physician Quality Reporting System (PQRS), Meaningful Use (MU), the Merit-based Incentive Payment System (MIPS), the Medicare Access and CHIP Reauthorization Act of 2015 (MACRA), and California's third-largest Medicare Shared Savings Program Accountable Care Organization (MSSP ACO) using nearly 100 EHR-based registries.

Dr. Sitapati's expertise includes board certification in clinical informatics and internal medicine, a bachelor's in engineering at Case Western Reserve University, a doctorate in medicine at Case Western Reserve University, coursework in clinical research at UC San Diego, business coursework at UC Los Angeles Anderson School of Business, EHR training in Epic as a physician builder, and Lean Black Belt training.

With more than a decade of experience in informatics-associated quality improvement, Dr. Sitapati brings substantial experience in using data to drive clinical workflows that improve care and ultimately provide healthier patient populations. She began this journey nearly 18 years ago caring for HIV/AIDS patients in inpatient, outpatient, and border care delivery sites. This evolved into a deep appreciation for the care continuum, complexity of multimorbidity, shortage of human health workforce, influence of social determinants, and remarkable foundational importance that registries can serve to anchor and improve care. In 2018, she received the UC San Diego Inclusive Excellence Award Recipients in recognition of the efforts of the Sexual Orientation and Gender Identity workgroup which she chairs. Dr. Sitapati has given much thought and daily iterative work to mastering patient-centered care delivery, implementation of meaningful risk acuity scoring, development of dynamic decision support, quality-driven care, and access to research. As a former member of the Agency for Healthcare Research and

Quality (AHRQ) health information technology study section and a current member of the National Comprehensive Cancer Network (NCCN) breast panel, Dr. Sitapati has experience in considering academic needs related to population health. Dr. Sitapati is the local investigator for the California Vital Records program and gives thought to the intersection between public- and health system–level data. She provides instruction in clinical informatics and Kelee meditation in the School of Medicine to physicians, pharmacists, and computer and computational scientists. From the perspective of research, she leads the local recruitment team for the National Institute of Health (NIH) precision medicine movement, All of Us, and thinks about the intersection between research and population health. Dr. Sitapati believes that medicine of the future will integrate research, continuous quality improvement, and population-driven healthcare delivery into the daily practice of medicine in remarkable ways to serve as the "penicillin" of the future by directing the right care to the right patient with the right resources.

Chapter 1

Introduction

As the practice of value-based care gains wide adoption, billions of dollars of government and insurer payments are contingent on quality reporting to demonstrate delivery of evidence-based care. Electronic health record (EHR) systems today provide increasing levels of clinical decision support and are the fulcrum for change at the heart of value-based healthcare delivery. In this context, we define applied population health as the use of the EHR system to identify patient cohorts in need of evidence-based interventions, and facilitate actions to address care gaps. The use of registries in the EHR has been transformative in the sense that we can identify and track groups of patients by diagnosis, treatment, enhanced demographics, and administrative relationships and efficiently drive appropriate action at the individual or group level. This is key to achieving economies of scale and delivering timely preventative care to keep patients well and prevent or slow their advance across the secondary and tertiary illness trajectory. The registries are not an end in themselves, but drive a population health engine that operationalizes clinical protocols, the "who, what, and when" of healthcare. The registry engine will drive the gears of standardized processes and workflows to deliver high-value care that reduces variance and waste. These will serve as foundational components to the future evolution of integrated digital health, precision medicine, and ever more sophisticated decision support.

Combining the people, process, and technology to deliver value-based care has proven to be a monumental effort. Pivoting from traditional fee-for-service to value-based care has the promise to more effectively avert poor healthcare outcomes and improve quality of life. This transformation of care delivery at a national scale pledges to keep people healthier through the judicious practice of evidence-based care and optimal deployment of limited clinical resources. Roots of this dissemination blossomed as a result of "value" visioning from key leaders such as Donald Berwick, who asserted that the triple aim of improved population health, improved patient experience, and reduced cost was not only possible but necessary. Subsequently, the recognition that doctors and healthcare workers were facing increasing challenges with the usability of EHR systems and meeting the new quality measurement practices resulted in a fourth aim: improved caregiver experience.[1] It takes just a single human story to move past the statistics and bring home the realities of provider burnout. A young primary care doctor recently shared this email:

> I receive 75–100 messages per day from or about my patients. It takes me about 5 minutes to respond to a message. This generates 6.5 to 8.3 hours per day of un-billable work amounting to a full workday for a normal person. The EHR trainer said that he has not seen anyone work faster; he could not even keep up with me. I am also seeing patients, writing notes, and reviewing charts.
>
> As a result of this much work, I sit in a chair and work every waking hour that I am not physically at work. This includes every weekend and every holiday. I have not stopped working long enough to eat food with my family or even open Christmas presents (it is now February). My daughter told me last week, "It is like you are an imaginary mommy." Being an imaginary person is lonely and unhealthy. As a resident, I worked a lot. I also had good friends, I did yoga, played with my kids, and volunteered as class parent. I was able to take good care of my patients and enjoy being a mother. I never got close to burning out. After 3 months under the load I described, I am completely burned out. This burden of work on physicians demands sacrifices in the quality of patient care, in physician health, and in the well-being of our children. This amount of work prevents me from doing the things I care about most: being an excellent doctor, a healthy person, and loving parent.
>
> —Imaginary Mommy, MD

Bending the curve on the healthcare quality–to–expenditure ratio, however, is recognized to require a fundamental "re-engineering" of healthcare delivery to support the practice of medicine and avert the unintended consequences faced by the "imaginary mommy."[2] The mere conversion of paper-based processes to electronic form is insufficient to achieve the quadruple aim. We need to vision, design, and shape enterprise-wide systems to thoughtfully direct and improve the efficiency and effectiveness of care delivery. Through the lens of our national healthcare system, financial opportunities and challenges are shaping the practice of applied population health as providers and patients experience it today. This handbook is designed to help large, complex health systems move the needle on quality measures and outcomes while preserving the dignity of patients and providers and the very important moments when they come together for healing and comfort. The primary audience for this book includes both clinical and nonclinical professionals with experience in healthcare delivery. Graduate students will gain a practical understanding of the professional roles engaged in this field to inform their career paths in medicine, nursing, allied health, healthcare administration, public health, clinical informatics, data analytics, or operations research with an emphasis in healthcare. As individuals coalesce into effective teams for population health care delivery, health systems will experience improved patient care, quality measure performance, and revenue from incentives and risk-based contracts.

The book is presented in three parts: 1) Fundamentals 2) Effective Delivery of Applied Population Health, and 3) Applied Population Health Today and Tomorrow, so that the reader may more easily find the material that complements their background and interests.

Part 1: Fundamentals

Value-based care seeks to achieve a quadruple aim of improving health outcomes and patient and caregiver experience, while concurrently reducing per capita cost. Policy, people, process, and technology are drivers of market-based healthcare reform to meet these challenges (Figure 1.1). Part 1 provides the reader with the background and common vocabulary that are prerequisite to understanding the effective delivery of applied population health presented in Part 2. We also believe that a shared lexicon of informatics terms will enable multidisciplinary teams to work together more effectively and productively to advance the overall state of practice.

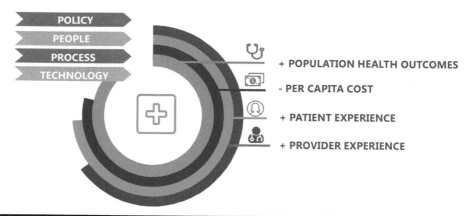

Figure 1.1   **Drivers of the quadruple aim for healthcare.**

Highlights of Part 1 include:

Policy   A brief history of the U.S. policies driving value-based
                   payment models
                   Quality measure use in pay-for-performance and risk
                   sharing programs
                   Value-based measurement framework

People   *Organizational characteristics*
                   Stepping stones to value-based care
                   Value improvement governance structure
                   Patient empanelment and attribution to define
                   doctor–patient relationships

                   Understanding patients and patient groups
                   Social determinants of health
                   New standards for race, ethnicity, and language
                   (REAL)
                   Data collection for sexual orientation and gender
                   identity (SO/GI)

Process	Sample population health protocol
	Technology flaws underlying healthcare waste
Technology	Introduction to the role of registries in value-based care delivery
	Taxonomy and ontology of health registries
Measuring the quadruple aims	Population health outcomes
	Per capita cost
	Patient experience
	Provider experience
Case studies	Provider engagement practices
	Collection of ethnic background data
	Doing the right thing with medication monitoring
	Use of Social Security decedent data in EHR registry

Part 2: Effective Delivery of Applied Population Health

When we formed the enterprise population health team in the information services department four years ago, we considered actionable registries in the EHR to be our prime deliverable followed by actionable clinical decision support. However, we grew frustrated with the difficulty of quantifying value with that approach. We had long lead-times for development of registries with large numbers of metrics, and there were disconnects between the registry build, quality measures, and clinical decision support. Gradually, we came to realize that applied population health methods are more effective when rolled out in the following order:

1. Identify the quality measure(s) to target for change
2. Build the registry with data elements needed for the measure calculations
3. Add clinical decision support and supporting workflows to drive performance
4. Build real-time dashboards for continuous process measurement

Highlights of Part 2 include:

Conceptual model	Applied population health technical foundation
Prototype system	Do-it-yourself quality measure management
Registry design principles	Transitioning from quality measures to registries
Second-generation clinical decision support	EHR tools that use the registry engine to drive care
Analytics dashboards	Innovative application of dashboards to: Track rolling performance measures in real time (365 day lookback) Demonstrate utilization and value of technology Co-locate quadruple aim outcomes

Along the way we'll include case studies to introduce readers to insights and tools for organizing and monitoring quality measure performance. "Field Report" highlights briefly encapsulate challenges and solutions based on our own experience. Exercises and discussion questions encourage individuals and/or small groups to develop innovative solutions. We encourage our readers to wrestle with these scenarios for a deeper understanding of the nuances in quality improvement projects and how each team member contributes within the bounds of available time and resources. The practice-based cases have no "right answers," but feedback from leading population health teams informs the discussion and analysis. Following are a few examples of questions and the concepts they inform.

Quality Program Manager

I'm responsible for meeting quality targets for 56 measures. Given the baseline and current performance, where do I focus my efforts?

Concept

Prioritization of competing quality measures can be guided by the relative level of difficulty of closing each care gap. One must also consider the impact of that effort upon patient cohorts.

Clinical Champion

I'm responsible for the cardiac measures, and I want an actionable registry to drive the work. How soon can you fulfill this request?

Getting value from information technology:
Frame IT requests in terms of the design goals and constraints, not the solution.

EHR Analyst

We met the goals, and the celebration has just ended. How are we going to make it easier to repeat or improve this performance next year?

Sustainable high-reliability systems: Registry-based EHR tools to promote standard work are effective in building highly reliable and sustainable processes.

Part 3: Applied Population Health of Today and Tomorrow

In Part 3, we draw lessons from firsthand experience with applied population health methods to vision the next generation of medical practice. This section begins with a review of successes, lessons learned, best practices, and ongoing challenges in applied population health today. We introduce the learning health system as a concept and a practice that will lead us to a future state based on good science and good evidence. The challenges encountered by population health programs today will form the basis of a call for action that will inform the training needs of our workforce of tomorrow.

Highlights of Part 3 include:

Population health of today

Use of the EHR as a "therapeutic"
Designing systems for people
Call to action

Learning health system

History and use of the learning health system in clinical practice

Population health of tomorrow

Scaling the deployment of health resources
Reduction of chronic disease burden through early detection, prevention, and management

Let's Get Started

We believe strongly in the necessity of bringing new methods and new voices to the interdisciplinary practice of applied population health and in the importance of a shared language and personal relationships to make this happen. We hope everyone interested in applied population health will find something in our menu of "appetizers," that is, our highlights, regardless of whether you're new to the field, expanding expertise in your current role, or preparing yourself for a higher level of professional competency. Thank you for sharing this journey with us . . . *Let's get started.*

FUNDAMENTALS

1

Chapter 2

Policy

Drivers for Value-Based Payment Models

Healthcare costs are "a hungry tapeworm on the American economy," according to Warren Buffet.[3] The Centers for Medicare and Medicaid Services report that in 2016 spending was 17.9% of gross domestic product (Figure 2.1). Amazon and J.P. Morgan Chase joined Buffet's Berkshire Hathaway to form Haven, a nonprofit healthcare venture. Atul Gawande, MD, MPH, promises to bring vision in the role of its chief executive officer as he has in his four bestselling books: *Complications, Better, The Checklist Manifesto,* and *Being Mortal: Medicine and What Matters in the End.* The company will focus on "technology solutions that will provide U.S. employees and their families with simplified, high-quality and transparent healthcare at a reasonable cost."[3] So, if everyone wants that, why is it so difficult to achieve?

Berwick cautioned that our traditional fee-for-service healthcare reimbursement model was in opposition to the aforementioned triple aim. He argued that payment for healthcare services without any direct linkage to quality and outcomes created market dynamics that encouraged hospitals to fill beds and expand services to protect profits and increase revenue.[4] Process improvement under that model could actually threaten profits and fail to foster improvement.

To achieve improvements in analytics, performance measurement, and care coordination, population health tools must continue to develop in sophistication, while also becoming easier to use. There is a knowledge

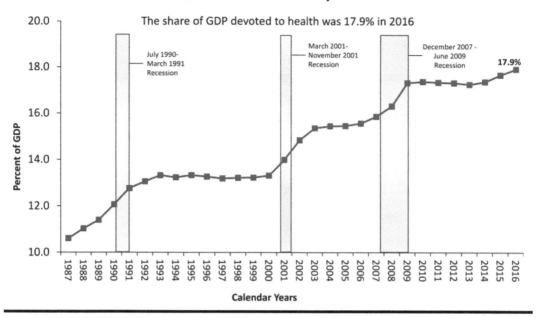

Figure 2.1   National health expenditures as a share of gross domestic product, 1987–2016.[5]

gap about what needs to be done and how to roll out successful programs.[6] In response, the U.S. government and private insurers are in a massive transition to new revenue streams for healthcare providers in the form of value-based programs with reimbursements tied to quality measures.

Payment reform has become a national reality, and the business case for the use of population health methods to drive healthcare performance has never been stronger. However, most health systems still support a mix of insurers. Over time, the decreased proportion of fee-for-service income has been steadily offset by quality incentive programs in the form of pay-for-performance and risk sharing contracts (Figure 2.2). As the payor mix at many healthcare organizations reaches or exceeds 30% full-risk payments, we are at a tipping point to realize the benefits of technical infrastructure, which includes electronic medical record systems and clinical registries.[7]

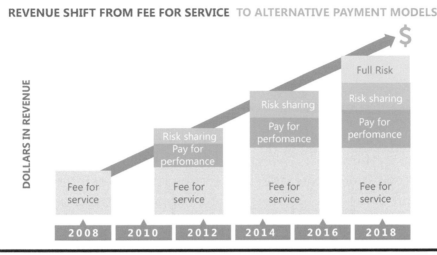

REVENUE SHIFT FROM FEE FOR SERVICE TO ALTERNATIVE PAYMENT MODELS

Figure 2.2   Revenue shift from fee-for-service to alternative payment models.

Pay-For-Performance (P4P)

Pay-for-performance (P4P) is a term that encompasses initiatives that provide financial incentives to healthcare providers for reporting improvements in performance of measures of quality, efficiency, and/or health outcomes. These programs can also impose financial penalties for failure to meet performance targets.[8] In addition to the Merit-based Incentive Payment System (MIPS) and Advanced Alternative Payment Models (APMs), Centers for Medicare and Medicaid Services (CMS) 1115(a) demonstration waivers are designating billions of dollars to states for Medicaid reform. A large portion of those funds are tied to quality indicators. California's five-year Medi-Cal 2020 Demonstration program includes $6.2 billion of initial federal funding to transform and improve the quality of care, access, and efficiency of healthcare services for 12.8 million members.[9] Roughly half of this sum is allocated to Public Hospital Redesign and Incentives in Medi-Cal (PRIME), which offers incentives to public hospitals for performance measures for quality and efficiency. California continues to lead the nation in healthcare transformation through the use of P4P programs. The March 2019 issue brief called "Journey to Value-Based Care" reports that "[i]n 2009, public health care systems in California had zero dollars tied to performance; today that figure is approximately $2.8 billion annually."[10] This analysis included whole-person care, PRIME, the quality incentive program, the global payment program, Medicare (Hospital Readmissions Reduction Program, Value-Based Purchasing, Hospital-Acquired Condition), and Medi-Cal Managed Care Pay for Performance (voluntary plan by plan).[10]

Risk Sharing Programs

A variety of accountable care organizations (ACOs), both public and private, have moved into risk sharing models under the Affordable Care Act (Figure 2.3). ACOs negotiate risk sharing contracts between the payor and the healthcare providers. One version of this model pays a fixed amount per patient to a medical group for care provided by their member physicians. A pool of money is set aside for the hospital (facility) charges for the ACO patients. If the physicians control the hospital costs through appropriate care management, they can share in a percentage of the savings. However, the characteristics of patient populations may affect utilization independent of the quality of care, and consequently many of these plans have risk adjustment formulas to account for these variables. While the minimum population deemed sufficiently large to spread risk effectively is 5,000, others would contend that this is much too low and may advocate for 500,000 lives.[11] Capitated plans vary in the amount of shared risk and whether that risk is upside only (incentives) and/or downside (penalties). Quality reporting enables a balance to be facilitated between maintenance of the quality of care in the face of cost-cutting pressure.

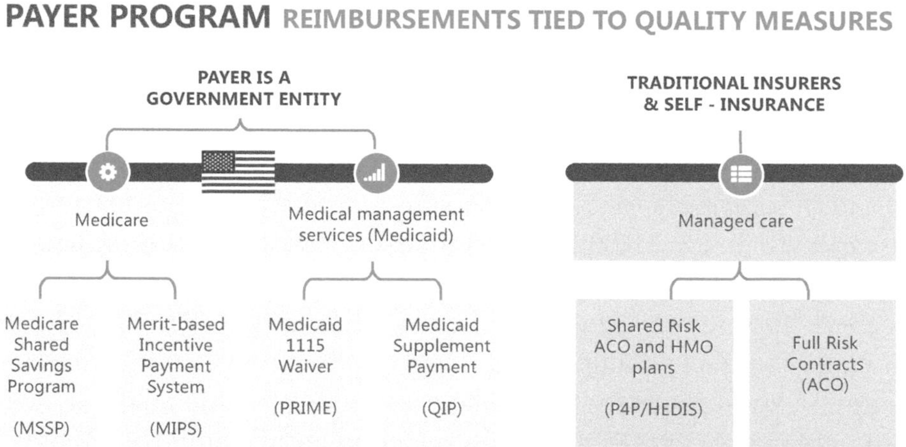

PAYER PROGRAM REIMBURSEMENTS TIED TO QUALITY MEASURES

Figure 2.3   Payor programs with reimbursements tied to quality measures.

CMS administers the Medicare Shared Savings Program (MSSP) ACO and Medicare Advantage. ACOs are groups of doctors, hospitals, and other health-care providers who come together voluntarily to give coordinated, high-quality care to their Medicare patients. The goal of coordinated care is to ensure that patients have access to the right care at the right time, while avoiding unnecessary duplication of services and preventing medical errors.[12] Medical management services are also available from Medicaid in addition to the Pay-for-Performance Demonstration Waiver programs. Traditional insurers and self-insured managed care plans include shared risk contracts in the ACO or health maintenance organization (HMO) models, as well as full-risk ACO contracts.

Risk Adjustment

Risk-adjusted payment helps organizations care for complex, high-cost patients. This structure encourages insurers to provide health insurance for patients with chronic health conditions, knowing that the payment will be commensurate with probable costs. CMS uses a hierarchical condition category (HCC) risk adjustment model to calculate risk adjustment factor (RAF) scores. This hierarchical risk adjustment model is intended to provide increased payments for Medicare patients with medical conditions predictive of higher healthcare costs.[13] The CMS-HCC model does not include acute services such as cancer, transplant, and other "acute" services, whereas the HHS-HCC model used for Affordable Care Act health plan premiums does.[14]

Savings

ACOs report significant gains in quality cost control with hospital services. The QUEST (Quality, Efficacy, Safety with Transparency): High-Performing Hospitals collaborative reports that its ACO hospitals saved an estimated $2.13 billion in costs and increased the delivery of recommended care to patients 90.5% of the time.[13] Over the 2010–2015 period QUEST members continued to show both quantitative and qualitative improvements in cost per discharge, improved patient experience, and unplanned readmissions.[15]

Healthcare Measurement Frameworks

Each quality measure uses an evidence-based clinical guideline to define "quality" for a specific healthcare service. The classifications of health quality measures rely heavily on Donabedian's conceptual model which categorizes healthcare evaluation into three categories: structure, process, and outcomes.[16] The model was originally utilized by the World Health Organization (WHO) over 30 years ago to evaluate the global state of medical systems. More recently, it has been adopted by the Agency for Healthcare Research and Quality (AHRQ) to define types of healthcare quality measures. In this model, **structure** is money, facilities, and personnel that create boundary conditions for the care delivery; **process** is what is actually done in the giving and receiving of care; and **outcome** denotes the effects of care on the health status of patients and populations.[16] CMS has expanded Donabedian's sequential construct to include the added patient experience dimensions. The 2019 MIPS Quality Performance Category Fact Sheet, lists seven types of quality measures for the Quality Payment Program (QPP): 1) process, 2) structure, 3) intermediate outcome, 4) outcome, 5) patient-reported outcome, 6) efficiency, and 7) patient engagement and patient experience.[17]

We propose a new value-based measurement framework that identifies the relationship between different types of measures in terms of pre-intervention, intervention, and post-intervention contexts, which was implicit in Donabedian's work (Figure 2.4). If we apply a systems approach, these measures do not stand alone, but are all reflective of data that may be collected about any given care process. The WHO used similar metrics to

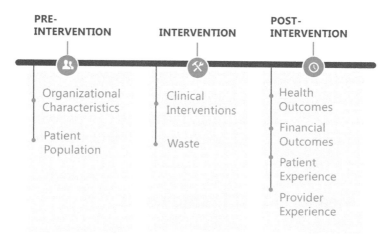

Figure 2.4   Value-based measurement framework.

evaluate how well national health systems controlled all-cause mortality, and we can apply this framework to something as simple as performing a risk assessment to reduce falls.

The pre-intervention context includes the unique characteristics of the organization and patient population that tend to make it easier or more difficult to meet quality program specifications. Examples include organization size, staffing, patient age, payor mix, and risk profile. The intervention phase focuses on the delivery of care, whether the clinical interventions meet evidence-based standards of care, and whether the process is optimized for minimal waste and maximum safety. Lastly, the post-intervention phase includes the quadruple aim outcomes of the collective clinical processes: health outcomes, financial outcomes, patient experience, and provider experience. Using the example of a population of type 1 and type 2 diabetics, we provide examples of measurements representative of the three contexts of the value measurement framework.

Pre-intervention context

- ■ Organizational characteristics
  - − Staff numbers and training
  - − Culture of quality
  - − Number of hospitals, beds, and clinics
- ■ Patient population
  - − Traditional demographics: age, gender, income, and education
  - − Incidence and prevalence of disease within the population
  - − Patient comorbidity
  - − Race/ethnicity/language and literacy
  - − Social determinants of health

Intervention context

- ■ Clinical intervention:
  - − Patients 18 years or older with type 1 or type 2 diabetes receive:
    - • Glycosylated hemoglobin A1c lab test every six months
    - • Microalbumin and creatine measurement (annual)
    - • Lipid measurement (annual)
    - • Blood pressure control (based on last measurement within year)

- Diabetic eye exam (annual)
- Diabetic foot exam (annual)

■ Waste: Rate of missing or manually entered laboratory values

Post-intervention context

■ Health outcomes (intermediate and long term)
  - A1c <8 (controlled)
  - Rate of microscopic proteinuria (urine)
  - Rates of dialysis and kidney transplant
  - Rates cardiovascular comorbidity resulting in heart attack and stroke
  - Rates of diabetic complications resulting in blindness or lower limb amputation
  - Mortality
■ Financial outcome: Cost of nursing time for post-discharge follow-up calls?
■ Patient experience
  - Diabetes distress scores captured using the Problem Areas in Diabetes Questionnaire (PAID)
  - Was healthcare accessible in a timely fashion?
  - Did your provider explain your health condition well?
  - Do you have access to clinicians, education and disease management tools through a patient web portal?
■ Provider experience
  - Is there a pharmacy or team-based workflow for diabetes management?
  - Do you have time for bathroom and meal breaks?

Published Results

Cardiac Health

Optimistic news is being reported on a number of interventions that have been successful in reducing overall cost while improving patient health at local, state, and national levels. One example is the Be There San Diego project, which reports "one in five fewer heart attacks" through patient activation and community-based intervention aggressively addressing blood

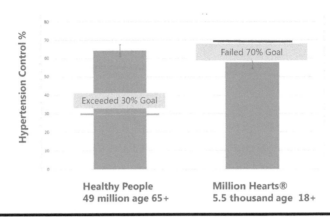

Figure 2.5   **Discordant national targets for hypertension control, 2016.**

pressure, blood sugar, and lipid levels. This resulted in an estimated savings of nearly $85.8 million locally on acute myocardial infarction alone.[18]

However, at a national level, the evidence around blood pressure control for prevention of cardiac events is mixed. Figure 2.5 compares the national targets and control of hypertension as reported by the CMS Medicare Quality Improvement Organization (QIO) and the Million Hearts initiative. The QIO reported high blood pressure control of 64.2%, exceeding the 30% target for 2016 by over 100% for a population of over 49 million people age 65 or older.[19] However, the Million Hearts performance for the same period was estimated at 57.7%, markedly under their 70% goal. High-performing providers serving 13.8 million patients were recognized by Million Hearts for controlling blood pressure for 70% or more of their patients.[20]

Facts such as these can be confusing when trying to compare achievements without a standard baseline, target performance goal, population, or measure methodology. The QIO and Million Hearts populations may be overlapping, with both contributing to the increase in performance. The longitudinal performance on hypertension and control reported by the National Center for Health Statistics (NCHS) tells a different story. The 2015–2016 rate of controlled hypertension is 48.3%.[20] Furthermore, the last significant change in the prevalence of controlled hypertension was from 1999–2000 (31.6%) to 2009–2010 (53.1%). *No significant changes in controlled hypertension were observed from 2009 to 2010 and from 2015 to 2016.*[21]

Nevertheless, mortality from heart disease has declined between 2006 and 2016 by 18% for males and 22% for females, which is encouraging overall.[22]

Tobacco Cessation

QIO also reports tobacco cessation interventions were provided for 75.7% of self-identified smokers, again surpassing the target (45%) by a wide margin.[19] However, national measures of smoking do show a persistent downward trend in tobacco use among adults, with the exception of people age 65 and over, who have a low smoking rate to begin with (Figure 2.6). To demonstrate that the QIO tobacco cessation intervention was effective in lowering the rate of smoking, we would need to know the smoking rate before and after intervention, and this information was not included in the report. Overall, the percentage of the U.S. population age 15 and over who smoke daily (11.4%) is well below the mean (16.6%) of eleven high-income countries, including the United Kingdom, Canada, Germany, Australia, Japan, Sweden, France, the Netherlands, Switzerland, and Denmark.[23] In that context, the cumulative efforts to reduce smoking rates over the last decade have succeeded, and this is indeed an important achievement for improving population health.

U.S. TOBACCO USE 2006-2016
BY AGE

ADULTS 65+ LOW, BUT RELATIVELY UNCHANGED

COMPARED TO REDUCTIONS 18-44
AND 45-65

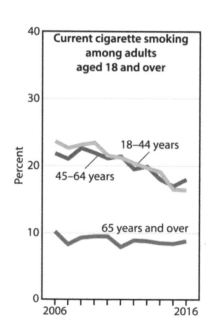

Figure 2.6   U.S. tobacco use by age, 2006–2016. Health, United States 2017, Chapter 3, Figure 5.[22]

Diabetes

Section 1115 Medicaid waiver programs have given the states opportunity to expand Medicaid services with matching federal funds. For more than a decade, California's safety net payments have been transitioning from volume to value. The PRIME program in California has implemented an ambitious portfolio of P4P metrics. As of year three, "[a]lmost all public health care systems [in California] are performing better than 90% of the country's Medicaid providers in managing blood sugar for patients with diabetes."[10]

Human Immunodeficiency Virus (HIV)

Pennsylvania's Chronic Care Initiative (CCI) also used a patient-centered medical home model to treat HIV-positive Medicaid patients with multiple comorbidities. The resulting savings of $214.10 per person as compared with the control group was realized through the shift of inpatient utilization to outpatient care.[24]

Benefits of Early Intervention

The lesson to glean from published success is that effective cost cutting is likely to be achieved by focusing appropriate care early in the disease or episode rather than denying access to service to care. This model results in early intervention, early management, and slowing or averting disease development and progression. The shift to payment for quality reporting is a difficult process, but it will likely continue because it has the potential to drive benefits for patients, healthcare systems, employers, insurers, and government through more thoughtful spending on healthcare. Not only do the measurement and reporting demonstrate that care is of high quality while costs savings are achieved, the detection of quality variance becomes a feedback loop for targeting quality efforts and human resources. In this way the people, infrastructure, and processes need to be able to address primary prevention for aversion and early detection, secondary prevention optimizing treatment and follow-up to reduce risk, and tertiary prevention where more complex and targeted services may be required. This prevention is also not along a specific domain, but rather along multiple interrelated domains that have complex synergistic interactions. The art and science of value-based care delivery are currently still young and are likely to continue to rapidly evolve. The winners will commit themselves to being better than everybody else at delivering healthcare. According to Scott Thompson, RN, MBA, and PRIME program manager at UC Irvine Health, health providers are being forced to make a choice.

> In my opinion, you can stay in the safe lane, the typical fee for service model with or without quality "bonuses." But the big moves are being made out there in risk-based contracting and people are making big bets on improved care delivery and outcomes as a financial strategy. You don't become better than everyone else cheaply. It takes investment and coordinated effort and an organizational approach.[25]

As value-based care becomes more prominent both as a care paradigm and a reimbursement philosophy, the number of organizations engaged in population health activities and the number of interventions within organizations are both growing rapidly. A HIMSS (Healthcare Information and Management Systems Society) survey of 104 technology leaders in U.S. hospitals found that the number of organizations with population health programs has grown from 67% in 2015 to 76% in 2016.[6] Healthcare leaders are sharing their successes and continuing challenges with population health and the quadruple aim. In the next section we will focus on the people who are coming together to build and engage in population health programs.

Chapter 3

People

Quality measures in the pre-intervention context of the value-based measurement framework are related to Donabedian's structure measures.[16] The Centers for Medicare and Medicaid Services (CMS) uses structural measures to "assess features of a healthcare organization or clinician relevant to its capacity to provide healthcare."[26] The CMS Measures Inventory Tools (CMIT. cms.gov) has a miscellany of structure measures ranging from "Adult Local Current Smoking Prevalence" to "Hospital Outpatient Volume on Selected Procedures" and "National Healthcare Safety Network (NHSN) Dialysis Event Reporting Measure." From a logical standpoint, we feel this category needs further clarification and focus beyond the size, number, and location of healthcare facilities. We believe that the primary modifiable measures in the pre-intervention context relate to people, and that they belong to two categories: organizational characteristics and patient population (Figure 3.1).

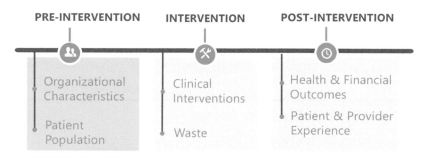

Figure 3.1   Pre-intervention measurements in the value-based measurement framework.

This chapter will focus on these groups who represent the human qualities of sociotechnical systems, and place constraints on what's possible within the intervention context.

Organizational Characteristics

The organization of people into highly functioning interdisciplinary workgroups, with well-defined roles and responsibilities, is a necessary precondition for sustained value improvement efforts (Figure 3.2). In this chapter we focus on the building blocks for driving change in high-performing healthcare systems: 1) engaged leadership, 2) data-driven value improvement workgroups, 3) clear provider–patient relationships through empanelment and attribution, 4) team-based care and care management, and 5) patient engagement (adapted from "The 10 Building Blocks of High-Performing Primary Care"[27]).

Engaged Leadership

Clinical operations executives set priorities and manage resources to support a portfolio of value-based initiatives for patient populations.

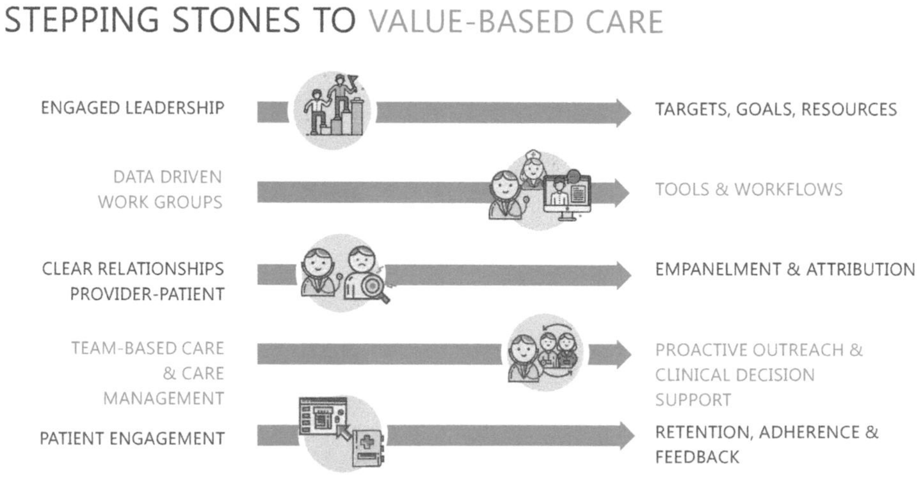

STEPPING STONES TO VALUE-BASED CARE

ENGAGED LEADERSHIP	TARGETS, GOALS, RESOURCES
DATA DRIVEN WORK GROUPS	TOOLS & WORKFLOWS
CLEAR RELATIONSHIPS PROVIDER-PATIENT	EMPANELMENT & ATTRIBUTION
TEAM-BASED CARE & CARE MANAGEMENT	PROACTIVE OUTREACH & CLINICAL DECISION SUPPORT
PATIENT ENGAGEMENT	RETENTION, ADHERENCE & FEEDBACK

Figure 3.2   Organizing people to drive change.

Source: Adapted from Bodenheimer, 2014

Whether the scale of programs is in millions of dollars over one to five years or more limited two- to four-month projects, organizations should be addressing population health in strategic planning as a key success factor for value-based care. The new care delivery paradigm requires a rethinking of organizational culture, structure, personnel, and compensation models. Organizational hierarchies and governance structures for leadership and decision-making may need to evolve as semi-autonomous projects are formed to meet the unique demands of specific quality measures. As organizations scale the size and number of projects, new governance structures are dynamically created to set the vision, prioritize effort, and remove obstacles and are dissolved when they are no longer needed. When projects are struggling to achieve their aims, governance is a likely cause. Although a one-size fits all approach will not apply to healthcare governance structures, there should be key lines of reporting from strategically prioritized projects to the executive team for informed decision-making. A successful governance structure that is both scalable and flexible receives vision and goals from an executive committee, is guided by a steering committee, has a program manager for day-to-day administration, and has workgroups for specific measures (Figure 3.3).

Figure 3.3   Value improvement project oversight, roles, and personnel.

Executive Committee

As executive teams address increasing regulatory requirements, patient safety, innovation, and market differentiation goals, a 5- to 10-year population health vision helps to anchor needed infrastructure toward these aims. Executives should periodically review progress toward those goals and execute key decisions while resolving obstacles and problems that arise along the path to develop a population health infrastructure[28] and assure adequate resources for success. Executives in the following roles commonly participate in this committee: chief executive officer (CEO), chief information officer (CIO), chief medical officer (CMO), chief nursing officer (CNO), chief medical officer of population health (CMO PH), chief medical information officer (CMIO), chief operating officer (COO), chief financial officer (CFO), chief quality and safety officer (CQSO), etc.

Steering Committee

A steering committee exercises its responsibility to triage, prioritize, and make decisions during weekly oversight meetings. Effective steering committees are agile and nimble in reviewing quality workgroup progress, pivoting available resources, identifying strategic partnerships for operational execution, communicating activities, and escalating issues that require executive oversight. Members would likely include physician leadership, program manager, information technology (IT) manager, and CQSO.

Quality Program Manager

The program manager's goal is to maximize the revenue recovery (earnings) from the quality program through the management of deliverables and timelines for multiple projects. Additionally, the program manager serves as the local liaison between what the external program requirements demand and what the local health system is working to achieve.

Workgroups

Data-driven value-improvement workgroups with expertise and focus on a particular quality domain, such as ambulatory cardiovascular care, should be formed with expertise to match the program deliverables. The program manager may participate in these meetings or may rely on one or more project managers to develop workgroup timelines and monitor status. Status updates, resource requests, and project dependencies are communicated to the program manager for review by the steering committee. Workgroups may be convened for short-term projects or may develop into standing committees to serve organizational needs. There may also be cases when the workgroups can be aligned with or incorporated into other internal programs within the same domain.

The programmatic efforts are championed day to day through the leadership of the steering committee and the activities born through efforts of the clinical workgroups. As a practical example, a cardiovascular **workgroup** may design a protocol for blood pressure follow-up that requires a hypertension registry and an outreach protocol to recall patients with high blood pressure. The **program manager** would present this proposal on behalf of the workgroup to the **steering committee** in order to help define the prioritization of the high blood pressure quality measure related to resource allocation. This type of proposal will likely require IT support, including electronic health record (EHR) build or ad hoc analytics, clinical staff support for outreach, and project management support. The steering committee would review whether the proposal takes precedence over a portfolio of other value-improvement projects queued up for resource allocation. Typically, the executive committee would not be involved in this decision-making. However, if the workgroup defined a need for transition or increase of current personnel, such as patient navigators for outreach, the **executive committee** would then evaluate the at-risk quality measure incentive payments in relation to the overall budget in order to determine whether to hire additional navigators or prioritize the outreach effort using existing personnel. These decisions result in both short-term tactical execution and longer-term infrastructure planning.

Data-Driven Value Improvement Workgroups

In the increasingly complex delivery of healthcare, value improvement workgroups are essential for the design and implementation of data-driven quality initiatives. Rather than committing to a single intervention to improve a measure, the groups commit to a measure goal and dynamically adapt one or more interventions to meet that goal. Typically, the measure performance alone is inadequate to guide a workgroup to the most effective intervention(s). The workgroup needs to know the current status and trending of at-risk measures, as well as performance drill-down by service location and provider to know where tactically to intervene. The workgroup may be convened for a single project or may develop into a permanent team focused on a particular medical specialty or process. The workgroups "must be interdisciplinary if they are to succeed with each team member participating equally."[29]

Clinical measure owner(s) are subject matter experts ultimately responsible for meeting specific measure targets in a clinically sound manner. Doctors are frequently chosen for this role, and co-ownership may bring additional perspectives and skills to a project. Examples of co-owners include primary care and/or specialist physician, psychologist, pharmacist, allied health professional, or registered nurse. These individuals are familiar with existing workflows and have relationships with key organizational stakeholders. The clinical leaders actively engage in tackling the organization's goals and become the face of the initiative locally. Clinical measure owners provide insight into the clinical accuracy of the data extraction. They rely on data to iteratively improve sustainable work processes to meet quality measures, lower cost, and improve patient and provider experience.

Applied clinical informaticist(s) bring the requisite skills to design enterprise-wide population health interventions. Physicians certified by the American Medical Informatics Association (AMIA) in informatics would be expected to have this training. However, this expertise may also be developed among allied health professionals, nurses, and systems analysts with EHR experience. They require deep organizational knowledge, as their work products will likely touch multiple operational and application teams. Whereas the measure owner possesses the expertise in what should be done, the informaticist has a broader vision how to build and implement new processes using technology tools. Required skills include workflow analysis, design of clinical decision support, user interfaces, risk acuity scores, and registries. They must be knowledgeable in the lexicons of standard health terminologies, analytics, data governance, leadership, and change management. A strong partnership between clinician and informaticist will provide a solid foundation for a value improvement team.

Separate and apart from the program manager is a **project manager**. Whereas the program manager is looking externally to the program requirements and coordination with the timeline of performance deliverables, the project manager is looking internally at selected projects and then managing task assignments, overall timelines, key dependencies and deadlines, meeting logistics, agendas, and communication back to the program manager. The project manager provides a communication channel between the clinical quality programs, clinical teams, operations, and quality teams. The project manager communicates objectives and timelines identified by a quality program manager and helps identify, coordinate, and accelerate project task completion to achieve aims.

Population health methods require a wider lens to consider all the **stake-holders** affected by process changes and to foster adoption in clinically meaningful workflows. Depending on particular projects, it is worthy to consider input/contributions from quality, contracting, care management, health information management, registration and scheduling, billing and compliance, and research. All applicable care settings should be included (ambulatory, acute care, procedural care), as well as transition of care or even community-based public health resources.

The minimum set of value improvement workgroup members and their tasks is provided in Table 3.1.

Table 3.1 Value Improvement Workgroup Members

Measure owner(s)	*Responsible for reaching measure goal* *Subject matter expert on clinical care and workflows* *Clinical protocol development* *Patient portal communications*
Applied clinical informaticist	Clinical decision support design Patient portal development User interface design Risk acuity and predictive models Registries Clinical terminologies (codes) Data governance
Project manager	Task assignments and deadlines Meeting logistics Agendas and minutes Status reports to the program manager.
Population health key stakeholders	Quality, contracting, care management, ambulatory/acute/procedural/transition care, health information management, registration and scheduling, billing and compliance, research, or even community-based public health resources
Information technology	EHR build Clinical decision support build Collection of new data in the EHR Registry build Operational reports Quality reports Process monitoring (dashboards, rolling measures) Data analytics External data management Training and communication

Table 3.2   Roles, Knowledge, and Skills Requirements for Population Health Technical Teams

Roles,	Knowledge, and Skills
Chief Medical Information Officer	Vision, direction, and oversight
Population Health IT Manager	Budget, program, and personnel management
Lead Population Health Architect	Registry infrastructure and risk scores
EHR Clinical Application Analyst	EHR workflows and user interface
Database Analyst	Quality reporting and analytics
EHR Reporting Analyst	Online patient engagement, messaging, and questionnaires
Patient Portal Analyst	Database design, external data, and patient matching

Organizations engaging in value-based care delivery frequently need to strengthen their **technical teams** to build efficient and effective population health tools (Table 3.2). Forming a dedicated population-health technical team is one solution that requires leadership and strategic planning. The informatics teams require cross-fit team members whose expertise spans multiple applications and clinical domains. Appendix C includes sample job descriptions for members of the population health team.

Adopting an enterprise-wide program for population health to support high-reliability clinical processes will require investment in resources that promise to accrue benefits from both the short-term, value-based incentive programs and long-term process control. Essential support for the development of a robust population health program may be cultivated with the presentation of a white paper to the executive team. Key elements of the Population Health White Paper (Appendix B) include organizational mission and vision as they relate to the population health framework, identification of the resource gap in terms of people and technology, defined measurable success goals, and roadmap with timeline.

Empanelment and Attribution

The recent emphasis on quality performance has led many organizations to rate providers and even adjust pay based on quality measure performance. It is not uncommon for a provider to question the fairness of this rating by stating, "those aren't my patients." To address this concern and ensure that the population health tools report the correct patients to their doctors for follow-up, an empanelment process must be established. From the care provider's perspective, the collective group of all the patients under his, her, or their care is called a panel, and active management of the patient–provider relationship is called empanelment. Attribution, on the other hand, is the algorithmic assignment of a care provider to a patient for the purpose of quality reporting. Both empanelment and attribution create the first link in a chain of responsibility for each patient. Manual panel management can be particularly important in specialty clinics because the patient–provider relationship may be less clear than that of the patient to their primary care provider. Examples in the table detail reasons to add, change, or remove a patient from a panel (Table 3.3).

This foundational cornerstone of the patient's healthcare team appears simple but is nuanced, is complex, and has deep ramifications. Establishment of a culture that embraces empanelment is essential to bring population health tools into the forefront. New programs starting a population health intervention frequently need to first establish the patient–provider relationships so that panel assignment is clear. Without accurate assignment of responsibility, patients may receive duplicate outreach from their providers or none at all. Keep in mind that attribution assignments may have legal ramifications, so attribution needs to be accurate and reliable.

Table 3.3 Patient Panel Maintenance Tasks

Task	Reason
Add to patient panel	— A new patient has established care and has not been assigned a care team relationship — An established patient has resumed receiving care by provider
Change patient to different provider panel	— The provider's schedule does not fit the patient's schedule — Personality conflict or patient reports difficulty communicating with provider — The patient is abusive or has violated behavioral or scheduled substance (such as opioid) contracts — The provider cannot provide the care that the patient needs — The patient prefers to see a male, female, or nonbinary provider
Remove from patient panel	— The patient has expired — The patient has moved out of the area — The patient is receiving care from an external provider — The patient was seen for a consult or procedure visit only — The patient was dismissed from the organization

Given that the manual maintenance of patient panel information can be onerous, provider performance on quality metrics typically uses automated **attribution** of a patient to primary care provider (PCP) based on care history. The CMS attributed provider is based on primary care services only. More than one attribution algorithm may be used in a single organization. For example, the following algorithm assumes that a patient can only have one attributed PCP and that patients dismissed from care by a provider (disempaneled) may not be reassigned to that provider.

- If a patient has had a completed visit with their current assigned PCP in the last 36 months, that provider is their attributed PCP.
- If a patient does not have a listed PCP or has not had a visit with their assigned PCP in the last 36 months, they are assigned the provider with whom they have completed the most visits.

If a patient has specialists on their care team, they are attributed to the provider from that team with the most visits per specialty. If the patient does not have providers from a particular specialty on their care team, they will be attributed to the provider with the most visits for that specialty. Mid-level providers (physician assistants, nurse practitioners, etc.) cannot be attributed as specialists.

Example:

- Dr. A is a cardiologist on the care team with whom patient had two visits.
- Dr. B is a cardiologist from same department who saw patient three times.

Patient is attributed to Dr. A due to care team inclusion.

Team-Based Care and Care Management

Traditionally, many healthcare organizations use a care model of one patient to one doctor who works with one nurse. Now team-based care is viewed as a necessity for many high-performing practices. Population health methods for panel management enable patients to receive proactive outreach from the clinic when evidence-based care is due or overdue. Routine functions not requiring clinical decisions can be carried out by unlicensed personnel using standing orders on approved clinical protocols.[30] The use of a care team to assist the provider with outreach to patients with care gaps reduces the overall cost of care by shifting routine, evidence-based care to frontline clinical staff like medical assistants (MAs), licensed vocational nurses (LVNs), registered nurses (RNs), or social workers (MSWs). The patient may have additional doctors and nurses, as well as other key clinical team members, such as pharmacy, psychology, navigation, case management, nutrition, quality nurse, and so on.

A transformation from traditional models to team-based care is a difficult process that affects every member of a clinic. People must be trained for new tasks and roles, and the hand-off and communication tasks are increased. A large regional Veterans' Health Administration study concluded that in the first two years post-implementation of team-based care, physicians' largely reported that they completed the majority of clinical tasks without the help of their teams.[31] In those same clinics, the majority of RNs and licensed practical nurses reported that they were relied upon for the same clinical tasks such as handling disability forms, responding to patient messages, and educating patients about medication or self-care. This raises interesting questions about the suboptimal understanding between nurses and PCPs regarding task allocation and the greater issue of physician dissatisfaction and burnout. A systematic review of the literature found that the prevalence of burnout exceeds 50%.[32] A call for action in the *Lancet* warned, "Physicians, disillusioned by the productivity orientation of administrators and absence of affirmation for the values and relationships that sustain their sense of purpose, need enlightened leaders who recognize that medicine is a human endeavor and not an assembly line."[33] Although this is a complex problem beyond the scope of this book, it is especially important for designers of clinical workflows and EHR tools to recognize and evaluate their impact on provider experience.

Promoting Information Flow Using a Communication Plan

Large, complex organizations are constantly evolving in response to new requirements, objectives, and targets. Careful planning of the flow of information will help leadership promote new initiatives and track consistent progress toward goals. How do these changes become integrated across an organization? One way is to establish communication and decision-making touchpoints that bring key individuals together on a recurring schedule to address a particular aspect of the innovation cycle.

OCHIN (Oregon Community Health Information Network) hosts a single shared instance of the Epic® EHR system for over 100 independent clinical organizations across the United States. Although site-specific customization is often possible to meet clinics' unique needs and workflows, there are areas of EHR functionality and content that must be shared across organizations. OCHIN's Epic system connects more than 10,000 providers across the country. As such, having a robust system of collective input and collaborative decision-making that includes providers' perspectives is critical.

CASE STUDY: PROVIDER ENGAGEMENT AT OCHIN

Erik Geissal, MD, FACP

The collaborative governance and development at OCHIN are anchored in a twice-monthly, two-hour interactive webinar series called the Primary Care Clinical Operations Review Committee (PC-CORC). This workgroup features presenters from OCHIN and member organizations and covers content including upcoming EHR changes, timely hot topics, significant clinical programs or campaigns, and updates from prior CORCs.

Along with the PC-CORC, there is also a Dental CORC to discuss issues related to Epic's dental module, a Population Health and Analytics CORC, a Behavioral Health CORC, and an Infectious Disease CORC. These specialty CORCs convene less frequently than the PC-CORC, typically monthly, but are important, as they allow for in-depth conversations on topics that may not be as relevant to the general clinical population.

While OCHIN strives to maintain the CORC structure to ensure collaborative-wide buy-in and input, we have learned there are longitudinal issues that are best solved in a series of ad hoc discussions with a few subject matter experts. For example, when OCHIN realized we needed to holistically rethink several build decisions around women's health, we developed an ad hoc group that met multiple times over several months. This group definitively tackled issues related to recording obstetric history, streamlining contraception ordering, and age limits around asking about pregnancy intention, among other topics. These ad hoc groups typically are composed of one or more OCHIN facilitators and 5 to 10 interested clinical members.

OCHIN has also been growing the Provider Builder Program, through which clinicians at a provider level (MD/DO/DMD/DDS/NP/PA) are trained at Epic headquarters to build functionality into the EHR, much like an analyst. OCHIN's Provider Builders, once certified by Epic, undergo extensive training on managing change within the EHR system and are paired with an OCHIN clinical analyst. These providers are given access to the development environment with the expectation that they will build content and functionality for their own organization. The added benefit of this program is that their work can be shared across the OCHIN collaborative if it is broadly applicable. Roughly one-quarter of OCHIN member organizations currently have a Provider Builder either certified or in training.

There is also a need for OCHIN to discuss high-level programmatic considerations with clinical executives at OCHIN member organizations. Led by OCHIN's chief medical officer, the Clinical Oversight Group (COG) is co-chaired by two medical directors from the OCHIN membership. Meeting online on a quarterly basis, the COG discusses a variety of technology-related issues, such as mitigation strategies for provider burnout, OpenNotes, and regulatory reporting.

Finally, to further engage with clinical staff, OCHIN hosts an annual three-day conference called the Learning Forum. All members are invited to travel to Portland, Oregon, to join a highly engaging set of presentations by OCHIN staff and members to collaborate, share best practices, and provide feedback.

CASE EXERCISE

Think of an organization you are familiar with, or plan a local site visit to study applied population health communication strategies. Then, complete Table 3.4 by entering the participants, meeting format, and frequency of regularly scheduled meetings/events to develop/disseminate organizational change. You may refer back to the OCHIN model for meeting formats, or use your creativity to adapt to the plan to local needs.

Table 3.4   Population Health Communication Plan

Purpose	Participants	Format	Frequency
Upcoming EHR changes Hot topics Clinical programs Quality campaigns			
Mitigation strategies for provider burnout OpenNotes			
Ad hoc longitudinal issues Specific topics: OB history data collection Streamlined contraception ordering			
Executive oversight			
Clinical oversight Regulatory reporting Local priorities			
Dissemination of best practices, networking			

Conclusion

Engaging executives in building a population health culture and creating functional teams that can convert vision into a transformative culture of value-based care delivery is necessary, yet not a sufficient first step. As a result of their efforts on pay-for-performance programs and risk-based contracting, a number of health systems are now adept at driving clinical processes to reliably cover the eligible population through the use of data-driven teams as described in this chapter. In the future, we expect health systems to more commonly deploy financial analysts for more sophisticated cost accounting and cash flow analyses of work processes and quality projects. Similarly, we expect the intersection between clinical research and value-based care to result in the addition of research analysts to quality workgroups to more scientifically evaluate clinical outcomes that may stretch beyond the single measurement year.

Understanding Patients and Patient Groups

The ability to define and manage groups of patients (cohorting) is of growing importance in healthcare delivery. Michael Porter and Elizabeth

Teisberg propose that health delivery should be organized into units by condition called integrated practice units (IPUs). These units then can better serve a distinct group of patients and be accountable to their outcomes and cost.[34] Consider, for example, patients with pulmonary embolus who have symptoms with walking due to shortness of breath. An IPU that is skilled in the management of pulmonary hypertension and the related risks from venous thrombosis can define the care plan and follow-up for that patient. According to the International Consortium for Health Outcomes Measurement (ICHOM), these outcomes should result in functional improvement and better foster the capability to lead normal and productive lives.[35] Implementation of this vision requires a technology platform that includes registries for robust cohorting functionality.

Social Determinants of Health

Increasingly, health systems and payors are interested in building systems to help address social determinants. It has been estimated that a substantial proportion of health behaviors and outcomes are influenced by environmental, social, and other factors.[36] Yet without systematic and standardized measurement of the social determinants of health, how can one address them? Today's EHRs are capable of discretely storing a variety of social determinants, including mental (stress, anxiety, depression), substance use (alcohol, illicit and prescription drugs, tobacco), economic determinants (food instability, access to fresh food, housing instability, inadequate transportation), violence, loneliness (social isolation), physical activity (fitness), and legal status (migrant, immigrant, etc.). Although these new categories of data are becoming more common in the EHR, practical considerations still abound, such as: 1) Would the patient, registrar, health navigator, or someone else complete the assessment? 2) Is the patient ready for additional services to address the barrier? 3) What are the possible unintended consequences of this data collection? 4) Who has access to this data? 5) Who from the health team or community is responsible to intervene when there are identified risks? 6) Is the current method of intervention making a difference?

Race, Ethnicity, and Language Standard

Race and ethnicity, once considered to be biologically determined at birth, emerge from geographic, social, and cultural forces and are potentially fluid.[37] The 2010 Census questionnaire was the original model for collection of the race and ethnicity data in certified EHRs. U.S. race and ethnicity will continue to be collected according to this definition at least through the 2020 Census for the purpose of distributing congressional seats and planning and allocating federal funds. Currently, most EHR systems follow some version of this standard, with minor variations in wording and grouping. The ethnicity question was asked first in order to group people of Hispanic, Latino, or Spanish origin (Figure 3.4). Answers of Yes were further categorized as Mexican, Puerto Rican, Cuban, or Another such as Argentinean, Columbian, and so on.

A second question, "What is the person's race," had 15 choices: White, Black, American Indian or Alaska Native, Asian Indian, Chinese, Filipino, Japanese, Korean, Vietnamese, Other Asian, Native Hawaiian, Guamanian or Chamorro, Samoan, Other Pacific Islander, and Some Other Race (Figure 3.5).

The Public Hospital Redesign and Incentives in Medi-Cal (PRIME) Medicaid Waiver program in California challenged participating health systems to adopt the CDC Race Ethnicity Categories (CDCREC). Unlike the one-level convention for race/ethnicity questions used in the Census, the CDCREC convention has a two-level hierarchy for race and ethnicity.[38] A new data field called "Ethnic Background" was deployed in the EHR to facilitate collection of CDCREC Level 2 details for both "Race" and "Ethnicity" (Figure 3.6). The approach avoided the reconfiguration of over 50 EHR computer interfaces, which would have been required if any codes were added to existing Level 1 race and ethnicity lists. The approach also improved the patient-centeredness of the data collection by combining detailed race (e.g., "Chinese") and detailed ethnicity (e.g., "Cuban") on the same list. A multiselect "Ethnic Background" enables a patient to self-identify (e.g., Hispanic Chinese Latin American Peruvian) outside the standard roll-up hierarchies.

Some health systems opted to collect the CDCREC demographic data on paper forms with over 50 options for ethnic background (Figure 3.7). A paper form somewhat limits the number of options due to space constraints. Legacy data already collected by health systems over the years to identify their local patient demographics may include options not offered in Figure 3.7. A fully electronic conversion to the CDCREC codes at our academic health center took approximately six months and included 133 options for ethnic background. Appendix A includes the mapping from legacy data to Level 1 race and ethnicity data. Also

CENSUS QUESTION FOR ETHNICITY DEMOGRAPHICS

IS THIS PERSON OF HISPANIC, LATINO, OR SPANISH ORIGIN?

- [ ] No, not of Hispanic, Latino, or Spanish origin
- [ ] Yes, Mexican, Mexican American, Chicano
- [ ] Yes, Puerto Rican
- [ ] Yes, Cuban
- [ ] Yes, another Hispanic, Latino, or Spanish origin- *Print origin, for example, Argentinean, Colombian, Dominican, Nicaraguan, Salvadoran, Spaniard, and so on*

Figure 3.4   2010 Census question for ethnicity demographics.

CENSUS QUESTION FOR RACE DEMOGRAPHICS

WHAT IS THE PERSON'S RACE? *Mark X in one or more boxes.*

- [ ] White
- [ ] Black, African American, or Negro
- [ ] American Indian or Alaska Native – *Print name of enrolled or principal tribe.*

- [ ] Asian Indian
- [ ] Chinese
- [ ] Filipino
- [ ] Other Asian – *Print race, for example, Hmong, Laotian, Thai, Pakistani, Cambodian, and so on.*

- [ ] Japanese
- [ ] Korean
- [ ] Vietnamese

- [ ] Native Hawaiian
- [ ] Guamanian or Chamorro
- [ ] Samoan
- [ ] Other Pacific Islander – *Print race, for example Fijian, Tongan, and so on.*

- [ ] Some other race – *Print race.*

Figure 3.5   2010 Census question for race demographics.

included is an ethnic background crosswalk to detailed mapping and conversion processes at that site.

The California PRIME experience with race and ethnicity data collection offers several lessons applicable nationally. First, a true standard for race

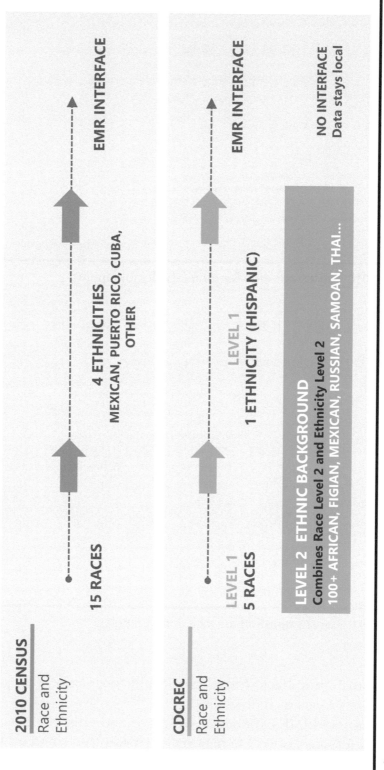

Figure 3.6   Race and ethnicity data conventions: 2010 Census versus CDCREC.

Now we would like you to tell us your **Race and Ethnic Background**. We use this information to review the treatment patients receive and make sure everyone receives the highest quality of care.

First, do you consider yourself Hispanic/Latino: ☐ Yes ☐ No ☐ Decline to state

Please tell us your **Race**. By race, we mean the major world group or groups from which your ancestors came.

☐ African American or Black	☐ Asian	☐ Decline to state
☐ American Indian or Alaska Native	☐ White	☐ Unable to respond
☐ Native Hawaiian or other Pacific Islander	☐ Other: _____	☐ Unavailable or unknown

We would like you to describe your **Ethnic Background**. By ethnic background, we mean the group or groups with whom you share your cultural identity or customs. *Please, check as many categories as you need to describe your specific ethnicity.*

☐ African	☐ Chicano	☐ Iranian	☐ Mexican American	☐ South American Indian
☐ Black or African American	☐ Chinese	☐ Israeli	☐ Mexican American Indian	☐ Taiwanese
☐ Alaskan Native	☐ Croatian	☐ Italian		☐ Thai
☐ Armenian	☐ Cuban	☐ Japanese	☐ Mien	☐ Tongan
☐ Arab	☐ Dominican	☐ Jamaican	☐ Native Hawaiian	☐ Vietnamese
☐ Asian Indian	☐ European	☐ Korean	☐ Other Pacific Islander	☐ Other: _____
☐ California Tribes	☐ Fijian	☐ Laotian	☐ Polish	☐ Decline to state
☐ Cambodian	☐ Filipino	☐ Malaysian	☐ Puerto Rican	☐ Unable to respond
☐ Central American	☐ French	☐ Micronesian	☐ Russian	☐ Unavailable or unknown
☐ Chamorro	☐ German	☐ Middle Eastern	☐ Samoan	
☐ Cherokee	☐ Hmong	☐ North African	☐ Scottish	
	☐ Irish	☐ Mexican	☐ South American	

Figure 3.7 Example of paper form collection of CDCREC data.

and ethnicity data collection in the EHR does not exist. There is wide variation in the implementation of data collection in the EHR both for reporting in government-funded research and for CMS billing and quality measure reporting. The implementation of many options for ethnic background would allow the roll-up of these categories to any level of aggregation desired for the purpose at hand, but managing lists of hundreds of options is difficult for EHR analysts, as well as for patients who may identify with multiple options or none. We found that patients who identified as belonging to black or white races frequently did not identify with any further detail for ethnic background. To facilitate the completion of the ethnic background information for these groups, it was helpful to add an option for "additional ethnic background details do not apply."

Lastly, the characteristics of the data collection should match the use case for the data. Whereas the political use case for census data is well defined, the use case for race and ethnicity in clinical records is more diffuse. Identified use cases include targeting culturally appropriate care, identification and mitigation of health disparities, and development of richer databases for medical studies inclusive of minority populations. There may be other use cases as of yet not identified or funded. There will likely be ongoing discussion around this topic for some time to come.

CASE STUDY: LESSONS LEARNED ON PATIENT PERCEPTION OF ETHNIC BACKGROUND

A case study on the implementation of the race, ethnicity, and language (REAL) demographic standard in the EHR system of an academic medical center illustrates the challenge of collecting detailed race information. Mid-year performance on a REAL data completeness quality measure for the PRIME program provides insight into the granularity of race data that has been collected to date. Patients pass the measure when all five data elements of the REAL standard are complete (general and detail race, general and detail ethnicity, and language).

EVALUATION RESULTS

Mid-cycle REAL data completeness post-conversion was 12%, with completion of detailed race being the primary reason for exclusion from the numerator. No more than 2% of the detailed races were documented for 86% of the measure population ("White," "Other or Mixed Race," "Black or African American," "American Indian or Alaska Native," and "Unknown"). "Asian" detail completion was 22%, and "Native Hawaiian or Other Pacific Islander" was 98%. Missing values at the general race and ethnicity levels were not significant.

CONCLUSIONS

Accurate demographic data entry is vital to identification of health disparities. Measurement incentives may promote accurate data capture. However, it is not clear how to appropriately credit the majority of the population who may self-identify as "American," "White," or "Black" with no further subdivision. We feel that this quality improvement effort highlights the need for further evaluation of demographic data collection, enhancement of the REAL standard, and data-informed benchmarks for demographic quality measures.

Sexual Orientation and Gender Identity

SOGI Standard

In order to provide care that is culturally appropriate and respectful, knowing whether a person's gender identity matches their legal sex is important. Additionally, sexual orientation, which may influence sexual behaviors and risk, is also clinically relevant. In modern EHR data, this information can be collected from patients as legal sex (male, female, nonbinary, unknown), gender identity, sexual orientation, sex assigned at birth, sex-related organ inventory, pharmacologic therapy, preferred name, and preferred pronoun. Keep in mind that local, state, and national terminology sets may vary in their depth and adoption of the specific terminology and mappings.

The collection of holistic demographic data at the same time as the more sensitive sexual orientation and gender identity questions may ease the process of data collection to a degree. The data collection form called REAL ME starts with the input of the patient's preferred name and then continues to the race, ethnicity, and language questions. The third part of the REAL ME form includes sexual orientation, gender identity, and sex assigned at birth. An enterprise-wide implementation and training effort helped clinical staff become more comfortable with asking these questions and explaining that patients had a right to refuse to answer them. The same data entry form was also offered in the patient portal for those who would rather type their responses than disclose them to a medical assistant or nurse.

Data collection efforts were successful in capturing the new sexual orientation and gender identity data for over 29% (11,268/37,790) of our University of California San Diego Health (UCSDH) PRIME-eligible population in the first year.

Finding and Addressing Health Disparities

Disagreements exist regarding distinctions between the terms "disparity," "inequality," and "inequity" as they are applied to healthcare and outcomes. A health disparity should be viewed as a chain of events signified by a difference in 1) environment; 2) access to, utilization of, and quality of care; 3) health status; or 4) a particular health outcome that deserves scrutiny.[39] When stratifying a quality measure by racial and/or ethnic groups, how do we know whether unequal performance between groups is significant and whether that a measurement that appears unequal is possibly unfair?

One method to evaluate a health disparity is to compare the differences between two groups within a race-stratified measure. The Chi-square goodness of fit statistic can be used to determine whether the distribution of the scores fits with the population distribution and whether or not those differences are statistically significant.[40]

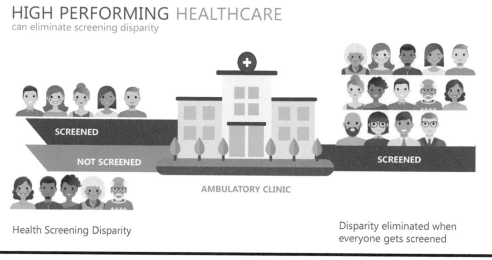

Figure 3.8 High-performing healthcare can eliminate screening disparity.

For example, to pass a common tobacco assessment and cessation measure, each patient is screened for tobacco use, and smokers are offered an intervention such as a referral to a smoking cessation hotline. In an experience at our organization, we documented that blacks were being screened and referred to a smoking cessation hotline at a lower rate than other races. To remediate this disparity, we implemented a high-reliability process to contact every person failing the tobacco measure. Starting with the black patients, the outreach nurse was able to contact each person with a tobacco care gap to offer the intervention. This technique quickly eliminated the disparity but also raised the overall performance. It is important to note that highly reliable healthcare processes help eliminate disparities by moving all patients in to a healthier status (Figure 3.8).

Patient Engagement

In the population health model, patients are not told what to do, but are engaged in decision-making that respects their wellness and lifestyle goals. At the minimum level of **engagement in care**, patients must show up for appointments. In chronic care management of HIV, **"retention,"** defined as a provider visit within a six-month period, has become an important quality metric, as it independently predicts failure to adhere to antiretroviral therapy, increased viral load (with corresponding risk of transmission), and mortality. Naturally, retention in care will vary based on a patient's chronic illness and multimorbidity. A study of a single urban academic clinic serving 2,776 active HIV-positive patients identified 25.8% (716/2,776) of patients who had not been retained in care.[41] The project located 87.7% of these patients of which 58.5% were actively in care at the end of the study.[41] Although this is a small study, it suggests a process to account for lost–to–follow-up patients and re-engage them in care or remove them from the active patient panel. From the perspective of payors and health entities bearing full-risk contracting, creating the right engagement in care is beneficial to all by improved screening, early detection, treatment goal achievement, and long-term relationships. Although charts may capture "the data," human relationships and understanding also are foundational for fostering long-term healing. Processes that help organizations maintain the right "stickiness" are likely beneficial to all.

Chapter 4

Process.

Clinical process measures are the bread and butter of healthcare quality measurement. The intervention context of the value-based measurement framework separates clinical quality measures from measures of waste, efficiency, and safety (Figure 4.1). Historically, healthcare efforts to avoid waste and improve efficiency have been carried out in separate silos from clinical quality improvement. Lean methods or similar process improvement approaches tend to focus on reduction in waste. The knowledge and methods required for process improvement overlap in these three areas, but often the goals differ. It should not be assumed that efforts to meet clinical quality

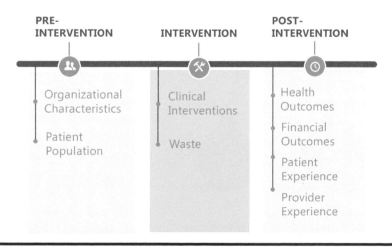

VALUE-BASED MEASUREMENT FRAMEWORK

PRE-INTERVENTION	INTERVENTION	POST-INTERVENTION
Organizational Characteristics	Clinical Interventions	Health Outcomes
Patient Population	Waste	Financial Outcomes
		Patient Experience
		Provider Experience

Figure 4.1   Intervention context of value-based measurement framework.

goals will automatically reduce waste. In fact, without careful planning and measurement, new clinical interventions to drive quality targets may actually raise the cost of care in the short term and possibly introduce wasteful practices. Just as a single health intervention has outcomes that can be assessed in the domains of the quadruple aim, health systems should move toward the integration of efforts to simultaneously evolve reliable, effective, safe, and efficient processes.

Clinical Interventions

Cascade of Care

Within the range of clinical interventions subject to value-based reporting, the cascade of care provides a way to view healthcare processes as a continuum from prevention to early identification, treatment, and recovery (Figure 4.2). The Cascade of Care model was developed for use in the diagnosis and treatment of HIV/AIDS. The National Institute on Drug Abuse (NIDA) recommends the cascade as a framework of care for opioid use disorder,[42] and it can be applied as well to population health activities. Prevention includes immunizations and interventions to reduce risk factors like tobacco use. Early identification helps identify patients with the target condition and engage them for treatment. Each treatment has a success rate such that the number of recovered patients is less than the number of those treated. The size of the drop represents the relative number of people in

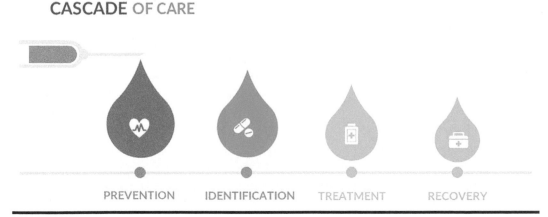

CASCADE OF CARE

PREVENTION   IDENTIFICATION   TREATMENT   RECOVERY

Figure 4.2   Cascade of Care model.

each group. For a given health condition such as hepatitis C, HIV, opioid use, etc., the prevention group will be the largest and will exclude patients who have been diagnosed with the condition. Similarly, when setting performance goals, the benchmark targets will also have a similar cascade, with higher expected completion rates for prevention and identification interventions than for treatment and recovery.

Prevention

Nearly everyone is eligible for prevention interventions to prevent injury and illness. They may be as simple as a reminder to wear seatbelts to more comprehensive recommendations for diet and exercise. In primary care the goal is to keep a person in a state of wellness. Immunizations directly improve the likelihood of the patient avoiding an illness, and other primary prevention interventions seek to reduce risk through early intervention of modifiable risk factors, often in the area of lifestyle and behavior changes. Screening for tobacco use and providing cessation interventions falls into the latter category. The delivery of prevention interventions to patients currently in care is largely the responsibility of the health system, although some patients may refuse. In general, high levels of completion are common for immunizations, screenings, and assessments.

Identification

In some cases, whole patient populations may be screened for a condition of concern. Patient questionnaires for universal depression screenings are relatively easy to administer and are deployed in this manner in some healthcare systems. In other cases, a smaller group of patients with higher-risk demographics, family history, or social history may be prioritized for screenings to identify the condition of concern. Laboratory screening tests such as those used for patients with diabetes (hemoglobin A1c) and heart risk (low-density cholesterol [LDL]) are also low cost and low risk. Performance measures for screenings can trend toward 100%. These types of activities are particularly amenable to efficiencies of scale, including automated reminders and bulk ordering via protocol.

Procedural screenings such as mammograms for breast cancer and colonoscopy for colon cancer have a higher cost and are perceived as more invasive. They also have inherent logistical barriers, such as making a separate appointment and scheduling time for the procedure. These barriers

FIELD REPORT

COLON CANCER SCREENING

Eligible patients age 50-75 years
must complete one of the interventions
during the measurement year.

Fecal occult blood test
Flexible sigmoidoscopy
Colonoscopy
FITDNA test
CT Colonography

Methods:

Registries, care alerts, call lists and order protocols
were used to increase screening rates.

Technical challenges:

- Legacy hospital data lacked discrete procedural name(s)
- CPT procedure codes were not available
- Overlapping codes that lack discrimination for accuracy
- Unclear selection of screening protocol
- Incomplete problem list documentation for patients with cancer exclusion

Figure 4.3   Field report: Colon cancer screening technical challenges.

reduce the rate of overall completion of procedural screenings. Technical challenges such as those described in our field report on colon cancer screening may also lead to the inability to accurately identify the completion of a procedure or exclude patients who already have the condition (Figure 4.3). Screening sensitivity and specificity indicate the ability of a test to detect a disease and to conclude with confidence that a patient can be excluded from having a disease based on a negative test. Generally, there are trade-offs between sensitivity and specificity, and neither will be 100%. Therefore, once a screening test has become positive, generally additional testing is required that is more invasive and costly to confirm whether the patient actually has the condition. For instance, a patient with an abnormal mammogram will undergo follow-up mammography with additional views, ultrasound, or magnetic resonance imaging (MRI) breast biopsy depending on the findings of a routine mammogram.

Treatment

Only a small proportion of those initially screened will be diagnosed with the condition and offered treatment. Treatment interventions vary in scope, difficulty, cost, and efficacy. Because there is a high degree of dependence on patient adherence and follow-through with treatment plans, these types of measures typically score lower than screening measures. Whereas screening protocols are standardized for large groups of patients, comorbidities, genetic factors, and even personal preferences may play a larger role in the development of a treatment regimen. Currently, population health methods are applied more successfully to standardized treatment protocols, and it remains a challenge to deliver and report personalized treatment plans. Nevertheless, quality reporting methodologies must evolve to address the reality that patients with high comorbidity and complex conditions should not simply be excluded from population measures but should have their own "normal." For instance, it may be more important to measure that some individuals have followed through with their personal treatment plans than to attest that they have achieved a particular standard of care.

Recovery

The recovery group will be the smallest of all. Behavioral and biological factors of the patient, as well as treatment efficacy, all play a part in whether the treatment is successful. HIV and hepatitis C are infectious diseases in which an undetectable viral load provides quantitative evidence of a successful outcome. However, with other chronic conditions such as diabetes, an intermediate outcome such as a controlled A1c, is not a true indicator of the overall course of the disease. Diabetes may predispose a patient to kidney failure, heart disease, and blindness as well. In such cases, it's not that our medical community doesn't know how to arrive at outcomes, but rather that within a single health system for any given treatment intervention, the quality reporting period may be too short, sample sizes too small, and individual multimorbidity too complex to draw defensible conclusions regarding the success of a treatment plan. Of course, health systems can provide some easy answers, such as was patient's A1c lab value less than 8 at the end of the measurement period? Was the blood pressure (BP) controlled as defined by a systolic BP less than 140 and diastolic BP less than 90 at the end of the measurement period? These are just snapshots of a longitudinal process that may have individual patients moving in and out of controlled states multiple times.

Harmonize Measures

If quality is viewed as both a healthcare deliverable and a revenue stream in the context of value-based care, then centralization and standardization of

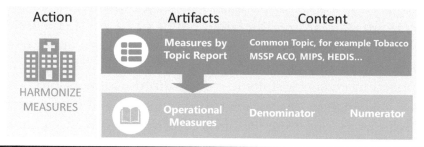

Figure 4.4   Harmonize measures.

applied population health activities across the organization become imperative. Population definitions and measure specifications that overlap yet vary across quality programs must be harmonized to develop *operational measures* that drive the clinical care delivery in the electronic health record (EHR) (Figure 4.4).

The extent of this phenomenon is described by quality program manager, Scott Thompson, RN, MBA:

> Between quality programs, we have about 150 unique measures that are reported over 250 times across the nine programs we're tracking. Resource planning in light of this overlap is significantly different than for unique, stand-alone measures. Information about the overlap helps with prioritizing measures that impact the most programs.[25]

The National Quality Forum (NQF) recognizes that variation in overlapping measure specifications can lead to "confusion about interpretation of measure results, inability to compare results across settings or populations, increased data collection burden, and even an adverse effect on the validity of a measure."[43] Measure specifications may vary somewhat in the rules to achieve a passing status in the numerator, yet clinicians within a health enterprise should be held to the same standard of care for all similar patients. The NQF guidance for measure harmonization was adapted for use in the EHR applied population health practice. The goal for the applied population health program is not to rewrite any of the overlapping measures, but to develop a harmonized operational measure set that will support consistent clinical practice, use of EHR tools, and reporting across an organization.

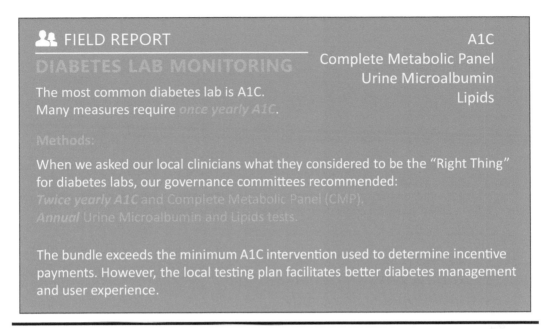

Figure 4.5   Field report: Diabetes lab monitoring.

Quality programs often include one or more quality measures requiring laboratory monitoring for patients with a diagnosis of diabetes. When designing work processes for clinical care, "doing the right thing" is an effective strategy for aligning clinical practice with measure goals. When clinical protocols, standard work, and decision algorithms are supported by individual clinicians, as well as their governing committees, a positive message of pride in providing the right care will strengthen efforts to drive quality performance independent of incentive payments or penalties (Figure 4.5).

Create a Population Health Protocol

Having agreed upon the operational measures, a population health protocol is needed to formalize the standard work, that is, work that is expected to be completed every time (Figure 4.6). Appendix E provides a template for documenting the five rights (i.e., the who, what, when, how, and by whom) for each measure. It includes a policy and a procedure, and clearly states the conditions concordant with state law under which registered nurses (RNs) may place orders for specific interventions based on clinical decision support in the EHR. For the purpose of registry design, the who, what, and when are the critical elements. We will return to the how and by whom when we discuss the clinical decision support tools later in this chapter.

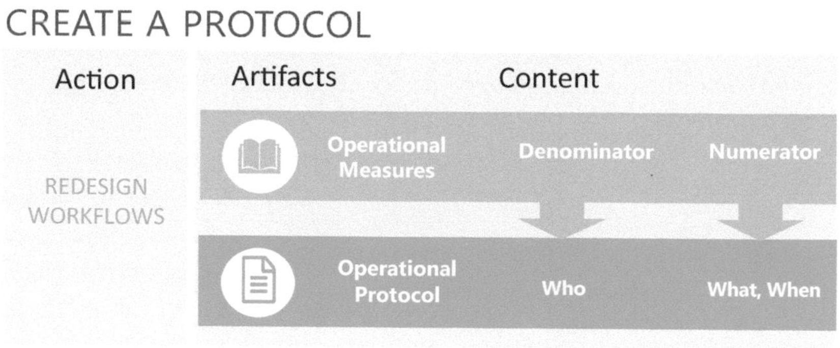

CREATE A PROTOCOL

Action	Artifacts		Content	
		Operational Measures	Denominator	Numerator
REDESIGN WORKFLOWS		Operational Protocol	Who	What, When

Figure 4.6   Create a protocol to deliver operational measures.

Who Signs the Order That Enables Bulk Processes for Population Health?

Protocol development required approval of the Quality department and primary care medical directors with relevant input from physicians in other disciplines. Initially, at our organization, the protocol was managed by the medical director at each practice. Due to inconsistent performance across the practices, the medical directors and clinical service chiefs agreed to central ownership by the clinically active Chief Medical Information Officer. This has proven the simplest method for signing the master order that enables protocol-driven activity.

How Do Nurses Function Using This Health Maintenance Protocol Process to Provide Bulk Activities?

Training on the policy and practice of bulk activities has been incorporated into the ambulatory care nurse orientation packet, and these trainings are set up by individual clinic managers for all new hires. Nurses who bulk-order under the ambulatory screening protocol must first pass a competency assessment and repeat the bulk order training assessment annually.

As an example, the following language in the Ambulatory Care Screening Order Protocol identifies **who** is covered under the protocol.

■ *All patients receiving ambulatory care* will be eligible for receiving appropriate health screening and monitoring tests.

Table 4.1   Screening Protocol Interventions and Frequency

Screening and Monitoring Tests	Test Ordered	Frequency
Wellness—All Active Patients		
Breast Screening	Screening Bilateral Mammogram	Annual
Colon Screening	Fecal Immunochemical Test (FIT)	Annual
Osteoporosis Screening	DEXA Scan	Once

■ The Screening Protocol Order is activated by completion of a signed order in the electronic medical record. *The active order enables tests to be ordered under the protocol by RNs.*

 The target population may be further refined for each metric to apply only to patients with a specific diagnosis like diabetes, cardiovascular disease, hypertension, etc.

What and When

The Ambulatory Care Screening Order Protocol lists the approved health screening and frequency. The following excerpt from the protocol shows the wellness category. Each category typically has its own registry. The intervention to be performed (**what**) is listed in the Test Ordered column of Table 4.1. The timing (**when**) is found in the frequency column.

CASE STUDY: DOING THE RIGHT THING . . . WITH MEDICATION MONITORING

Patients taking statins are recommended to complete annual lipid and liver function testing. In order to streamline the workflows, we chose to enable bulk ordering of lab tests for thousands of patients with just a few clicks. The timing of the bulk orders was related to the condition, and we became concerned about patients who had multiple conditions. For example, if a patient had diabetes and was also on a statin, would they need multiple trips to the lab to draw all the necessary tests? Would they miss important additional tests that are also due to be completed?

Discussion questions:

1. How would you resolve the potential conflict in timing of the lab tests for patients with diabetes and on statins?
2. What are the possible patient benefits of using applied population health methods monitoring other medication such as warfarin? (Hint: Search for warfarin.)
3. In your personal experience, are compliance rates for medication monitoring routinely measured by health systems? Should they be monitored? Why or why not?

Direct and Indirect Interventions

Clinical interventions encompass a wide range of health services that include physical examinations, laboratory tests, procedures, medications, etc. In value-based care, whatever is reported and incentivized can be referred to as the primary intervention. Indirect interventions include the tasks that must be completed as a prerequisite or that support the completion direct intervention in some way. Understanding all of the steps required to complete a direct measure such as a lab test or examination is the first step to analyzing potential indirect interventions, including automation such as alerts, bulk orders, and messaging. Associations between common direct and indirect population health interventions are illustrated in Figure 4.7. For example, the population of patients with diabetes is to receive direct interventions of A1c and LDL lab tests every year, and a prerequisite task is to place the orders to perform that test. Automation of the order process through protocol-based bulk orders will ensure that any failure to meet this measure is not due to missing orders. However, the order does not guarantee that each patient with an order will understand and remember that they need an office or lab visit to monitor their condition. A supportive task of bulk electronic messages may also be automated to increase the likelihood that the tests will be completed on schedule. Even without reminder messages, there is a measurable probability that the lab tests will be completed, but chances are improved with the messages. Automation of indirect interventions may be a cost-effective way to improve the completion of chronic care regimens, but automation is not always required. Physical screenings such as diabetic foot

DIRECT AND INDIRECT HEALTH INTERVENTIONS

📊		Indirect Measures	
		Prerequisite	*Supportive*
🧪	Lab test (A1c, LDL)	Lab Order	Bulk electronic reminder messages
🩺	Exam (Vitals)	Appointment	Direct mail reminder
💊	Procedure (Colonoscopy)	Insurance Authorization	In-clinic Poster campaign
➕	Med Management (Statin)	Referral to pharmacist	In-clinic pharmacist consultations

Figure 4.7   Associations between common direct and indirect population health interventions.

exams cannot be completed without an appointment, and personal outreach from clinic staff may be the preferred method for some providers to meet this requisite intervention. A birthday card sent to a patient with a quick reminder to schedule an appointment would serve as another type of supportive intervention. For every direct clinical intervention, there may be one or many indirect interventions, and the challenge is to iteratively improve the workflow processes to the point that direct measure performance meets the goal in a sustainable way.

Value Improvement Cycles

The work of driving healthcare value through continuous value improvement cycles is inherently different from traditional quality programs that only judge a health system's performance through a limited sampling of retrospective measurements. The latter practice of yearly reporting gives no visibility to the trajectory of performance over time. Compare the longitudinal performance of the two measures in Figure 4.8. On the retrospective annual quality report, both measures finished the reporting year above the target threshold, although their paths were very different. Measure A, screening for clinical depression, started the year as a failing measure, as this was a new practice. Early in the measurement year, a timer was added to the depression screening questionnaire so that it would automatically appear along with the other routine check-in question whenever it was due. We use the term, "timer" to refer to an automated intervention scheduling tool in the EHR (see chapter 11 The When: Intervention Scheduling). This change in the standard work performed at office visits was immediately reflected in improved

HIGH RELIABILITY PROCESSES TREND TOWARD 100%

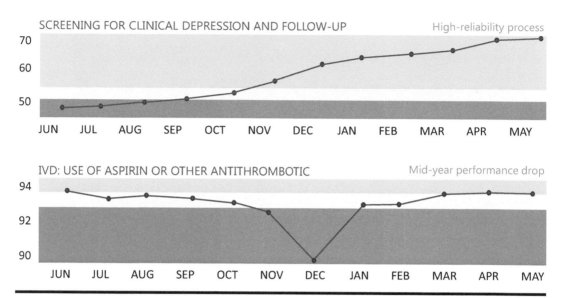

Figure 4.8 Longitudinal performance measurement reveals patterns that can't be seen in annual quality reports.

depression screening scores. The improvement continued throughout the year at a nearly constant rate and will naturally trend toward 100%. With the timely prompting of the EHR, the longitudinal measurement reflects a highly reliable process at work. In contrast, Measure B, use of aspirin for vascular disease, began the year in a passing state due to the efforts applied in the previous reporting period. Unlike the simple timing requirement for the depression screening, the aspirin measure required a higher level of clinical decision-making. The EHR decision support for this measure used registries to find patients with ischemic vascular disease who were not already taking aspirin and a time to indicate that an assessment for aspirin therapy was recommended. An RN was temporarily assigned to review patients flagged for assessment. The nursing intervention was very successful, yet without operational funding to sustain the intervention, the follow-up on the intervention waned mid-year. When it became apparent that the technology was not self-sustaining without the nurse intervention, the aspirin outreach was restarted, and the high level of performance was restored. It is worth noting that quality incentive programs pay for performance after the fact and only if successful. There may be little or no funding in the operational budget dedicated to building the quality infrastructure and maintaining the staffing to deliver sustainable performance. Consequently, the organization may temporarily prioritize quality efforts, pirating people (time, energy, focus) to achieve the goals. Once the race to finish is over, however, people return to their customary tasks. Without meetings, leadership, a commitment to sustainability and prioritized time to remain engaged in the quality activity, the performance is likely to trend downward from peak performance. The result is a great deal of stress and effort applied for a short period, contributing to fatigue and burnout.

The stale construct of retrospective measurement is insufficient to efficiently and effectively drive quality. In contrast, the goal of modern high-reliability process design is to build standard work processes expected from everyone, every time. Similar to other industries, modern continuous quality improvement considers process, demand, and resourcing so as to iteratively adjust the approach.

Iterative learning cycles combined with continuous process measurement are effective tools for achieving sustainable, high-reliability population health interventions. Just as a continuous flow of information helps the body adjust to changes in the environment or level of activity, population health systems rely on continuous process measurement to regulate the timing of health screenings, wellness interventions, or chronic care management such as laboratory tests or medication management.

A conceptual model of a value-based learning cycle illustrates how measurements are compared to a quality goal to determine whether a value improvement project is needed (Figure 4.9). The baseline is the reference measurement at the start point used for comparison to future performance. If the baseline measurement is greater than or equal to the quality goal, in other words "passing," an abbreviated cycle of process measurement and evaluation will commence. As long as future measurements meet or exceed the goal, then no further improvement efforts are required. However, if the measurement at baseline or at any time in the future falls short of the goal, then actions to improve the process and/or measurement commence. Upon implementation of the improvements, the process and/or measurement will reach a new state, and a new round of measurements will again be compared to the goal. The learning cycle continues until the process reaches a steady state or the time and resources to fuel the cycle run out.

One cycle of improvement may be enough to meet and maintain a process at the quality goal, but quite often, multiple improvement cycles are needed. Because quality programs evaluate performance on a yearly basis,

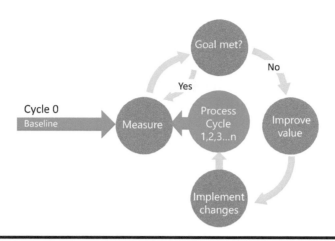

Figure 4.9 Value-based learning cycle.

there is a constant race against the clock. If the time runs out before the performance measure crosses the goal line, then the providers will lose incentive dollars. Additionally, the cost of process improvement is a function of time and is a costly endeavor due to the human resources required. The longer it takes for quality teams to organize, study the process, gather data, design, build, train, and implement a process improvement, the higher the manpower component in the project cost. Anything that can be done to increase efficiency in the learning cycle will increase the likelihood of meeting the goal within the measurement period and also frees up resources to apply to other improvement projects.

Technology Flaws Underlying Healthcare Waste

Bending the curve on the healthcare quality–to–expenditure equation, however, is recognized as requiring a fundamental "re-engineering" of healthcare delivery. Recent studies show that inadequate, unnecessary, uncoordinated, and inefficient care, when combined with suboptimal business practices, may waste on the order of $1 trillion.[6] A 2007 Commonwealth Fund report concluded that the following strategies for reducing the cost of care would be effective and politically popular: "1) eliminating duplicative or unnecessary care and reducing administrative overhead; 2) preventing illnesses

TECHNOLOGY FLAWS UNDERLYING HEALTHCARE WASTE

COMPLEXITY
Why have one
way when we
can have 10?

MISSINGNESS
If I can't find it, the
data's not there

MECHANIZATION
If it works for the
computer, it's fine for
human use

Figure 4.10   Technology flaws underlying healthcare waste.

or complications and detecting conditions at an early stage; 3) avoiding unneeded hospitalizations; and 4) enhancing the productivity and efficiency in the provision of care."[44] These strategies have motivated the growth in regulatory reporting and healthcare quality measurement ever since.

The Lean approach to process management popularized by Japanese auto production is one of several methodologies adapted to address these healthcare goals. The method employed may be less important than the consistent application of a common approach within an organization, and gains are likely to be temporary without the development of technological solutions that make the right action the easiest course of action. Less attention has been paid to the technology flaws underlying healthcare waste: complexity, missingness, and mechanization (Figure 4.10).

Why Have One Way When We Can Have 10?

Complexity flourishes in siloed systems when technological solutions are addressed at the level of a single requester or department without including a broader contingent of stakeholders. As organizations grow, process design often becomes distributed to many individual analysts, whereas a more centralized design process may lead to greater standardization. Complexity and redundancy often go hand in hand. For example, within one health system, we found 12 ways to capture information on advance directives within the EHR. Quality reporting on the completion of advance directives within such an environment is challenging, but so is the data governance effort to convert to a standard data collection process. Complexity of the health lexicon is another example. In the standard practice of diagnosis terminology maintenance, it is quite common for disease concepts to be mapped to thousands of diagnostic terms, and the maintenance of value sets for clinical decision support and quality reporting is a daunting task, which deserves to have its own tools, training, and specialists. The reduction of complexity through data governance and/or the development of computerized tools to manage complexity should be a guiding principle for health systems.

If I Can't Find It, the Data Aren't There . . .

Missingness is the result of both fragmentation of the EHR market and poor data governance within an organization. Years of experience validating quality measures leads us to believe that performance on quality measures is often significantly underreported due to the difficulty of extracting data from the EHR. The reasons for "missing data" include lack of interoperability, inability to interpret free-text clinical notes, lack of data standards for data collection and coding, and work processes that fail to capture the data necessary for process measurement and management. When weighed against the cost of data collection and curation, the cost of missing data can lead to the loss of quality incentive revenue and the waste of resources deployed to solve problems that don't exist or aren't as bad as they seem. In a data-driven organization that recommends and delivers health interventions based on the care history recorded in the EHR, "missing" or "misplaced" data drive waste and have the potential to affect patient care.

If It Works for the Computer, It's Fine for Human Use . . .

Mechanization is a term that captures the failure of healthcare systems to address human needs and constraints in the construction of a complex sociotechnical system. The timeless scene of Lucille Ball trying to keep up with the conveyor belt in the candy factory conveys the sense of machines pushing workers past their capacities. If you haven't seen it or want to see this classic again, search YouTube for "Lucy candy." The assumption that humans can and will always conform to computer demands has underpinned the lack of attention to human factors and usability in healthcare system design. In a sociotechnical system, strengths and limitations of both human beings and computer technology must be addressed for optimal system performance.

Automation that addresses a need with technology support can be powerful and cost-effective. However, in the rush to meet the demands of the growing number of quality reporting requirements, time and resources were generally not allocated to anticipate or correct human factors problems with cognitive load, interruptions, visual complexity, and workload. The impact of poor design can lead to suboptimal performance, burn-out and potentially medical errors.

Fortunately, through innovative strategies, thoughtful design, and effective governance we can begin to remove the burden of complexity, missingness, and mechanization. Health registries provide one way to organize and standardize health data.

Chapter 5

Technology of Health Registries

The term "registry" can be used to refer to any database storing clinical information as a by-product of patient care, but the ambiguous use of the term impedes our ability to retrieve information and study specific types of registries.[45] Registries in the Operational Domain (Figure 5.1) inform and guide clinical care. Actionable registries (A) comprise a subset of operational registries that are embedded within the electronic health record (EHR). This architecture supports greater functionality and increases the efficiency of interventions. Standards of care are interpreted and approved locally, and the resulting clinical protocols inform the design of clinical decision support based on registry inclusion. Quality measurements may be made directly from the actionable EHR or from a data warehouse in which the data storage architecture facilitates quality reporting. The data from the quality measurement process drives the value improvement cycles toward the quality reporting performance targets.

Research registries (B) collect and aggregate observational data by topic or condition. Data collected for the purpose of quality measurement in the operational domain are also a source of practice-based evidence. However, no observational data may be used for medical research without the approval of an institutional review board, which reviews research projects involving human subjects.

REGISTRIES IN EVIDENCE-BASED MEDICINE

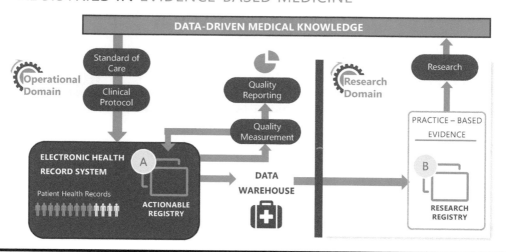

Figure 5.1   Actionable (A) and research (B) registries in evidence-based medicine.

Early Operational Registries

The first operational registries began to inform clinical practice in the mid-1990s with the early adoption of EHR systems. Dr. Lucy Savitz, director of Kaiser Permanente Center for Health Research, Northwest, shared that experience in an interview with the authors:

> Early on, two very visionary physicians at Intermountain Healthcare, Brent James and Dave Burton, did a key analysis of all the work processes in healthcare across the continuum. They identified 140 processes which they organized ultimately into eleven clinical program areas similar to service lines such as cardiovascular, primary care, and women and newborns. Registries were created within these program areas, but they were in silos. You would have one registry that dealt with diabetes, for instance or another for kidney disease (or any other condition). But there was no way to link patients with multiple conditions across the registries. Nevertheless, they were used in clinical decision-making, and could be categorized as operational registries.
>
> Lucy Savitz, PhD, MBA[46]

Actionable EHR Registries

Amy and Barbara began their first dive into custom registry design in 2012 in the EpicCare Ambulatory application developed by Epic Systems (Madison, Wisconsin). They struggled to explain to colleagues how their new HIV registry was different from other familiar registries. Drolet and Johnson's definition of medical data registries (MDRs) was empirically derived through the identification of common characteristics shared by MDRs. Those included mergeable data, dataset standardization, rules for data collection, observations associated over time, and knowledge of outcomes.[45] Panzer et al. used the term "deep registry" to describe the type of registry needed to meet the increasing demands for quality measurement.[47] Terms like "EHR registry" and "actionable registry" provided a context and use case. Ultimately, the attributes of this "new" type of registry are best captured by the phrase "Sustainable Timely Operational Registry in the EHR" (STORE). These registries contain data collected directly through the routine delivery of clinical care and are **sustainable** because there's no incremental cost or time for data entry. They are **timely** because the data are available within minutes after entry. This is a significant advantage over claims data that may not be available until 90 days after care is delivered. These registries are **operational** in the sense that they can be used to inform clinical decision-making in day-to-day operations. Finally, they are **embedded in the EHR** and use the master patient index to link everything together (Figure 5.2).

SUSTAINABLE TIMELY OPERATIONAL REGISTRY IN THE EHR: STORE

Sustainable
No extra cost of data entry

Timely
Up-to-the-minute information

Operational
Used daily in clinical operations

Registry
(in the)

EHR Supports value at scale through
- Immediate access to the whole patient chart
- Links clinical decision support to measurement
- Populates dashboards
- Bulk activities

Figure 5.2 Sustainable Timely Operational Registry in the EHR.

Regardless of the underlying medical conditions, chronic care management programs face the common challenge of monitoring a cohort of patients to ensure they are reevaluated at regular intervals and that treatments are effective based on quantitative measures. The use of registries enables the identification of a group of patients at risk for multiple adverse outcomes and creates the opportunity for efficient and directed intervention when there is a care gap between the patient's current treatment state and the protocol. Due to the very real impact on human resources, patients, and payors, actionable registries require the same high level of accuracy that has typically been associated with clinical decision support.

The Spectrum of Registries

The EHR has evolved to include sophisticated tools for managing patient populations at the health system level. Registries function as customizable indices to patients with common characteristics and can facilitate actionable tasks, while collecting and displaying quality data for a wide array of care settings and conditions. The spectrum of registries (Figure 5.3) available within an EHR continues to expand, increasing our ability to fine-tune

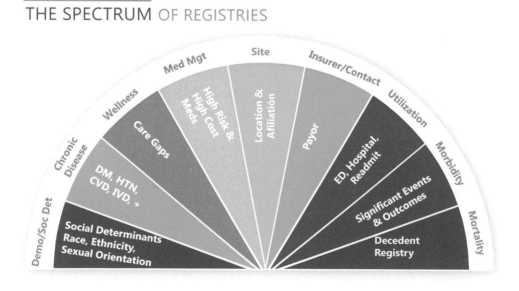

Figure 5.3   The spectrum of EHR registries.

cohort identification and intervention. These include from the far left of the figure:

- Race, ethnicity, and language; social determinants of health
- Wellness
- Chronic disease such as hypertension, coronary artery disease, and diabetes
- Medication management for high-cost biologics, high-risk anticoagulants, opioids, etc.
- Business, facility, and site for segmentation by tax ID of affiliates or operational units
- Payor segmentation for fee-for-service, shared-risk, full-risk, and managed care
- Active patients and utilization of inpatient and emergency services
- Morbidity such as dialysis, amputation, and re-operation
- Mortality data from public decedent records

Maintaining our focus on registries that exist within the EHR, we review here the spectrum of registries used for wellness and prevention, chronic care delivery, medication management, administrative tasks, significant events, and outcomes.

Active Patient Registry

Inclusion: Seen in Past 1,095 Days (Three Years)

The primary purpose of registries in the EHR is to drive clinical outreach, interventions, and decision support. Therefore, the purpose of the active patient registry is to restrict the cohort to individuals who are more likely to be alive and still eligible for services from the health system based on encounter history. Inclusion is defined as not deceased, not a test patient (used by the technical team), not limited life expectancy, and has completed a person-to-person encounter in the last 1,095 days (three years). For example, office visits, hospital admissions, and e-visits count, but automated outreach does not. The active patient registry serves as a single-point filter to restrict cohort inclusion in other registries and streamline the maintenance to a single inclusion rule. Due to the size of this registry, this is kept fairly minimal in terms of content and is only updated every 14 to 30 days. However, patients who newly arrive for service will be added immediately.

Payor Registries

Inclusion: Enrollment File from Payor

Payor registries serve an important role in the identification of risk-based contracts based on actual payor enrollment files. They identify patients who may be included in value-based programs such as Medicare Shared Savings Program (MSSP), Merit-based Incentive Payment System (MIPS), Medicaid Waiver, and shared- or full-risk contracted care. Enrollment files, typically uploaded monthly, serve to more accurately segregate cohorts for particular risk outreach or performance attribution. They contain essential information for quality programs that require the inclusion of all enrollees in quality metrics, regardless of whether they have actually had a visit with the health system. These registries often track metrics and utilization related to specific contracts. Payor registries may also be *skinny*, meaning that they primarily exist for grouping and filtering patients and contain few, if any, metrics.

Managed Care Registries

Inclusion: Enrollment File from Payor

When managing a portfolio of risk-based contracts, it may be advantageous to use managed care registries to house key metrics and data related to risk, utilization, and empanelment. For example, metrics may include risk scores, emergency utilization, hospital utilization, care management, panel assignment, and so on. Similar registries can be used to manage any care services contracts for which an enrollment file is available. In some cases, additional services are provided to patient populations based on an internal risk score threshold. In all of these cases, a registry of patients identifies groups for whom care delivery, quality performance and outcomes are tracked separately from the general population.

Affiliate Registries

Inclusion: Affiliate ID (per Contract)

Healthcare consolidation is creating opportunities for private physician practices to affiliate with a larger health system for improved quality of care delivery and subsequent contracting opportunities. One of the benefits is shared access to technology and expertise in population management and value-based care. Affiliates may be offered the same electronic medical record system as the parent health system at subsidized rates, or they may select to continue on their own EHR platform. When the same EHR is used, access to shared patient charts or shared quality reporting is greatly facilitated. Affiliate registries are a critical tool in managing these relationships and helping to segment the data.

Acute Care Registries

Inclusion: Acute Setting Utilization

Health systems can benefit from registries for emergency and hospital admissions for clinical purposes and quality reporting. These acute care setting registries can identify patients to drive clinical pathways, bundled payments, and clinical decision support. Because hospital billing lags patient discharge by weeks, the ability to capture admissions and discharges in real time via EHR registries provides a much earlier view of patient utilization for health systems sharing risk with insurers. Admissions and readmissions can also then be harnessed to indicate clinical outcome measures as evidence of chronic disease exacerbation or adverse drug events.

Post–Acute Care Registries

Inclusion: Service at Post-Acute Setting

Information about the disposition of patients unable to return home or receiving home health services can be important for case managers, care managers, chronic care programs, bundled payment programs, quality reporting, and business relationships with post-acute providers. Appropriate supportive care can help prevent readmissions and facilitate the patient's path to recovery. In a society that increasingly medicalizes the process of death and dying, the transition to and facilitation of hospice services can improve the last days of a loved one. Much of this information has yet to be captured in standardized ways, yet this is an area that is likely to grow in importance. Examples include registries for skilled nursing, assisted living, home health, and hospice.

Primary Care Registry

Inclusion: Active and Assigned to Primary Care Provider Within the Organization

The primary care provider (PCP) is associated with a primary care department internal to the health system. Academic medical centers may also include patients with primary care residents (PCR) internal to the health system. Clearly defining the attribution to primary care clarifies who will be eligible to receive ongoing wellness assessments and interventions that are not typically extended to patients solely referred for a one-time visit to a specialist or to have surgery, then return to a PCP outside the health system. This registry will be intersected with other registries to drive outreach to patients who have active care gaps for wellness screenings or chronic care management.

Wellness and Prevention Registries

Inclusion: Active, Not on Hospice, Age

The wellness and prevention registries drive clinical outreach and interventions, so only alive, active patients are included based on encounter history. These registries are typically used to target primary prevention efforts to the general patient population, primary care, or patients who are at risk for developing chronic disease based on clinical assessments or family history. Patients may be excluded if they are on hospice or have limited life expectancy. These are often segmented using age parameters to increase computer processing efficiency by segregating data relevant to children from the adult screenings. The composition of the health system demographics and focus of outreach may influence segmentation. We opted not to segment genders and believe that with inclusion to a nonbinary community, this selection further simplifies activities that may cross gender assignment. Examples of wellness registries include Wellness All 0–17, Wellness All 18–39, and Wellness All 40+. Metrics may include key demographic, payor, and acuity or risk scores. Additional registries relevant to the wellness and prevention types include the following that may be included in your architecture.

Patients at Risk

Inclusion Examples: Obesity (BMI >= 30), Pre-Diabetes (A1c 5.7–6.4), Cancer Prevention

Patients with known risk factors can be identified for referral to specific programs to address conditions. For example, obesity is a treatable condition and a risk factor for diabetes, heart disease, and sleep apnea. This registry is used to drive clinical decision support as well as to identify risk.

Diabetes is a condition of poor control of blood glucose (sugar) levels. The diagnosis of diabetes is based on the glycated hemoglobin A1c test that measures the average blood sugar levels for the past two to three months. Normal levels are below 5.7 percent, and results between 5.7 and 6.4 percent are considered **pre-diabetes**. These patients can benefit from weight loss, healthy eating, exercise, and possibly medication to prevent their average blood sugars from moving into the diabetic range of A1c 6.5 percent and over, where secondary complications are more likely.[48]

Pancreatic cancer has a high mortality rate with 9.3% survival after five years (2009–2015).[49] The pancreatic cancer prevention registry captures observational data in discrete data elements to facilitate a screening and monitoring regimen for these patients at risk and facilitate data contributions to larger research registries. Inclusion is based on pancreatic cysts, chronic pancreatitis, family history of pancreatic cancer, and genetic studies. It tracks both existing data through ICD coding and data that has been manually added, such as genetic and imaging-based risk assessments.

Chronic Condition: Diabetes, Hypertension, Coronary Artery Disease, etc.

Inclusion: Active Diagnosis Codes (ICD)

Within a health system, registries are used to monitor that patients sharing a common chronic disease receive the standard of care defined in an evidence-based protocol. The chronic disease registries are likely the most beneficial to a patient cohort driving secondary prevention and management to a group of patients with risk already identified. The use of registries enables the identification of a group of patients at risk for multiple adverse outcomes and creates the opportunity for efficient and directed intervention when there is a care gap between the patient's current treatment state and the standard. A population health registry integrally embedded in an EHR system enables orders and messages to be placed at larger increments, typically hundreds to thousands, referred to as bulk orders and bulk messaging via the EHR patient portal.[50] In order to fine-tune the outreach, chronic care registries are typically tiered under an active patient registry. This is aimed to limit the outreach, engagement, and attribution to patients who have received services in the past three years. In addition to chronic care management, these registries can calculate acuity scores, promote patient engagement, trigger clinical decision support, and provide continuous quality management through 365-day rolling metrics that can be displayed on real-time dashboards with patient-level drill-down reports to quality, which can drive clinical quality measures. Due to the very real impact on human resources, patients, and payors, inclusion in these registries requires the same high level of accuracy that has typically been associated with clinical decision support. Frequently, quality measures may lack appropriate sensitivity to be used in clinical operations. For instance, a patient with steroid-induced temporary high glucose may be included in the measure set; however, monitoring by A1c, diabetic foot, urine, and eye exam would not be indicated.

Most chronic care registries use diagnosis coding to define the cohort. This is by choice, as it infers a diagnostic decision made by a licensed healthcare provider. Therefore, use of lab or procedure-based data may not generally be a standard approach to cohorting. For example, what if a patient has a positive test for hepatitis C antibody screening? Is this a false positive? What about the hepatitis C RNA? What if the patient is on treatment and the viral load is undetectable? What if the patient is not aware of the diagnostic test result? Use of diagnosis is more likely to have included a diagnostic evaluation where a decision was made and the patient has been informed, although this is not always the case.

In order to set the cohort, the inclusion rule must be clearly defined. Most commonly, the cohort is defined by diagnosis using either one problem list diagnosis or two encounter diagnoses. The reason for duplicative encounter diagnoses is related to the misattribution from diagnosis error, which also commonly occurs when ordering tests, such as a patient with chest pain getting an electrocardiogram (EKG) who lacks coronary disease but is having indigestion. Additionally, vague code sets or symptoms may frequently be best left out of disease-based registries. The delicate balance of crafting an inclusion rule requires a trade-off between sensitivity and specificity.

Examples of chronic condition registries include the following:

Diabetes: type I and type II
HIV
Chronic kidney disease
Chronic obstructive pulmonary disease
Asthma
Hypertension
Heart failure
Ischemic vascular disease
Depression

Registry Suites

Some conditions lend themselves to a suite of registries because the management, treatment, and quality measures vary greatly between subsets of patients, who may share laboratory sets, procedures, risk scores, and other values in the metric set. For instance, the ischemic stroke registry and the hemorrhagic stroke registries can be rolled up into an all-stroke registry.

Within the domain of liver disease, for instance, care may be relevant to many provider types, such as primary care, hepatology, infectious disease, and transplant. Additionally, there are overlapping conditions in the domain such as viral (hepatitis A, hepatitis B, hepatitis C) or states of the liver (cirrhosis, end-stage liver disease). The condition of interest, the inclusion criteria, and the count of a sample population are in Table 5.1.

Within the suite of chronic disease management registries can also be the Medicare risk adjustment factor (RAF) registry. Keep in mind that RAF scoring includes hierarchical condition codes for 79 condition categories established by the Centers for Medicare and Medicaid Services (CMS) that nationally have been areas of resource utilization for Medicare patients. This coding schema is a methodology that tries to enable adjustment of payments for care to more difficult cohorts. As a registry, RAF can provide insight into comorbidity, but keep in mind that this may not include less common variants and illnesses that are more common to youth.

Table 5.1 Liver Registry Suite

Condition	Inclusion Rule	Patient Count
Hepatitis A (acute)	ICD diagnosis	220
Hepatitis B	ICD diagnosis	2,316
Hepatitis C	ICD diagnosis	5,166
Cirrhosis	ICD diagnosis	4,985
End-stage liver disease (ESLD)	ICD diagnosis	3,621
All liver disease	Diagnosis or inclusion in any of the other liver suite registries	13,056

Medication Management Registries

Inclusion: Active Medication

Medication registries offer an opportunity to improve the safety related to drug therapies. Eligible medications include those that have routine Food and Drug Administration (FDA)–recommended monitoring and are used in high volume. Others include lower-volume medications that may have catastrophic safety implications. Patients with an active medication or prior dosing that poses ongoing risk are included in the cohort. Medication registries can also store information collected outside the EHR such as opioid prescriptions filled by pharmacies. In the future, medication registries could routinely capture patient-entered data on efficacy and/or automatically interface with surveillance systems for adverse drug events.

Type of medication—Anticoagulants

Inclusion: Patient on Warfarin

The anticoagulant medication warfarin (trade name Coumadin) helps prevent blood clots and is generally safe to use so long as there is appropriate monitoring and caution with drug interactions. Each patient has a uniquely titrated dose that is determined based on laboratory monitoring. However, illness, diet, drug interactions, and other patient factors can affect the pharmacokinetics of this medication and hence the therapeutic window. Most patients on this medication receive regular lab tests to determine if medication adjustments are necessary, but sometimes they forget or choose not to complete tests. A warfarin registry can help track which patients may be overdue for their tests (to trigger outreach action), when the last test was performed, and whether other monitoring labs have been completed.

Another feature of this registry is that it can manage anticoagulation provider attribution, efficiently alerting the correct team when a patient is due for a care intervention.

Type of medication—Chemotherapeutic

Inclusion: Patient on Anthracycline

Patients who receive anthracyclines as part of their chemotherapeutic cure for cancer may subsequently develop heart failure resulting in decreased ability to ambulate and complete daily activities. The American Society of Echocardiography and the European Association of Cardiovascular Imaging issued a consensus statement recommending echocardiogram imaging for patients who have received a class of chemotherapy medication called anthracyclines.[51] The development of heart failure from anthracyclines increases with cumulative dose. The purpose of the anthracycline registry is to track the lifetime anthracycline dose of patients and record the completion of monitoring using echocardiograph results for patients with significant exposure.

Type of medication—Intravenous Antimicrobial

Inclusion: Patient on Outpatient Parenteral Antibiotic (OPAT) Therapy

As value-based care delivery moves to increase the number of patients receiving subacute services from home, the value of developing an ambulatory antibiotic registry has grown. An outpatient approach to antibiotic therapy allows patients to return home quickly while providing substantial cost savings for all parties involved. The OPAT registry is a means to temporarily cohort patients receiving intravenous treatment as an outpatient to help ensure that the duration is appropriate, follow-up is timely, and key laboratory tests related to safety are being monitored. Use of ambulatory antibiotics has increasingly become the standard of care for a wide range of infections such as wound infection, bone infection, and a variety of others. However, patients on this program require strict monitoring to ensure they receive continuous care, and complications require early intervention. Use of the OPAT registry and outreach program also enables the infectious disease clinicians to closely monitor patients for less costly treatment, as well as proactively monitor the therapeutic response to help reduce admissions and readmissions for decompensation.

Table 5.2   Patient-Based Registry for Hypertension

Patient	Inclusion	Metric
Patient A	HTN diagnosis: I10	Last systolic blood pressure: May 22, 2019, SBP 155
Patient B	HTN diagnosis: I10	Last systolic blood pressure: March 5, 2018, SBP 138
Patient C	HTN diagnosis: I10	Last systolic blood pressure April 13, 2017, SBP 120

Patient-Based Registries

The registries we've discussed so far are all patient-based, meaning they have one record per patient. Table 5.2 provides an example of this type of registry. Patients A, B, and C are included in the hypertension registry based on diagnosis I10, and each metric stores only the most current (last) value. In this example, it's the systolic blood pressure.

Event-Based Registries

In the journey across the wellness to sickness continuum, significant events can signal the transition from primary to secondary or tertiary care. Significant events may be new, first-time events or may be decompensation from a chronic condition. Examples could be a patient with hyperlipidemia that then results in a first-time acute myocardial infarction (AMI) episode that may then subsequently lead to heart failure, where readmission is common. The patient may have multiple episodes of diagnoses, but the anchoring significant event may be more difficult to define at a population level. Causality may not be correctly inferred and has to be carefully defined at a patient level. The data may reveal an aggregate level of cohorts with intersecting morbidity. A solution to the challenge of sequencing, time, and repeat events in outcomes is the event registry. The design of the event registry enables key anchoring dates to be noted, as well as duration from event to subsequent outcome. A variety of inclusion criteria may be used to populate this type of registry, but the data structure must place the event on a time continuum, with the possibility for recurrence. We can express this in data processing terms by saying that the key for event registries includes time, and hence a patient may have more than one row. Examples of event registries can include adverse drug event, postprocedural morbidity, acute utilization, and catastrophic outcomes (loss of limb, loss of sight, etc.).

Table 5.3 Event-Based Registry for Acute Myocardial Infarction

Patient	Inclusion	Metric: Date of AMI Event
Patient A	AMI diagnosis: I21.9	May 22, 2019
Patient A	AMI diagnosis: I21.9	March 5, 2018
Patient A	AMI diagnosis: I21.9	April 13, 2017

As shown in Table 5.3, one patient can have multiple rows. Each row corresponds to a series of heart attacks (AMI diagnosis I21.9) that occurred over a period from April 13, 2017, to May 22, 2019. The longitudinal event view of health data is more common in medical research databases but has been increasing in use within the EHR.

Decedent Registry

One of the more important outcome-related events is mortality. Hospitals must update the EHR patient status to deceased when a death occurs. However, the EHR patient status may never get changed to "deceased" for persons who died outside a hospital or at a different hospital. Accurate patient status and date of death information in the EHR add value to an organization's population health program by excluding deceased patients from patient outreach workflows and providing accurate patient mortality outcomes. As EHR data are aggregated for research purposes, the exclusion of information from public death records threatens the accuracy of research findings on mortality.[52]

Death data are stored in two national databases: the Social Security Administration's Death Master File (DMF) and the Centers for Disease Control's National Death Index (NDI).[53] Although there are concerns about its completeness, the DMF is relatively easy to procure and can be used to update the patient status in an EHR.

In summary, a variety of different registries can be designed to help improve care delivery and assignment of patient attribution and outcomes with use of EHR-based registries. These are fairly new in development in the past one to two decades and are likely to continue to mature in order to help improve the dexterity of care delivery, as well as the reflection on both expected and unexpected outcomes.

CASE STUDY: USE OF SOCIAL SECURITY DECEDENT DATA IN AN EHR REGISTRY

A health IT project request form was submitted in June 2016 for the update of patient status in the Epic EHR based on the Social Security Death Master File obtained through the National Technical Information Service at www.ntis.gov/products/ssa-dmf/. The project team included representatives of health information management (record management), EHR interface team, decision support, population health, compliance, data security, and EHR vendor support. The research team was informed to ensure no duplication of effort.

The package included the file layout, security policies from the issuing agency (NTIS), and information on the monthly electronic updates. The base file includes the national listing of all Social Security Administration–reported deaths from 1934. The initial analysis of the data matching Social Security number (SSN) and name matched on 172,328 patients. The patient load and update were piloted in a test environment. In February 2017, a mass update successfully changed patient status from alive to deceased for approximately 4% of patients (120,678 of approximately 3 million).

The effort of this task was over 200 hours over a period of nine months.

Discussion Questions:

1. What types of validation would you perform to ensure that truly alive patients weren't marked as deceased?
2. Although California does allow the use of a limited set of death data from the Vital Statistics Office, the patient SSN is not included. How would you perform patient matching without a SSN?
3. What steps would promote the routine updating of EHRs based on public vital statistics?

Registry Architecture

It is the combination of multiple registry types within a common architecture that empowers and organization to manage patient populations

(Figure 5.4). Patient status and coverage registries identify groups of active and deceased patients and their connection to payors, accountable care organization (ACO), affiliates, managed care, and quality programs. For the active enrolled populations, the quality and efficiency registries track quality and efficiency related to ambulatory care, including; wellness screenings, chronic care management, medication management, and outpatient procedures. These services may be provided in the care setting of ambulatory primary care or specialty clinics, or for patients in post–acute care, such as a skilled nursing facility. Utilization and episodes track the significant events that precipitate emergency or inpatient admissions. Tracking these events on a timeline and linking related care in episodes (like a pregnancy or a heart attack) allows the longitudinal analysis of care.

When operational registries are built within the EHR, they facilitate standard definitions of disease states and simplify access to curated data from the health record. Most importantly, the integrated architecture facilitates action based on registry inclusion, exclusion, or metric value. Although our examples focus on a registry architecture integral to the EHR, an alternative design may establish registries in a system layer outside the EHR. The latter approach may be particularly appealing for affiliate groups in which the members use many different EHR systems.

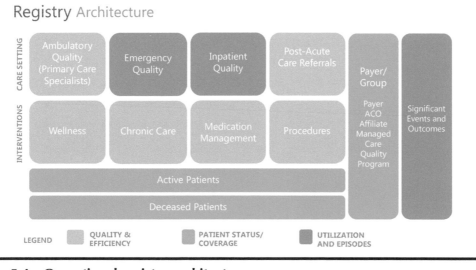

Figure 5.4   Operational registry architecture.

Registries: From Taxonomy to Ontology

A taxonomy of registries is included in the Agency for Healthcare Research and Quality's (AHRQ's) *Registries for Evaluating Patient Outcomes: A User's Guide, Third Edition*. The guide presents categorized patient registries based on how the populations for the registries are defined: product registries, disease or condition registries, health services registries, and combination registries.[54] In 2015, the term "registry" or "registries" was found in 47 articles in the *Journal of the American Medical Informatics Association* (JAMIA).[55] Upon review, we concluded that there was no reference to operational registries during that year but did find an additional registry category of public registries developed by the government in the interest of public health (epidemiology) and healthcare payments (CMS). The birth and death records contained in state registries also fall into the public registry domain because they provide information useful for patient identification and mortality data that are important for outcome studies. We have therefore extended the AHRQ registry taxonomy to include the additional categories of Public Registry and Operational Registry (Figure 5.5). A public registry may include vital statistics of birth and death. An operational registry is a combination patient/health services registry that is used for direct patient care.

TAXONOMY OF HEALTH REGISTRIES

Figure 5.5   Taxonomy of registries (adapted from Gliklich et al., 2014).

Further analysis of the corpus of JAMIA registry articles led to preliminary work on the development of classes, subclasses, and properties for a prototype health registry ontology (Table 5.4). Like a taxonomy, an ontology defines classes with associated attributes. Unlike a taxonomy that enforces hierarchical relationships (trees), ontology properties link classes together through action verbs to create a semantic network that can be useful in information retrieval tasks. Semantic searches use the meanings and relationships to retrieve data. It is hoped that through the further development of registry ontologies, we will improve the science of health registry design and use and lay a stronger foundation for the use of aggregated clinical data for the development of a national learning health system.

Table 5.4   Health Registry Ontology: Proposed Classes, Subclasses, Properties, and Instances (Barbara Berkovich 2018)

Classes/Subclass	Properties	Instance
Health Registry	Financed by	*Registry_Owner:* health system third-party vendor government professional societies
Health Registry	Aggregates	*Health Data Domains:* patient demographics enhanced demographics (REAL/SOGI, social determinants) genomic data assessments vital signs utilization history (visits, admissions) product data service provider data billing data clinical outcomes patient reported outcomes
Health Registry	Classified as	*Registry Type:* product registry patient registry disease or condition registry health services registry hybrid registry public registry sustainable timely operational registry

(Continued)

Table 5.4 Health Registry Ontology: Proposed Classes, Subclasses, Properties, and Instances (Barbara Berkovich 2018) (Continued)

Classes/Subclass	Properties	Instance
Health Registry	Governed by	*Governance Structure:* shared brokered federated single user
Health Registry	Used for	*Registry Purpose:* research postmarketing surveillance statistical reporting clinical care
Health Registry	Used by	*User Type:* researchers public health workers clinicians patients
Health Registry	Includes	*Condition of Interest:* diabetes heart disease kidney disease pregnancy opioid use knee replacement products etc.
Health Data Domains	Stored in	*Storage Architecture:* spreadsheet data mart research network electronic health record online health data sites (e.g., patientslikeme)
Health Data Domains	Conform to	*Data Standards:* ICD International Classification of Diseases SNOMED Systematized Nomenclature of Medicine LOINC Logical Observation Identifiers and Names Codes CPT Current Procedural Terminology OMOP
Health Data Domains	Collected from	*Data Source:* observational data (direct clinical care) administrative data (billing records) research data (collected for the sole purpose of a research study) external data (retrieved from another health system) patient-reported data

Table 5.4 (Continued)

Classes/Subclass	Properties	Instance

Registry Purpose	Subject to	*Data Use Laws:*
		HIPAA (Health Insurance Portability and
		    Accountability Act for healthcare providers)
		Common Rule (created IRBs—institutional review
		    boards—for human subjects research)

Patient	Contributes	*Health Data Domains*
Patient	Consents to	*Data Use restrictions*

Chapter 6

Measuring the Quadruple Aims

Approximately one-third of the measures in the National Quality Forum Quality Positioning System (QPS) search tool (www.qualityforum.org/QPS) are labeled outcome measures. For a true understanding of how healthcare delivery processes affect outcomes, there needs to be a linkage between the two. Furthermore, each healthcare process has all four quadruple aim outcomes; clinical, per capita cost, patient experience, and healthcare provider experience (Figure 6.1). This chapter offers ideas and resources for outcome assessment.

Health Outcomes

Although intuitively simple, measuring health outcomes is astonishingly difficult. The Outcome Measurement Framework (OMF) from the Agency for Healthcare Research and Quality (AHRQ) further categorizes health outcomes as survival, clinical response, events of interest, and patient reported.[56] According to Wikipedia, a health outcome is a "change in the health of an individual, group of people or population which is attributable to an intervention or series of interventions."[57] The measurement of outcomes typically requires a pre-intervention measurement (baseline) followed by one or more post-intervention measurements that show a change that can plausibly be attributed to an intervention. The post-intervention outcomes can be measured immediately after the intervention (proximal) or after a

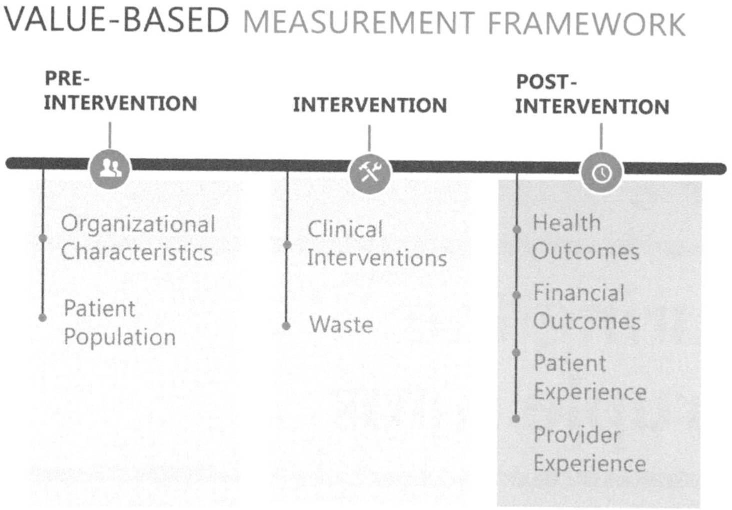

VALUE-BASED MEASUREMENT FRAMEWORK

Figure 6.1 Post-intervention measurements in the value-based measurement framework.

longer period of time (distal). For example, to evaluate the effectiveness of a smoking cessation intervention, a proximal outcome would be a change in status from smoker to nonsmoker, and a distal outcome would be a lowered rate of lung cancer among smokers.

The ability to compare outcomes across registry populations is hampered by a lack of consistent definitions. The Evidence-based Practice Center's Methods Workgroup defined minimum measure sets (MMS) in five clinical areas: (1) atrial fibrillation, (2) asthma, (3) depression, (4) non–small cell lung cancer, and (5) lumbar spondylolisthesis.[58] They found it necessary to convert narrative (free-text) measure specifications to codes and value sets for the extraction of data from the EHR. Code mapping is a time-consuming and error-prone task. Even the combined efforts of informaticists and clinical domain experts do not ensure that the intended data will be extracted from the correct location in the electronic health record (EHR), or even that they exist in a retrievable format within the EHR. Overriding all of these challenges is that "ICD-10 was not initially designed to ensure sufficient specificity to inform action, whether at the individual or population level."[59]

National Quality Forum

The National Quality Forum QPS search tool at www.qualityforum.org/QPS includes search filters for outcome measures. A search on March 25, 2019,

Table 6.1 National Quality Forum–Endorsed Outcome Measures Retrieved from QPS

Measure Type	Result Count	Examples
Outcome	316	Hospitalizations; readmissions; mortality; smoking prevalence; and a number of assessments, labs, and vitals
Outcome: PRO-PM	34	Patient-Reported Outcomes in Performance Measurement are patient questionnaires focused on the care experience
Outcome: Intermediate Clinical	12	Population-level HIV viral load suppression, gout: serum urate target Proportion with more than one emergency room visit in the last days of life

returned 316 outcome measures, 34 patient reported outcomes, and 12 intermediate clinical outcomes. Together, these represented one third of the 1085 measures in the QPS tool (Table 7.1).

International Consortium for Health Outcomes Measurement (ICHOM)

ICHOM is committed to developing and sharing international standards sets to identify what should be systematically tracked in connection with a medical condition such as back pain, diabetes, or coronary artery disease. Each set includes the full care cycle for the medical condition, risk factors, clinical outcomes, and patient-reported outcomes to capture the burden, functional status, and quality of life. Details of what, how, and when to measure provide clear instructions so that results can be compared across multiple sites. Data collection can be as simple as pen and paper, kiosks, or third-party services, or can be fully integrated into an EHR.[12] Over 25 standard sets are available at www.ichom.org, including diabetes, chronic kidney disease, heart failure, and breast cancer, and more are in progress.

Per Capita Cost

Measuring financial outcomes may seem relatively straightforward. However, keep in mind that the true cost of care can be difficult to discern as it relates to particular services for particular patients from particular providers. Imagine today that you need to have a dose of chemotherapy. The cost components will include expenses from the ambulatory visit (front desk, team, physician), laboratory (front desk, phlebotomist, and clinician), infusion center (front desk, licensed nurse, registered nurse, physician, pharmacist), pharmaceutical, information services, facilities, and supplies and that is not all! Service charges are generally a poor indicator of actual cost. The contracted rates for some components will also vary the reimbursements for billable charges. How do you really measure key components, draw conclusions about outcomes, and reduce waste?

Calculation of before/after costs for data collection activity can be approximated using wages. For example, if a new depression screening is being considered for adoption, what are the economic implications around that implementation? The clinical case seems appropriate, as it is estimated that for every $1 spent on mental health for patients with major depressive disorder, there is an additional $6 of cost related to suicide, workplace, and comorbidity expenses.[61] To now consider the cost of screening for depression using a survey, we have the following analysis. The data collection cost in wages for the collection of 30,000 depression surveys on paper is compared with online portal data collection in Table 6.2. For a paper survey, the estimated licensed vocation nurse (LVN) cost for collection of 30,000 surveys at five minutes each is $37,500. The data entry by LVN for 30,000 surveys at three minutes each is $22,500. Review of 3,000 surveys (10%) by a doctor at three minutes each is $15,000. The total cost in wages expended for the

Table 6.2 Cost Comparison for Data Collection of 30,000 Surveys (Paper vs. Patient Entered)

Topic	Estimated Costs	Estimated Wages $US
Paper-based surveys		
Administer surveys	Licensed vocational nurse @ $15/hour 30,000 patients @ 3 min/patient	37,500
Clinical data entry	Licensed vocational nurse @ $15/hour 30,000 patients @ 3 min/patient	22,500
MD review	MD $100/hour 30,000 patients @ 3 min/ patient	15,000
	Recurring annual wages for paper survey	**75,000**
Patient-entered digital surveys (via patient portal)		
IS analyst build and reporting	500 hours EHR analyst @ $50/hour	25,000
	One-time wage for secure online survey	**25,000**

paper survey is $75,000. If we administer the same survey to 30,000 patients via patient-entered data in the patient portal, we have a one-time EHR analyst wage of $25,000. There are no recurring charges, and the survey is scalable, meaning that it's the same cost whether we are surveying 30,000 or ten times that number. The challenge for population health systems is to drive the transaction cost to zero and relieve healthcare workers of routine administrative tasks.

Patient Experience

Operational processes should be informed by patient experience. Optimally, data would include from both quantitative and qualitative information that is both ad hoc and systematically collected. At the moment, engagement of patients with patient advisory boards and patient experience teams can vary. Inclusion of patients on population health design teams is not common. Typically, instead, standardized assessments of patient experience are purchased by a third party. Consumer Assessment of Healthcare Providers and Systems (CAHPS) is an AHRQ program that develops surveys that focus on aspects of healthcare that consumers are best qualified to assess. These surveys are available for free and cover topics like ease of access to care and patient experience.

> Users of CAHPS survey results include patients and consumers, health care providers, public and private purchasers of health care, health care accreditation organizations, health plans, and regional improvement collaboratives. These individuals and organizations use the survey results to evaluate and compare health care providers and to improve the quality of health care services.
> About CAHPS www.ahrq.gov/cahps/ retrieved March 25, 2019

Collecting patient feedback through local survey and advisory groups is also important. The patient experience is molded by their participation in their care. Modern EHRs enable patients to actively track and manage their care. Population health tools in the EHR provide static and dynamic opportunities to engage patients in their care delivery. For example, patient experience is enhanced by access to condition-specific material and access in their web portal. Population health tools also enable targeted and direct outreach with patients that help them better self-manage care.

Provider Experience

Many health systems now collect data on provider experience in response to a growing awareness of provider burnout. Provider experience can be measured with a physician burnout survey or a variety of other tools. Surrogates for experience can include turnover; after-hours and weekend work (controlling for work that is assigned in these time blocks); clinical efficiency, including note length, delinquencies, and message volumes for non–face-to-face work; and task time recorded in EHR time stamps. There is a body of literature on the human factors of EHR use. Unfortunately, methods and instruments for evaluating usability are not widely used. There is little generalizable evidence to compare provider experience using centralized patient outreach, supportive care teams, population health tools, and clinical decision support that drives care. Because of the wide variation in practice both between and within healthcare organizations, population health teams are encouraged to develop innovative metrics to better understand the impact of their EHR system changes on providers.

EFFECTIVE DELIVERY OF APPLIED POPULATION HEALTH

2

Chapter 7

Chapter 7

Applied Population Health Technical Foundation

The technical infrastructure required to drive healthcare to established performance goals requires a higher up-front investment than for retrospective quality reporting, but the benefits are sustainable performance and high-reliability care. Necessary components of the infrastructure include:

■ A rigorous system of measure documentation and version control of measure code
■ An operational metric set that sets local protocols at the lowest common denominator for redundant measures or clinical guidelines
■ A set of 365-day rolling metrics for continuous process measurement
■ An analysis and reporting system for summarizing the quality performance by program, with on-demand drill-down to the service, clinic, and provider levels

Underlying the value-based measurement framework discussed in Part 1 is the applied population health technical foundation. As with the measurement framework, there are unique tools and methods in the technical foundation that apply to three distinct contexts: 1) pre-intervention, 2) intervention, and 3) post-intervention (Figure 7.1).

In the **pre-intervention context**, a quality measure management system facilitates enterprise-wide financial and tactical planning, governance, and resourcing related to quality programs. The purpose of the system is to enable central aggregation of the key information specific to each quality

Figure 7.1 **Applied population health technical foundation.**

program. Reports and analytics from this system inform enterprise-wide process design and can provide insights to optimize revenue contingent on quality performance. Although measure management systems are not universally recognized as an integral feature of the population health infrastructure, they are of particular importance in complex multiprogram health systems with dozens of clinical domains and hundreds of value-based quality measures. In Chapter 8, we will discuss commercially available quality measure management solutions and introduce a do-it-yourself measure management design that provides a low-cost alternative.

The **intervention context** is where operational registries and their related clinical decision support facilitate the management of patient cohorts. Registry architecture may vary by vendor and must be responsive to the local design requirements at an organization level. However, most systems drive action by clinical teams across care settings and specialties, engage patients, and automate higher-reliability processes. Chapter 9 describes how quality measure specifications inform the design of electronic health record (EHR) registries and provides an overview of second-generation clinical decision support, including intervention timers, dynamic order sets, bulk actions, and risk stratification.

The **post-intervention** context relies on analytics dashboards to provide the feedback loops for rapid quality improvement and sustainable quality control. Dashboards drawing on business intelligence systems and sophisticated EHR reports are now a primary means to communicate business information and are replacing static paper-based and/or columnar reports. Display of a visual summary of information enables quick assimilation of the data. When more details are required, dashboards can dynamically pan and zoom across large data sets to focus on the data of interest. Chapter 10 discusses common features of measure performance dashboards, as well as the novel application of dashboards to track technology use and quadruple aims.

Chapter 8

Quality Measure Management Systems

The pre-intervention phase of the technical foundation focuses on getting ready to measure. That may seem strange, since all health systems are already reporting a wide range of quality measures. However, to meet the high level of reporting demands, organizations must standardize, reuse, and scale the decision-support and reporting infrastructure in order to achieve economies of scale. In other words, we must step back and develop an enterprise view of all the reporting requirements across all programs and care settings. For health systems providing a full spectrum of care and managing a complex payor portfolio, a single enterprise-wide quality measure management system is required that is distinct from but integrated with the performance reporting infrastructure. Such a system provides value by improving:

- Management of budgeting, resourcing, and incentive capture for quality programs
- Accuracy and timeliness of quality measurement: ensuring measure specifications and targets are current and submissions are timely
- Strategic alignment of quality program goals and priorities
- Cross-pollination via enterprise level teams, resulting in breaking down silos for more efficient use of data, value sets, and skills
- Scaling of the portfolio of quality assets related to workflows, analytics, and auditing

- Harmonization of measures and standard practices for a unified patient and provider experience
- Completeness by improving the accessibility to capture and manage internal measures critical to clinical practice that may not be formally included in external quality programs

What Is Healthcare Quality Measure Management?

Electronic health record (EHR) vendors and third-party applications offer a variety of tools for managing quality program specifications, benchmarking, and reporting. Historically, functionality focused on regulatory quality reporting siloed by program. While the ability to access quality program measure specifications and program-compliant value sets within the EHR represents a big step forward, it falls short of a fully integrated and customizable solution for enterprise quality program management. Healthcare systems need a one-stop shop with robust quality improvement functionality, but today many must combine health management tools, EHRs, and business intelligence tools to effectively address this challenge.[62]

A summary of available information on healthcare quality management systems is provided by KLAS Research, a provider of analysis and reports on the healthcare technology industry (www.KLASresearch.com). Search the KLAS website for "quality management" to retrieve the latest vendors, products, and blogs. This source may not be complete, but finding vendors online can be confusing because the search terms lack specificity. The July 3, 2019, results of a Google search for "healthcare quality measure management system" returned a mix of links covering several unrelated topics.[63] Only one of the first page of Google results, Change Healthcare, offered a software solution for quality program management. Their system offers features that are essential to a robust management system, including 1) computing quality metrics across multiple programs and 2) choosing meaningful measures to drive informed business decisions[64] (Figure 8.1).

In contrast to the well-targeted search results for Change Healthcare, the range of results provide an illustration of the lexical challenges in researching this type of system—for example, the paid advertisements for quality management systems linked to solutions not specifically targeted for healthcare. A featured link provided information on the Centers for Medicare and Medicaid Services (CMS) Measures Management System, which is not designed for health enterprise requirements.[65]

Take Control of Quality Programs

Compute quality metrics across multiple programs, enabling seamless management of successive versions and updates.

Choose meaningful measures that best reflect the care your organization provides. Provide critical quality data to drive informed business decisions.

Figure 8.1   Change healthcare quality measure insights.

Source: © *Change Healthcare Inc. Used with permission.* Available from: www.changehealthcare.com/solutions/quality-measure-insights (2019).

Do-It-Yourself (DIY) Quality Measure Management

An alternative to a vendor solution is a DIY quality measure management system. An enterprise quality management system can be developed internally by most organizations in four steps: 1) identify and enter quality programs; 2) add the measure numerator and denominators; 3) add new measure classifications; and 4) execute consolidated and program-specific reports (Figure 8.2).

The specifications for the system tables, data dictionaries, and instruction are in Appendix D. The technical steps are listed here:

Step 1. Build the quality program table and enter program details related to deadlines, potential revenue, count of measures, and links to official program documentation.

Step 2. Build the quality measure table based on the measure specifications document and supporting category tables.

Step 3. Add new measure classifications for intervention domain, scope of practice, and difficulty.

Step 4. Create and distribute quality program management reports.

The following four reports serve to illustrate the utility of the data provided by the measure management system. For each, we identify who is likely to use the report and the types of questions the reports can help answer.

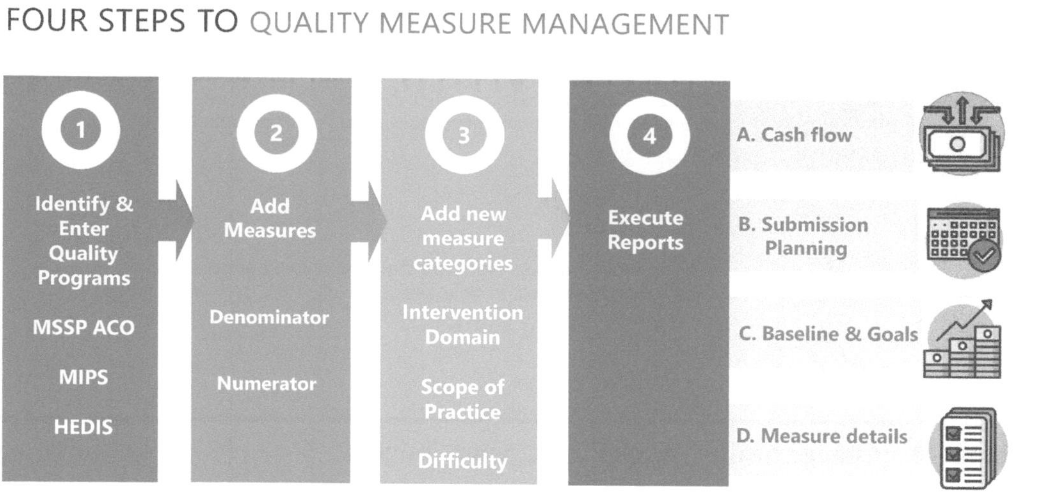

FOUR STEPS TO QUALITY MEASURE MANAGEMENT

Figure 8.2   Four steps to quality measure management.

A. Quality Program Cash Flow Report

The quality program cash flow report in Figure 8.3 supports the activities of the executive leaders, quality program steering committees, and program managers related to budgeting, resourcing, and incentive capture for quality programs. This report shows all active quality programs across the enterprise sorted by business entity, for example, hospital, physician group, and capitated care plans. The key to the quality program table comprises the business entity, quality program, and reporting period, as indicated by the key symbol in Figure 8.3. Each combination of these values has a unique row in the report, which also displays the date that each submission is due. The maximum upside and downside for total quality incentives and penalties is followed by the approximate day that incentives or penalties are paid. A view of the anticipated cash flows is important for business planning. However, the "value" of a program may extend beyond specific dollar incentives. Value may also include improved clinical outcomes, public recognition of high-quality care, improved business practices, or be contractually required. If an organization chooses to assign a market value to reputation or the gain or loss of a contractual relationship, we recommend that a consistent valuation methodology be used for all programs.

QUALITY PROGRAM
CASH FLOW REPORT

BUSINESS ENTITY 🔍	PROGRAM 🔍	PERIOD 🔍	SUBMIT	MAX UPSIDE	MAXDOWNSIDE	PAYMENT
Capitated Care	MSSP ACO	2018	03/22/19	500,000	-120,000	10/15/2019
Capitated Care	MSSP ACO	2019	03/22/20	500,000	-120,000	10/15/2020
Hospital	CALIF PRIME	DY14	08/30/19	25,000,000	0	12/1/2019
Hospital	CALIF PRIME	DY15	08/30/20	20,000,000	0	12/1/2020
Physician Group	MIPS	2019	03/31/20	5 PERCENT	0	1/1/2021

Figure 8.3 Quality program cash flow report.

Questions answered by this report:

How much revenue is expected to be available and when?
What is the potential downside risk if we don't submit or perform poorly?
What level of resources might be justified in pursuing the program goals?
What is the relative resource allocation across the programs?
Where might there be opportunities for improving value at scale?

B. Quality Program Submission Planning Report

The quality programs submission planning report (Figure 8.4) supports the activities of the program steering committees, the program oversight, and information services. The purpose of the report is to identify major deadlines for quality reporting submissions and estimate resource requirements. Active and future submissions are sorted by submission date and method along with the total measure count for each program/year/method combination. Besides the simple count of measures, it is also helpful to drill down to the individual measures and sort by topic to find measures that are repeated across different programs. Measures overlapping multiple quality programs will significantly affect resource planning and may rise to the top of the priority queue. This report also identifies the program manager and the submission team. The submission team may be composed of internal staff, consultants, or third-party vendors. The rightmost column includes hyperlinks

QUALITY PROGRAM SUBMISSION PLANNING REPORT

DUE	PROGRAM	PERIOD	METHOD	CNT	PGM MGR	SUBMISSION TEAM	HYPERLINKS
08/30/19	CALIF PRIME	DY14	Manual	56	Dave	CAREDRIVER TEAM	http://www....
03/22/20	MSSP ACO	2019	CAHPS Survey	10	Vicky	EXPERIENCE TEAM	http://www....
3/22/20	MSSP ACO	2019	Claims	6	Vicky	CLAIMS-BASED TEAM	http://www....
3/22/20	MSSP ACO	2019	Web Interface (SQL)	9	Vicky	CAREDRIVER TEAM	http://www....
03/31/20	MIPS	2019	eCQM	6	Mark	CLAIMS-BASED TEAM	http://www....
08/30/20	CALIF PRIME	DY15	Manual	56	Dave	CAREDRIVER TEAM	http://www....

Figure 8.4 Quality program submission planning report.

to program specifications and benchmark documents to help ensure that the submission teams are always working to the correct version.

Questions answered by this report:

When is each program submission due?

What are the correct program specifications for any given submission?

Which program manager and team will be involved?

Which measures will be satisfied by the direct transmission of the raw data (via claims, survey data collected by vendors, or through designated organizations)?

Which measures require custom calculations or programming prior to submission?

Do I have enough lead time with my current staffing to meet the submission deadlines?

The submission methods vary based on the quality program and type of data. Examples include:

■ *Consumer Assessment of Healthcare Providers and Systems (CAHPS) survey data.* Medicare Shared Savings Program (MSSP) accountable care organization (ACO) patient/caregiver experience measures are assessed using CAHPS survey data. The acronym CAHPS is a registered trademark of the Agency for Healthcare Research and Quality (AHRQ) that developed this survey instrument. More information is available at www.ahrq.gov/cahps/about-cahps/index.html.

■ *Claims.* Some measures are automatically computed from claims data and do not require any submission processing by the healthcare organization. MSSP ACO measures related to cost and utilization of acute services such as care coordination and patient safety measures fall into this category.

■ *Web interface.* A web interface is a common way for providers to submit their scores. Each organization first translates plain-text measure specifications into computer code and algorithms. The measure scores are then submitted online. To standardize the calculation of quality measures, some programs are transitioning to the submission of the underlying data rather than the calculated measures. The CMS Web Interface is such a data submission mechanism for ACOs and groups of 25 or more clinicians to report quality data to the quality payment program.

■ *Electronic clinical quality measures (eCQMs).* eCQMs use the quality reporting document architecture (QRDA) or other structured methods to extract EHR health data to be used in measure calculations. The benefits of this submission format include:
  – Use of detailed clinical data to assess treatment outcomes
  – No manual chart abstraction
  – Automated reporting for provider organizations
  – Access to real-time data for bedside quality improvement and clinical decision support

   CMS is making efforts to standardize eCQMs across multiple quality programs. An enterprise measure management approach works well for these measures, since the eCQM is the target, not each individual program measure. More information is available at https://ecqi.healthit.gov/ecqms.

■ *Qualified clinical data registry (QCDR).* QCDR is a designation for approved vendors that can develop and/or submit measures to CMS on behalf of other health providers. These organizations may include specialty societies, regional health collaboratives, large health systems, or software vendors working in collaboration with one of these medical entities.[66] QCDR is not to be confused with the sustainable timely operational registries in the EHR, which link directly to real-time clinical decision support.

■ *Application programming interface (API).* CMS offers tools for industry developers to integrate their quality software directly with CMS applications and data. For more information see https://qpp.cms.gov/developers.

C. Quality Baseline and Goals Report

The steering committees, program managers, and workgroups can use the baseline and goals report in Figure 8.5 to answer the following questions:

> *Which measures are pay for reporting only (any reported score is above goal)?*
> *Which measures are at risk?*
> *At baseline, how many additional patients must pass the numerator to achieve the measure goals?*

Baseline

A sample of this report for the MSSP ACO shows the denominator, numerator, and base rate (also referred to as baseline) for each measure. The base rate is typically equal to the previous year's performance. Program specifications will define the exact base rate calculations for each measure. Here's an example of the base rate calculation for ACO-13 Falls: Screening for Future Fall Risk.

Baseline Denominator: 10,000
Defined as Medicare ACO patients age 65 and older with a visit in the previous measurement year
Baseline Numerator: 8,000
Defined as Medicare ACO patients age 65 and older who had a fall risk screening in the previous measurement year
Baseline Rate (numerator ÷ denominator) 8,000 ÷ 10,000 = .80 or 80%

Base rates for each measure are entered into the quality measure table as soon as the responsible team can compute the scores.

Goals

Each measure has two columns to express the goal as shown in Figure 8.5. The **Goal** column is based on the 90th percentile rate from the MSSP benchmark document,[60] and this value is manually entered into the measure table of the DIY system. The use of percentages for scoring facilitates comparison between multiple organizations of different sizes. However, internal quality teams need to estimate the human effort needed to move the baseline rate to the external goal. The **Patients to Goal** column is the number of patients that must convert from numerator negative to positive to meet the

QUALITY PROGRAM
BASELINE & GOALS REPORT

MEASURE	NAME	DENOM	NUMERATOR	BASE RATE	PATIENTS TO GOAL	GOAL	PAY_FOR
ACO-13	Falls: Screening for Future Fall Risk	10,000	8,000	80.00%	1,073	90.73%	Performance
ACO-14	Influenza Immunization	10,000	6,000	60.00%	3,000	90.00%	Performance
ACO-17	Tobacco Use Assessment and Cessation Intervention	10,000	7,800	78.00%	1,431	92.31%	Performance
ACO-20	Breast Cancer Screening (Mammography)	5,000	4,500	90.00%	0	90.00%	Performance
ACO-27	Diabetes Mellitus: Hemoglobin A1c Poor Control	2,500	300	12.00%	-50	10.00%	Performance
ACO-40	Depression: Remission at 12 Months	1,000	500	50.00%	0	N/A	Reporting
ACO-42	Statin Therapy for Prevention and Treatment of Cardiovascular Disease	500	300	60.00%	0	N/A	Reporting

Legend

Base rate does not meet goal
Base rate meets external goal
Base rate exceeds goal

Figure 8.5   Quality program baseline and goals report.

goal. If we continue the example for the ACO-13 Falls: Screening for Future Fall Risk, the external goal is 90.73%. To find the number of patients who must close this care gap to achieve the 90th percentile, perform the following calculations:

1. Divide the goal (90.73%) by 100 to determine the passing rate for the goal, and multiply by the denominator (10,000):
   (90.73% ÷ 100) × 10,000 = 9,073.
   Numerator positive goal: 9,073

2. Subtract the numerator positive at baseline (8,000) from the numerator positive goal (9,073):
   9,073–8,000 = 1,073
   Patients to Goal: 1,073

It is important to note that the "patients to goal" value at baseline is not an absolute number of patients required to pass the measure. Measure denominators frequently include encounter conditions that require patients to be treated by the reporting organization within the measurement year. Some patients leave the organization and new patients arrive, and the denominator is constantly shifting. Consequently, the *rate* of care gaps must be reduced so that the gap of 1,073 patients from our example is closed.

The program steering committee and executive team may choose to establish tougher internal goals to provide a cushion in the event of minor changes or adjustments to the reportable rate in the final submission. In addition to fluctuating denominators, complete enrollment files, payor claims files, and accurate analytical reporting may not be timely. For this reason, the creation of internal targets can help ensure success by creating an over-achievement in the rolling 365 day performance rates.

D. Quality Measures Details Report

The quality measures details report (Figure 8.6) may be used by the quality program manager and quality teams to provide insights into the following questions:

Which measures align with clinical priorities?
What subject matter and/or technical expertise is required?
What is the relative level of difficulty?

Three new columns—intervention domain, scope of practice, and difficulty—were manually added to the quality measure management tables to populate this report.

QUALITY MEASURE DETAILS REPORT   *Legend   LVN — Licensed Vocational Nurse / PharmD — Pharmacist / MD — Medical Doctor

MEASURE	NAME	INTERVENTION DOMAIN	SCOPE OF PRACTICE*	DIFFICULTY
ACO-13	Falls: Screening for Future Fall Risk	Assessment	LVN	Easy
ACO-14	Influenza Immunization	Immunization	LVN	Easy
ACO-17	Tobacco Use Assessment and Cessation Intervention	Assessment	LVN	Easy
ACO-20	Breast Cancer Screening (Mammography)	Procedure Order	RN (Protocol)	Moderate
ACO-27	Diabetes Mellitus: Hemoglobin A1c Poor Control	Lab Order	RN (Protocol)	Difficult (clinical)
ACO-40	Depression: Remission at 12 Months	Questionnaire	PATIENT	Difficult (process changes)
ACO-42	Statin Therapy for Prevention and Treatment of Cardiovascular Disease	Medication	PharmD, MD	Difficult (process changes)

Figure 8.6   MSSP ACO 2019 measure details report.

Table 8.1   Intervention Domains

Intervention Domains	Examples
Demographics	Age, homelessness, ethnic background, sexual orientation
Discrete data entry in the EHR	Forms (advance directives) and/or assessments (fall risk)
Examination	Diabetic foot exam
Immunization	Influenza
Lab order	A1c, HIV viral load
Medication management	Is on aspirin, Is on opioid
Medication reconciliation	Medication reconciliation performed post-discharge
Outreach	Phone calls and/or patient portal messages
Procedure order	Tobacco referral
Questionnaire	Patient-entered data such as PHQ-9 depression screen
Referral to specialist	Referral order
Vitals measurement	Blood pressure

Intervention domain: Understanding the primary intervention domain helps with planning for enterprise workflows. For example, there may be one preferred method for chart entry of screening data used in quality measures. Lab orders should have a standard workflow for completion and reporting of discrete, quantifiable results. Early identification of the intervention domain can frequently lead to improved work processes for customization of EHR build and prioritization of tasks related to quality programs. The intervention domain table in the quality measure management system is shown in Table 8.1.

Scope of practice: Similarly, early identification of responsibility by role will provide important information about scheduling and staffing. A primary goal of workflow design is to assign tasks so that each person is performing at the top of their license or scope. In other words, the doctors shouldn't take on all the new tasks. If a measure calls for a routine order, perhaps a nurse should perform that task as a protocol order. Wherever possible, nonlicensed tasks such as communication and outreach tasks should be automated or scaled using technological processes. Insight into upcoming workflow changes may result in shifting of task responsibilities or new hiring. Changes in human task assignments often need several months of lead time, and the measure details report can provide early insight into upcoming demands.

Difficulty: Ranking measures by level of difficulty informs the tactical prioritization of work. In some cases, it may make sense to complete the easier measures and then try to tackle the more difficult ones. A different strategy would be to start work on the difficult measures first to allow more time to work on them during the measurement year. We suggest a three-level ranking; easy, moderate, and difficult.

Easy measures include tasks that can be completed by the staff so that the healthcare organization has direct control over success or failure. Health screenings delivered within a routine office visit such as questionnaires, laboratory tests, or clinical assessment (e.g., blood pressure) are examples of easy measures. Education, training, and follow-up would also fall into this category. Although large numbers of patients may receive these interventions, high-reliability processes can push the rate of completion toward 100%.

Moderately difficult measures require patient compliance and effort to complete a lab or procedure. Although evidence indicates that interventions such as colonoscopy and mammogram provide positive health benefits over the long term, completion of these procedural interventions may add time, risk, and/or expense to patient care in the short term. There is shared responsibility for the completion of these interventions by the provider (who orders the intervention), the patient (who receives the intervention), and the insurer (who pays for the intervention). Because of the increased reliance on patient compliance, these measures typically score lower than measures for office visit assessments. Patient activation is a factor in the completion of the intervention, and the level of patient activation can itself be measured by a standard screening instrument called Patient Activation Measurement (PAM).

Difficult *clinical* measures require long-term patient care and compliance, such as A1c lab result below 8.0 or blood pressure below 140/90. These require a series of visits, staff attention and interventions, patient understanding, compliance, and lifestyle change. Clinical outcomes often fall into this category and are affected by nonmodifiable variables such as genetics, patient demographics, comorbidities, and social determinants of health, as well as the range of treatment response. It may take a long time and high levels of clinical resources for certain individuals to meet these goals. Once a patient has achieved a goal, there is no guarantee that the passing state will persist through the measurement year. Patients who have met a goal may revert back to a failing state due to a number of factors, including natural disease progression.

Difficult *process* measures require changes to organizational work-flows or systems. These measures may require additional resources such as nursing staff, case managers, or navigators to deliver the interventions. Perhaps extra lead time is required to engage third-party services to deliver the intervention. EHR customizations may take weeks or months from the time of request to implementation, and workflow training also adds to the burden of process changes. For example, the ACO-42 Statin Therapy measure has workflow requirements that make it a difficult process measure. First, providers (or clinical decision support) must recognize who should be screened for statins. A chart review is conducted to confirm that there is no contraindication to statin use. The patient is contacted to propose pharmacologic therapy with statins. There may be documentation in the clinical notes providing evidence that the doctor and patient have had this conversation before, but many clinical decision support systems in use today don't process free-text information. In total, these requirements indicate a need for widespread process changes involving the EHR, as well as extra manpower to deliver the intervention.

CASE STUDY: TACTICAL PLANNING FOR QUALITY PROGRAMS

Scott Thompson, RN, MBA

Role: Quality program manager

Concept: Learning to assess the relative difficulty of measures provides a tactical advantage in prioritizing tasks and resources in large quality programs.

Background: The Public Hospital Redesign and Incentives in California Medi-Cal (PRIME) program is a quality/value program managed by the California Department of Health Care Services (DHCS) based on funding provided by the federal Affordable Care Act as part of the expanded payments for Medicaid programs. In the fourth year of the five-year program, there are 56 reportable PRIME measures that focus on elements of primary care, specialty care, and in-patient perinatal care.

Each year the reporting goals change to reduce gap between performance and goal by 10% until the 90th percentile is reached. Once the baseline performance and new goals are established, the inpatient and ambulatory teams begin to develop their tactical approach to meeting those goals.

CHALLENGE

You are the program manager with the task of determining how to organize efforts to maximize financial performance for the year. You have just received the baseline and goals report (Figure 8.7). All measures are pay-for-performance, and you know the incentive dollars at risk for each measure.

CALIFORNIA PRIME-YEAR 4 BASELINE & GOALS REPORT

MEASURE	NAME	DENOM	NUMERATOR	BASE RATE	PATIENTS TO GOAL	GOAL	AT RISK $
Project 1.1 Integration of Physical Health and Behavioral Health							
1.1.1	Alcohol and Drug Misuse Screening	30,000	300	1.00%	2,700	10.00%	300,000
1.1.5	Screening for Clinical Depression and follow-up	20,000	8,000	40.00%	1,000	45.00%	300,000
1.1.6	Tobacco Use Assessment and Counseling	30,000	29,100	97.00%	300	98.00%	300,000
Project 1.2 Ambulatory Care Redesign: Primary Care							
1.2.1	Alcohol and Drug Misuse Screening	30,000	300	1.00%	2700	10.00%	300,000
1.2.4	Diabetes Poor Control (A1c > 9)	3,500	600	17.14%	75	<15.00%	300,000
1.2.5	Controlling Blood Pressure	10,000	7200	72.00%	-200	70.00%	300,000
1.2.7	Ischemic Vascular Disease Patients on Aspirin or other Antithrombotic	3,000	2610	87.00%	60	89.00%	300,000

Figure 8.7   PRIME year 4 baseline and goals report.

Discussion questions

1. Based on the criteria presented, assess the level of difficulty for the following measures and explain your rationale. Assume the screenings are simple questionnaires.
   1.1.1 Alcohol and Drug Misuse Screening
   1.1.5 Screening for Clinical Depression and Follow-up
   1.1.6 Tobacco Use Assessment and Counseling
   1.2.1 Alcohol and Drug Misuse Screening
   1.2.4 Diabetes Poor Control (A1c >9)
   1.2.5 Controlling Blood Pressure
   1.2.7 Ischemic Vascular Disease Patients on Aspirin or Other Antithrombotic
2. Based on Figure 8.7 what other data might you consider for prioritizing efforts?
3. Considering the incentive dollars at stake, how much would you be willing to spend on each measure to achieve the goal?
4. Which measure would you work on first? Why?

Chapter 9

EHR Population Health Projects

As we move into the intervention context of the technical foundation (Figure 9.1), we dive deep into the heart of the population health system. The integration of electronic health record (EHR) population health tools into a complex system design to drive healthcare delivery is an emerging art. As the technology advances, a suite of tools that were developed independently are being linked together to create unprecedented synergies of cohort management, intervention scheduling, bulk ordering, messaging, patient engagement, and continuous process measurement.

To deliver the promised value, we must design population health projects to move a quality measure to a goal within a time-bound period. Once the

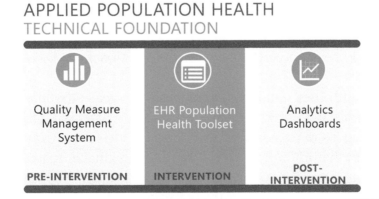

APPLIED POPULATION HEALTH
TECHNICAL FOUNDATION

Quality Measure Management System	EHR Population Health Toolset	Analytics Dashboards
PRE-INTERVENTION	INTERVENTION	POST-INTERVENTION

Figure 9.1   Technical foundation: Intervention context.

system reaches that goal, the infrastructure, decision support, and measurement are in place to ensure the continued delivery of high-reliability care. Failure is not an option. If the goal is not achieved as planned, then Agile improvement cycles can continue to refine the technological and human elements in the process until it reaches the desired state. Without this laser-like focus on the goal, healthcare will continue to build incomplete, ad hoc systems without the necessary redundancy and structure to close the gap if plan A fails.

Judicious Use of Redundancy

Standard work processes are a useful tool for ensuring uniform delivery of evidence-based care. However, variation is a theme in life, as well as in complex care delivery. Consider the possible interactions that occur in busy clinical settings:

> Jane Late requested a same-day appointment with two hours' notice. She arrived 15 minutes after the start time due to transportation problems. Jane was not included in the morning review of care gaps, since she was a late addition to the schedule. By the time she was in the exam room, it was already 5 minutes after her 20-minute appointment was scheduled to end. She had not seen a doctor for six months and was feeling quite short of breath upon her arrival. When it was discovered that her oxygen saturation was running low at 90%, that issue was prioritized for the day's care. Her diabetic eye and foot exams were not completed. Additionally, Marsha Ontime was disappointed that her exam started 20 minutes late and was anxious to return to work. After a few minutes with her provider, she asked to forego counseling about her colonoscopy and breast screening so she could get back to the office.

Population health uses multilayer strategies to increase the likelihood that patients will follow up on their care and that providers will close any outstanding care gaps during and between the face-to-face encounters. However, we understand that in the real world there are justifiable reasons that standard work may remain incomplete. The ability to query the status of care gaps monthly or yearly and perform outreach, bulk orders, and messages to close those gaps is what ultimately delivers the high-performance care.

CASE STUDY: AUTOMATED CLINICAL DOCUMENTATION PROJECT

Failures can provide the best opportunities for learning. The following case study outlines a failed informatics project aimed at automatic note generation for a complex diagnostic decision-making scenario. Table 9.1 contrasts the project development efforts with lessons in the framework of Lean methodology.[67]

Table 9.1   Lessons Learned in Clinical Documentation Project

Background	Lean Lesson
In 2014, an academic obstetrician approached a loosely knit siloed population health informatics team to solve a problem around inefficient and non-standardized documentation of their perinatal high-risk ultrasounds. The goal of the eight-week project would be to template a note for documentation of twin pregnancies in the EHR. It was believed that discrete data could generate a standard note based on ultrasound examination results. Furthermore, the data collection would be standardized for research purposes.	Established urgency and vision
Working alongside the obstetrician, the team built a clinical note generation script that could collect data entered by the clinician and computer generated a clinical note that included numeric calculations and a suggested diagnosis. The build was complicated. The note generation tool had to linguistically accommodate various clinical scenarios, numbers of fetuses, and genders. A risk score based on measurements was to drive clinical decision-making.	Failure to establish a quick win, unclear scope and feasibility
After nearly eight weeks of full-time effort, the first product was ready for user testing by additional physicians. These physicians did not share the vision and had strong opinions on why they preferred to continue their practice of individual narrative note writing.	Failure to include leadership and stakeholders early
Division-level leadership support was solicited and achieved, but the uptake did not occur. There were no escalations. A few clinicians adopted the process, but there was very little utilization.	Failure to demonstrate measurable use and impact on outcomes
The OB ultrasound scripting tool was never adopted as part of routine practice, and the project was scrapped six months later.	Failure to anchor into culture

Case Questions

1. It's quite easy in hindsight to recognize a failure. How might you have defined success for this project in a way that is measurable and time-bound?
2. Review Figure 9.2. In which quadrant would you place the clinical documentation project (A, B, C, or D)?
3. For project prioritization purposes, which quadrant of the project complexity versus patient volume matrix would be most favorable for a population health project?

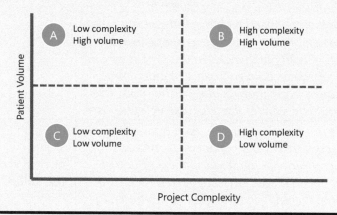

PROJECT COMPLEXITY VERSUS PATIENT VOLUME

Figure 9.2   Project complexity versus patient volume matrix.

Best Practices for Population Health Projects

To deliver value at scale, we are entirely rethinking the packaging of population health projects into second-generation clinical decision support systems with closed-loop feedback and continuous measurement. Only the most important measures deserve this level of effort, such as harmonized operational measures with the associated population health protocols. Looking beyond the relatively limited scope of national quality measures, this method can be applied to any critical process to increase patient safety, improve efficiency, or reduce waste.

Scoping a population health project can be challenging because the best results may require the integration of a registry engine with a suite of seemingly disparate tools. The architecture behind this new form of integrated clinical decision support is invisible to the clinical users. Requests for population health tools are often vague, for example, "I want a registry." Similarly, the governance structures to scope and prioritize these projects may not exist, or the newly formed population teams may not be integrated into existing governance bodies, leading to ineffective resource utilization and increasing the likelihood of failure. The following best practices will give you the best chance of success for your population health projects.

- Use the incentive structure and governance around quality programs to drive your project requests.
- Define success measures and collect baseline data.
- Include quadruple aims in outcomes measurement: Improved clinical care at lower cost that improves the patient's and provider's experience.
- Form data-driven value-based workgroups that include multiple perspectives to fine-tune the solutions. Include experts in clinical practice and technical design.
- Once the design is finalized and approved, the project is ready to be prioritized for EHR analyst build time.

Population Health Project Request Form

A population health project request form supplemented by checklists can early on establish the justification and intervention parameters that are required for scoping. Figure 9.3 Elements of a population health project illustrates how a request and its checklists: 1) Justification; 2) Intervention; and 3) Project Management to capture the information necessary to define socio-technical process changes that may include a registry, risk score, intervention timer, order, and work queue.

We will review the key elements of each section and describe their role in establishing a foundation for a successful intervention. The complete Population Health Project Request form may be found in Appendix F.

Intervention Project Request

A request cover sheet begins with requestor's contact information and sponsorship. Often, project requests will include many interventions and a sweeping statement that the requested changes will improve process efficiency, clinical outcomes, etc. The Situation, Background, Analysis, and Recommendation

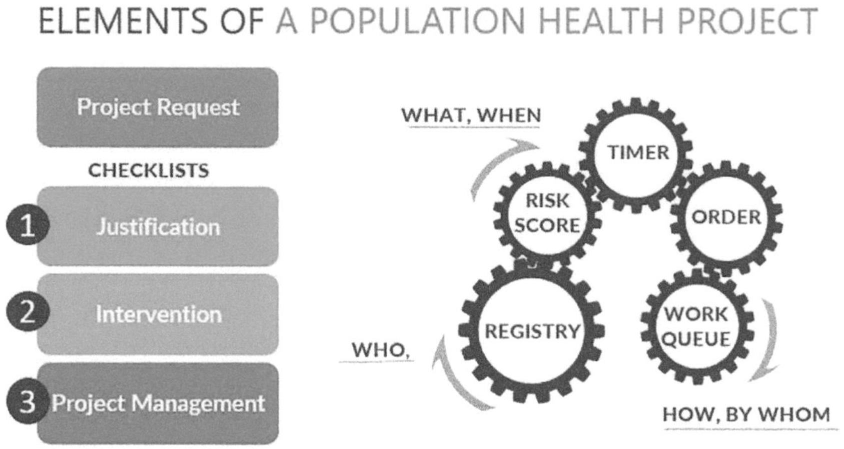

ELEMENTS OF A POPULATION HEALTH PROJECT

Figure 9.3   Elements of a population health project.

Table 9.2   Situation, Background, Assessment, Recommendation (SBAR)

Situation: *What is the justification for this new metric and/or registry?*	**Background:** *What relevant factors or challenges led up to this request?*
Assessment: *How will this metric and/or registry improve the current situation and quality performance?*	**Recommendation:** *Please attach any additional information that will help in describing/scoping the effort.*

(SBAR) defines the rationale for the request (Table 9.2). It is critically important that each SBAR be limited to one primary intervention. A one to one relationship between a project and a success metric will ensure that effort is expended only where it will produce measurable results. This approach will facilitate the prioritization of projects by outcome, reduce waste, and increase the rate at which agile, incremental changes can be operationalized.

1) Justification checklist

The justification section grounds the project with a clear statement of the quality measure that will be used to define success. Although baseline data may not be available at the time of request, there should be a plan to obtain them. Key questions to be defined in the justification include:

Quality Measure(s): *What measure(s) are you planning to change with this intervention?*

Rationale: *What are the clinical, quality, and/or financial goals and supporting evidence for the intervention? Attach guidelines, studies, etc., to support the rationale.*

Baseline Data: *Describe the baseline data if you have them, or the plans to obtain them.*

Measure Target: *What is the goal for the quality measure change and over what period of time?*

2) Intervention Checklist

The intervention checklist conforms to the conceptual framework for effective clinical decision support interventions.[68] The framework developed by Osheroff et al. includes five elements that must be defined correctly: target population (**Who**), primary intervention (**What**), recurring frequency (**When**), CDS method (**How**), and responsibility (**By Whom**).[68] What does clinical decision support (CDS) have to do with all of this? First-generation CDS was characterized by alerts that would fire during a face-to-face encounter between one provider and one patient. The technical foundation of EHR population health tools supports a second generation of CDS that both suggests and enables action supporting population health in the EHR. These newer tools have two unique qualities. First, they can be used both *during* and *between* face-to-face encounters. Second, they allow a provider to update either a single patient record or, more efficiently, multiple patient records simultaneously. The collection of this information at the outset of the project will speed data collection for design specifications and help avoid the dreaded scope creep.

3) Project Management Checklist

The project management section identifies project stakeholders and Quadruple Aim outcomes in the clinical, quality, financial and experience domains. Checklist items include:

Primary stakeholders: *Who are the primary group(s) or committee(s) that have a stake in this new workflow?*

Established level of consensus? *Do stakeholders all agree on need and priority?*

Financial cost/benefit: *Consider project costs, changes in work effort, waste reduction, etc.*

Patient experience: *What changes will the patient perceive?*
Impact on provider/caregiver experience: *Predicted changes to tasks, efficiency, usability, etc.*

CASE STUDY: REGISTRY PROJECT REQUEST

New legislation dictates that all attending clinicians in California regularly login to the state database of Schedule II, III, and IV controlled substances using the prescription drug monitoring program (PDMP) to evaluate whether patients on chronic scheduled substances are seeking multiple providers for prescriptions. The local anesthesia pain team approaches the information services team to see whether an opioid registry can help to service better monitoring and tracking of patients on controlled substances. Today, they have use of orders to attest PDMP access, pain agreement contract, and electronic controlled prescribing.

INTERVENTION PROJECT REQUEST

The narrative above provides sufficient information to complete the SBAR in the project request form.

Situation: What is the justification for this new metric and/or registry? State of California mandated controlled substance attestation and increased scrutiny on oversight of chronic opiate use.	Background: What relevant factors or challenges led up to this request? Providers need to more closely monitor and attest to opiate dispense behavior.
Assessment: How will this metric and/or registry improve the current situation and quality performance? At a patient level, monitoring practices anticipated to deter drug-seeking behavior. Physicians will benefit from CDS to indicate when PDMP attestation is due. Dashboards and reports will enable organizational oversight and auditable evidence of compliance with state regulations.	Recommendation: Create the opioid registry to track monitoring and attestation status for patients on Schedule III, and IV medications. During office visits, alert providers when attestation is due. Provide dashboards to show organizational compliance, and drill-down reports prioritized by dosing to identify patients who need monitoring and follow-up.

The state PDMP website states that all patients on controlled substances schedule III and higher need to have documented review of the PDMP records at prescribing and every 4 months. We use an order to attest review of the PDMP record. This information is used to complete the justification checklist.

1) JUSTIFICATION CHECKLIST

Quality Measure(s): Percentage of ambulatory patients on schedule III and IV opioids with a PDMP attestation order within the preceding 4 months.
Rationale: See State of California Cures Website https://oag.ca.gov/cures
Baseline Data: Baseline reports show 40% of patients met requirement prior to law being in effect.
Measure Target: Increase to 100% performance before the end of calendar year.

2) INTERVENTION CHECKLIST

Who (Denominator): Active patients with an active order for an ambulatory opiate in the past 120 days.
What (Numerator): The attestation order has been completed in the past 120 days.
When (Timing) When the attestation order is missing or expired.
How This will be achieved using an intervention timer that drives an alert during the office visit and a patient list who is due at the provider and clinic level.
By Whom: The attestation is required by the prescribing clinician.

3) PROJECT MANAGEMENT CHECKLIST

Primary stakeholders: The chronic opiate committee serves as the task force to launch new quality programs in opiate prescribing. The clinicians are represented by two team members who work with the build team. The executive team including CMO and CIO are included as key stakeholders.

Established level of consensus? There is agreement on the approach but there is concern about the workload and conflicting project prioritization.

Patient experience: Patients are concerned about stigma of being perceived as drug addicts.

Impact on provider/caregiver experience Clinician documentation is onerous, and this is one more task for them to complete.

Financial cost/benefit: This is a regulatory requirement and the automated solution improves the efficiency and compliance.

CASE EXERCISE:

Complete the SBAR, Intervention and Justification Checklists in Appendix F for the following scenario.

Your physician group participates in an Accountable Care Organization with capitated plan benefits. The ACO Medical Director has initiated a social intervention to connect homeless patients with local housing services. A registry will track all ACO patients without a valid home address. Admitted patients in the homeless registry will be added to a work queue to receive the housing intervention. Goal is to reduce emergency and hospital utilization for this group by 30% within the first year of the program.

Chapter 10

The Who

Cohort Management with EHR Registries

Registries are cohorting tools that help to identify groups of patients with shared characteristics and needs. The applied population health approach uses the registry inclusion rules to govern population definitions and registry metrics to drive consistent decision support and clinical practice across an organization. When used to operationalize quality measures, registries provide the segmentation of particular groups of individuals by age (screening and providing immunization by age), disease (diabetes, heart failure, ischemic vascular disease), and medication risk (anticoagulant, chemotherapeutic associated with heart failure, etc.). Throughout this chapter, we will define the technical steps that are needed to support a population health intervention.

The registries used to define "The Who" in the protocol fall into four types previously described in the spectrum of registries in Chapter 5: Active patient, Wellness and Prevention, Chronic care, and Medication registries. Whereas Chapter 5 introduced individual registry categories, this chapter will explain how a thoughtful registry architecture facilitates flexibility in defining operational cohorts through the intersection of multiple registries. The use of the Active Patient Registry, Wellness, Chronic condition and Medication registries in combination are described as they support the Ischemic Vascular Disease intervention described in the upcoming case study. The Active Patient Registry is used in combination with the other registry types as a filter to ensure that patients reminders and care messages are sent only to patients meeting the active criteria as shown below.

Active Patient Registry

Patients must meet the following criteria in addition to the age criteria in order to belong to an active patient registry:

■ Patient is not deceased
■ Patient is not a test patient (used by technical team)
■ Patient does not have limited life expectancy
■ Patient has had a person-to-person encounter at our facility in the last 1,095 days (three years)

Wellness and Prevention Registry

The wellness and prevention registries identify patients for primary prevention efforts in the general patient population, primary care, or patients who are at risk for developing chronic disease based on clinical assessments or family history. Patients are excluded if they are on hospice or have limited life expectancy. An organization may choose to have a single wellness registry or may segment them for more efficient computer processing. Wellness screenings for children and adolescents are quite different for adults, and similarly older adults have more recommended screening than younger adults. Therefore, our registry design for wellness included an all age registry and three sub-registries:

■ Wellness All
  – Tobacco screening
  – BMI screening
■ Wellness 0–17 year old
  – Gonorrhea and Chlamydia Screening (sexually active)
■ Wellness 18–39 years old
  – Gonorrhea and Chlamydia Screening (until age 24 or later if at risk)
  – Influenza Immunization
  – Human Papilloma Virus Immunization
  – Tetanus Diphtheria Pertussis Immunization
■ Wellness 40 and over years old
  – Breast Screening (Women 50–74 years)
  – Colon Screening (50–75 years)

   – Osteoporosis Screening (Women 65 and older)
   – Influenza Immunization
   – Pneumonia Immunization

For each screening or immunization, the registry contains a metric recording the latest completion date, from which it can be determined if the patient has completed all recommended screenings or has one or more care gaps.

Chronic Condition Registry

Once a patient is diagnosed with a chronic disease, evidence-based interventions are intended to defer or prevent disease progression and complications. "The Who" in this case, is patients diagnosed with these conditions. Implementation of the Ambulatory Care Health Screening Order Protocol relies on five chronic condition registries: Diabetes, Cardiovascular Disease, Hypertension, Chronic Kidney Disease and Depression. Inclusion in the registry is generally based on an active diagnosis on the problem list or two encounter diagnoses. The exception is the Depression registry which will also include patients with a high score on a depression screening assessment.

Medication Registry

Some medications have known risk of side effects or adverse events. Patients taking these types of medications may be placed on a routine monitoring schedule to reduce that risk. Other medications require regular monitoring to ensure that dosages stay within a therapeutic range.

   "The Who" for Laboratory Monitoring for Safety of Persistent Medications includes patients with an active ambulatory medication order for Digoxin, Angiotensin-Converting Enzyme Inhibitor, Angiotensin II Inhibitor, certain types of diuretics, statin or thyroid replacement therapy.

   Further information on medications registries for Warfarin, Outpatient Parenteral Antibiotics and Anthracycline may be found in Chapter 5 in the Spectrum of Registries section.

CASE STUDY: COMPLEX COHORTS ACO-30 ASPIRIN THERAPY FOR ISCHEMIC VASCULAR DISEASE

The process of building an inclusion rule may be relatively straightforward when finding patients with a single condition such as diabetes or hypertension. However, an architecture using multiple registries may more advantageous in some cases. For example, patients with known ischemic vascular disease (IVD), coronary artery bypass graft (CABG), or percutaneous coronary intervention (PCI) may be at risk for significant ischemic events such as heart attack and stroke. The field report shown in Figure 10.1 identifies the seven registries used in combination to find the IVD cohort who may be eligible to receive aspirin or antiplatelet medication.

If the three categories of risk, (IVD, CABG, and PCI) were combined in a single registry, use would be limited to a single quality measure. However, as three separate registries, each is capable of triggering clinical decision support or serving as an outcome measure in addition to its use in the original IVD measure. Similarly, the hospice and hemorrhage registries can be used in multiple measures and decision support rules as inclusion, exclusion, or outcome measures. The IVD quality measure calculates the rate of at-risk patients on aspirin/antiplatelet or antithrombotic medications for the purpose of risk reduction.

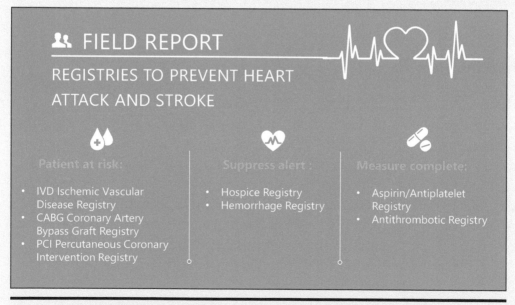

FIELD REPORT

REGISTRIES TO PREVENT HEART ATTACK AND STROKE

Patient at risk:
- IVD Ischemic Vascular Disease Registry
- CABG Coronary Artery Bypass Graft Registry
- PCI Percutaneous Coronary Intervention Registry

Suppress alert :
- Hospice Registry
- Hemorrhage Registry

Measure complete:
- Aspirin/Antiplatelet Registry
- Antithrombotic Registry

Figure 10.1   Field report: Registries to prevent heart attack and stroke.

Chapter 11

The What and the When

Building the Feedback Loop

Whereas "The Who" identifies the target population, "The What" and "The When" define the interventions and timing. The application of the technical components to operationalize these concepts is summarized in Table 11.1. If we follow the columns from top to bottom, we see that The Who in this example is patients with hypertension, and a registry inclusion rule will identify the cohort. The What is a Complete Metabolic Panel (CMP) blood test. A registry metric in the hypertension registry will track when this test was last completed. The When is the schedule for this intervention, and in this case the test is annual. An intervention timer is used to schedule the intervention. Each day, the timer updates the status to indicate whether the current status is not due, due or overdue. The next sections will go into more detail about The What and The When and how the use of registry metrics and intervention timers has implications for precision medicine.

Table 11.1   Application of Technical Components

Concept:	The Who	The What	The When
Example	Patients with hypertension	Complete Metabolic Panel (CMP)	Annual
Technical Component	Registry Inclusion	Registry Metric(s)	Intervention Timer

WHO'S ON ASPIRIN?

MORE THAN 1200 TYPES

ST JOSEPH LO DOSE 81MG PO CHEW
ST JOSEPH LOW DOSE PO
QC ASPIRIN LOW DOSE 81 MG PO CHEW
BAYER BACK & BODY 500-32.5 MG PO TABS
BAYER BACK & BODY PO
EQL HEADACHE RELIEF EX STR PO
H-E-B ASPIRIN 81 MG PO TBEC
H-E-B ASPIRIN PO
SB ASPIRIN ADULT LOW STRENGTH 81 MG PO TBEC
QC ENTERIC ASPIRIN 325 MG PO TBEC
EQL EFFERVESENT COLD RELIEF PO
QC ENTERIC ASPIRIN PO
SB ASPIRIN ADULT LOW STRENGTH PO
HM MIGRANGE RELIEF 250-250-65 MG PO TABS
GOODSENSE ASPIRIN 325 MG PO TABS

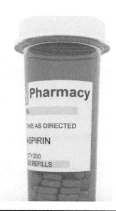

Figure 11.1   Registry helps standardize the list of over 1,200 aspirin-containing medications.

The What: Registry Metrics

Registry metrics organize the information required to compute numerator completion for quality measures. They keep track of interventions so that we can readily determine the last time an intervention was performed as well as the result. For example, a lab metric will store the last A1c lab test, the date it was completed, and the result. An immunization metric will store the last flu shot administered and the date.

Registries also provide a way for a health system to centralize and standardize clinical definitions such as the list of medications containing aspirin. There are over 1,200 types of aspirin, many in combination products. The effort to review this list is considerable, as the commonly available value sets may lack the sensitivity and specificity to support clinical decision-making at a very high level of accuracy (Figure 11.1). The use of a registry metric such as "on aspirin" improves data governance and enables clinical decision support algorithms and quality measures to apply a consistent determination of whether a patient meets a particular criterion.

The When: Intervention Scheduling

Registries are very good at tracking target populations and indicating whether interventions are complete. In order to drive the closure of care gaps, a timer helps ensure that interventions are completed according to schedule. For example, influenza immunizations are yearly, and tobacco use assessments

Table 11.2   Functions of a Robust Population Health Timer

Role	Function
Patient	Shows the current status of planned care and any upcoming assessments or tests due
Care Managers	Indicates which patients are overdue or due soon for population health interventions to facilitate bulk orders and messaging
Care Team	Indicates which assessments and tests are due for patients being seen today

are every 24 months. A robust population health timer uses the same information about the timing of interventions to perform different functions for the patient, care managers, care team, and providers (Table 11.2).

Precision Medicine

The intervention scheduling tool is the mechanism for a pivot from the population best practice to the individual needs of each patient. Consequently, the tool needs to be able to turn on or turn off an intervention for a specific individual. This concept of finding the right patient within the registry and then applying a timer to help with the appropriate scheduling can be taken one step further. As an example, "Jenny" is a 15-year-old who has familial adenomatous polyposis, which in classic form carries nearly 100% chance of imparting colon cancer due to a particular genetic mutation. In this case, the precision medicine approach would result in modification of the colorectal cancer screening plan to begin earlier and continue at a much more frequent rate. The ability to adjust standard national protocols for high-risk individuals is essential to the personalized approach of precision medicine. A personalized intervention plan can be constructed with linkages between registries, intervention timers, and clinical decision support to enable population-level outreach that is in accordance with individual needs.

> ### CASE STUDY: COMPLEX MEASURES ACO-17 TOBACCO ASSESSMENT AND CESSATION
>
> Complex quality measures are frequently built to combine concepts of screening and intervention for patients with risk. For example, a single measure for depression screening and follow-up is a complex measure with two components: 1) screening and 2) follow-up.

Another example of a complex measure is ACO-17 Tobacco Assessment and Cessation, which measures patients who were screened for tobacco use at least once within 24 months *and* who received tobacco cessation intervention if identified as a tobacco user. Two separate processes for assessment and cessation counseling need to be performed in sequence to pass the numerator requirements. Figure 11.2 shows how this measure was resolved into ACO-17A Tobacco Assessment and ACO-17B Tobacco Cessation. When complex measures are reduced to simple measures, a clearer picture of the work process performance emerges. If remedial action is required for the tobacco measure, the simple measures will help determine whether to target the initial screening, or the cessation intervention. In some cases, both processes may need remediation and improvement.

FIELD REPORT

REDUCE COMPLEX MEASURES

COMPLEX ACO-17 Tobacco Assessment and Cessation

Screened for tobacco use every 24 months AND
Tobacco users receive cessation intervention

SIMPLE ACO-17A Tobacco Assessment

Tobacco assessment documented in EHR during current or prior measurement year

SIMPLE ACO-17B Tobacco Cessation Intervention

Tobacco users have cessation intervention during measurement year.
Includes: referral to quit-line, order for cessation medication, or completed order for tobacco counseling

Figure 11.2 Reduce the complex tobacco measure into two simple measures.

Chapter 12

Applying Clinical Decision Support

Workflow Modeling

Once the registry engine and timer are in place, the design focus transitions to the workflow. This is the exciting part of the process when the patients, providers, and technology all work together to get the job done. Let's assume that our evidence-based healthcare goal for patients with hypertension is to complete an annual blood test. The primary process measure for this intervention is that active patients with diagnosed hypertension have at least one resulted complete metabolic panel (CMP) lab test within the measurement year. We chose this for our example because lab-based measures are fairly common, and the population health methods for this measure would apply equally well to diabetes A1c, HIV viral load, cardiac lipid panels, etc. One small study of 93 patients age 70 and older reported an error rate of 6.1% for 132 lab orders.[69] Systemic reasons cited included failure to order lab tests, failure of the lab to perform all ordered tests, and lab result not filed in patient chart.[69] Figure 12.1 shows the task dependencies of a simplified lab test workflow using hypothetical data.

The humans in this process are the patient, provider, and phlebotomist. These individuals must come together to complete a visit and a blood draw. A patient appointment must precede a visit. An order must precede the blood draw. The blood sample must precede the result, and the result must be recorded in the electronic health record (EHR) in such a way that our quality measure program recognizes it and counts it as numerator

ROUTINE LAB SCREENING SIMPLE WORKFLOW MODEL

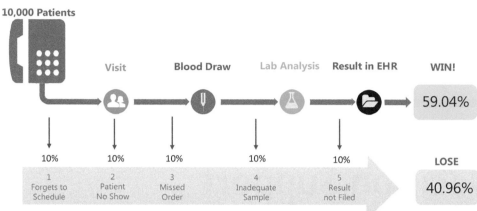

Figure 12.1 Routine lab screening: Simple workflow model.

complete. If all that happens for every patient in the target population (denominator), then the measure score will be 100%, yet that is a rare accomplishment.

In real life, if each patient had one chance to pass through this sequence of steps within a year, there would be some that drop out along the way. The large arrow at the bottom of Figure 12.1 identifies five reasons a patient might fail to complete a step:

1. Patient forgets to make an appointment.
2. Patient doesn't show up for appointment, or the provider has an emergency and bumps the patient.
3. Provider forgets to place the order, or the patient is treated for an urgent matter and routine testing is deferred.
4. The blood draw is missed, or the sample is insufficient, spoiled, or misdirected.
5. The lab result was delivered on paper (handheld or fax) and didn't get entered into the system.

Let's assume 10,000 patients require this test, and 90% of the patients complete each step successfully. How many would end up with a numerator positive score? Table 12.1 shows at each step the reduction in the size of the cohort of patients that can pass the numerator for the lab test quality measure. For example, only 9,000 patients schedule appointments.

Table 12.1   Five-Step Lab Test Workflow

Step	Cohort size before	Percent complete	Cohort size after	Status
1	10,000	90%	9,000	schedule appointment
2	9,000	90%	8,100	complete an appointment
3	8,100	90%	7,290	order for a blood test
4	7,290	90%	6,561	have blood sample tested
5	6,561	90%	5,904	lab result in the EHR

The remaining 1,000 cannot complete the test if they never schedule and appointment. Following this logic 8,100 patients will complete an appointment. Of those, 7,290 patients will receive an order for a blood test. Of those, only 6,561 patients will have the blood sample tested, and 5,904 patients will actually have the lab result stored in the EHR by the end of the measurement period.

Although each step in the process is performing at a relatively high rate of 90%, the compounding effect of sequential failures reduces the final score to 59.04%! Even though the completion rates are hypothetical, a few important conclusions can be drawn from this logical model. The complexity of clinical care delivery, as assessed by the number of actors and number of steps in the workflow, reduces the likelihood of completion. Certainly, the provider who is performing at a 90% order rate cannot be blamed entirely for the low-quality score of 59.04%. If we changed only the rate of order completion to 100% in this model, the overall score would increase to 65.61%, assuming 10% drop-out rate for scheduling and visits. We can conclude from the existence of multiple points of failure that multiple changes in our process would be required to raise the overall score.

This is representative of the types of quality issues managed in clinical care, and this is where population health methods can make a huge difference. What if you could use population health tools to ensure that 100% of eligible patients got an order for the CMP? Let's explore how we could accomplish that feat. Suppose we had a dynamic smart set in the office visit workflow so that every patient who was seen by a provider received an order for a CMP if it was due. That would effectively change the provider order completion to 100%. If we also used a population health protocol to allow the nurses to bulk-order the CMP when it was due and message the patients to direct them to the lab for their tests (without an appointment), we

ROUTINE LAB SCREENING WITH POPULATION HEALTH WORKFLOWS

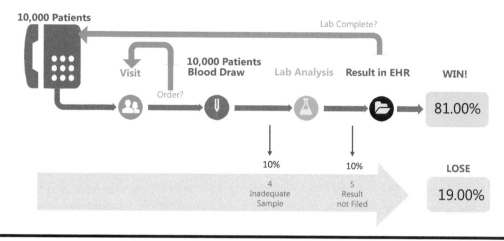

Figure 12.2 Lab screening workflow.

Table 12.2 Five-Step Lab Test Workflow after Population Health Intervention

Step	Cohort size before	Percent complete	Cohort size after	Status
1	10,000	100%	10,000	schedule appointment
2	10,000	100%	10,000	complete an appointment
3	10,000	100%	10,000	order for a blood test
4	10,000	90%	9,000	have blood sample tested
5	9,000	90%	8,100	lab result in the EHR

would ensure that 100% of eligible patients received an order, boosting the final score to 81% (Figure 12.2).

We repeat the step-by-step analysis of the lab workflow under the new assumptions (Table 12.2). Of the 10,000 patients, 9,000 would have the blood sample tested, and 8,100 would have a lab result in the EHR by the end of the measurement period.

Each local healthcare organization has heterogeneous patient populations and process workflows, and the reported results cannot be generalized to other sites. Therefore, it is advisable to perform internal audits to develop the actual probabilities of the completion of each task. One of the benefits of continuous process measurement is that once the computer configuration is in place, simulation models can use real-time task completion rates to predict changes in the final process measure.

Discussion Questions

1. According to the calculations in Table 12.2, 81% of patients will pass the lab test measure if every eligible person received an order (for test and blood draw). If the clinics hired phlebotomists so that each person who had an order also received a blood draw during their appointment, what would be the estimated measure rate?
2. This simplified case study lists five reasons that patients didn't pass the numerator conditions. Name some other reasons that might prevent patients from completing their scheduled care.

Ambulatory Care Screening Order Protocol

An Ambulatory Care Screening Order Protocol (ACSOP) describes in detail the policies, definitions, and protocols for routine population health interventions including bulk orders (See template in Appendix E). The ACSOP must activated individually for each patient by a signed order in the EHR by a licensed physician or advanced practice provider (pharmacist, nurse practitioner, or physician's assistant). This signed order is valid for five years. Patients who have the ACSOP order are then eligible for individual or bulk orders and messages by nurses acting on the protocol. Screenings included in the protocol fall into the categories of wellness, diabetic patients, hypertension, medication safety and contra-indication of anticoagulants (Table 12.3).

Both dynamic orders and bulk orders were used in the preceding example to improve the completion rates for laboratory tests. The following sections describe in more detail the typical use case and how these population health order tools work.

Dynamic Orders

Dynamic orders are used to close all care gaps for a single patient during a scheduled encounter. They are similar to standard order sets that are frequently used by clinicians to quickly locate a set of commonly used interventions during an encounter. However, for a population of patients with established protocols, the dynamic order set automatically selects topics that are flagged by the population health timer as due or overdue. It provides a pre-flight checklist tailored to the individual needs of a

Table 12.3 Interventions on Ambulatory Care Screening Order Protocol

Eligible patients must be in specified registry as well as Active Patient Registry, and must have an active population health screening order	
Registry	**Intervention**
Wellness	
	Procedure: Cancer screening (breast mammography, colon FIT test)
	Procedure: Osteoporosis (DEXA scan)
	Tobacco assessment & cessation
	Lab tests: Gonorrhea and Chlamydia
	Depression PHQ2 assessment
	Immunizations: Influenza, Pneumonia, Human Papilloma virus, Diphtheria-Tetanus-Pertussis (DPT)
	Vitals: Elevated BMI (consult order to Nutrition)
Diabetes	
	Lab tests: A1C, Microalbumin, Lipid, Comprehensive Metabolic Panel (CMP)
	Examinations: Eye Screening, Monofilament foot test
	Vitals: Blood pressure screening and control
	Diabetic Education/Referrals
Cardiovascular Care	
	Lab test: Cholesterol Screening (Lipids)
	Assess statin use in cardiovascular disease (CVD)
	Assess aspirin, antiplatelet and anticoagulant use in ischemic vascular disease (IVD)
Hypertension	
	Vitals: Blood pressure monitoring with recorded BP in a face to face visit
	Lab test: CMP
Chronic Kidney Disease (Stage 3 and higher)	
	Lab Tests: Urinalysis, Complete Blood Count (CBC) with differential, CMP
Medication Registries	
Digoxin	
	Lab Tests: Digoxin level and Comprehensive Metabolic Panel (CMP) lab tests
Angiotensin-Converting Enzyme (ACE) Inhibitor or Angiotensin II Inhibitor	
	Lab Test: CMP
Loop, potassium sparing, and thiazide diuretics	
	Lab Test: CMP

Table 12.4   Dynamic Order Set for Scheduled Screenings

Population Health Dynamic Order Set	*Patient 1 Male Age 56*	*Patient 2 Female Age 45*	*Patient 3 Female Age 82*
Breast Cancer Screening—mammogram		Due	Complete
Colon Cancer Screening—colonoscopy	Overdue		
Osteoporosis Bone Density Screening—DEXA Scan			Overdue
Tobacco cessation referral order		Due	
Influenza immunization	Complete	Complete	Due

patient. The population health order quickly sets up orders for interventions due now. This feature saves time by automating the task of assessing whether the measure is due for a particular patient, and reduces missed opportunities to close care gaps during office visits. Table 12.4 lists five orders from the population health order set. The order status for each of three patients is shown in the columns on the right.

The dynamic order set would select the following orders for each patient:

Patient 1: 56-year-old male: colonoscopy
Patient 2: 45-year-old female: mammogram, tobacco cessation referral
Patient 3: 82-year-old female: DEXA scan, influenza immunization

Bulk Orders

Bulk orders are used to close a single care gap for the entire target population at once, and can deliver real value at scale. In our first use of these tools, a bulk order for a tuberculosis test was created simultaneously for a group of patients, and bulk patient portal messages alerted those patients to the new order. The bulk actions for orders and messages were completed in eight hours, whereas in the previous year this work had required 80 hours of dedicated per diem nursing effort to place the orders one by one. However, the success of these powerful tools requires people, process, and technology to work together in a complex system driven by a registry engine.

Key Technical Components That Require Support of the EHR Team

1. Build the ambulatory care screening order to be signed by a licensed physician or nurse practitioner to initiate the ambulatory protocol. We recommend centralizing the ordering process with the chief medical informatics officer or designee.
2. Build a primary care registry that includes active patients with a primary care physician working within the organization. The registry will have metrics for the last date and result of each screening order in the protocol.
3. Set up the intervention scheduler to evaluate whether the screening order is due, overdue, or due soon based on the frequency stated in the protocol. This status is then recorded in the registry next to the last date and result of the screening.
4. Activate bulk ordering to close any care gaps that may be identified by the ambulatory protocol.
5. Build a template for bulk messaging patients regarding new orders in their patient portal accounts and what they should do to complete those tasks. Patients with a "Do not contact" flag in their chart are not included in the bulk messaging activities.

Key Operational Steps in Building This Process

1. Maintain a careful empanelment process for primary care. Patients should typically not be assigned to a primary care provider without first being seen/established in the practice because this triggers inclusion in the primary care registry.
2. Build and have approved a health maintenance protocol that abides by state law and organizational policies.
3. Train and educate the staff who are using this bulk ordering and messaging process formally, including face-to-face training, with attestation of the completion of this training annually.
4. Monitor the use and uptake of the protocol at least quarterly.

Chapter 13

Calculating Risk

Risk scoring is used widely in healthcare for both financial and clinical applications. Chapter 2 introduced the concept of risk-adjusted payment in shared-risk payment models. This practice recognizes that patients with serious conditions utilize more healthcare resources than average, thereby warranting payment adjustment. Risk stratification is quite different, in that it prioritizes the delivery of healthcare services to patients based on a quantitative score.

Risk Adjustment Registry

Centers for Medicare and Medicaid Services (CMS) uses a hierarchical condition category (HCC) risk adjustment model to calculate risk adjustment factor (RAF) scores. The RAF score is based on a statistical model in which the projected spend of a Medicare beneficiary is tied to information in the patient chart. RAF scores are the sum of the demographic components of a patient's risk such as age, gender, disability status, and comorbidities. The HCC algorithms weight patient diagnoses based on the relative utilization of Medicare services for patients with one or more specified conditions. RAF scores are adjusted such that 1.0 represents the average projected spend for all patients in the upcoming year. For example, beneficiaries with a RAF score of 1.5 indicate a projected spend 50% higher than the average beneficiary for a given enrollment type. A RAF score of 0.9 indicates a projected spend 10% less than the average beneficiary. The computation of the RAF score within the EHR utilizes a registry to identify the disease groups to which a patient belongs and the roll-up of the score. Although the RAF scoring methodology was developed for Medicare patients, we have chosen to extend this scoring method to the entire active adult population within the EHR system.

Risk adjustment questions:

1. What does it mean if a patient's RAF score is 0.6?
   a. It is projected that the patient's care would cost 60% *less* than the average beneficiary for their enrollment type.
   b. It is projected that the patient's care would cost 60% *more* than the average beneficiary for their enrollment type.
   c. It is projected that the patient's care would cost 40% *less* than the average beneficiary for their enrollment type.
   d. It is projected that the patient's care would cost 40% *more* than the average beneficiary for their enrollment type.
2. Does the RAF score accurately reflect the relative amount of clinician time required for each patient visit?
3. Does the RAF score accurately reflect the relative spend for a single accountable care organization (ACO) adult population age 18 to 64?

Risk Stratification

Risk stratification is a method for targeting a subset of patients for an intervention. If the intervention requires human effort, the threshold for action must match the capacity of the staff available to perform the intervention; either the intervention or the staff must be scaled to achieve success. For example, it's counterproductive to refer 1,000 patients to a health coaching program that can only serve 500. In the setting of capitated payments or value-based care, the size of the patient cohort will inform the costs and resources required to carry out the intervention, whereas medical complexity, multimorbidity, and social determinants will affect the intervention design and likelihood of success.

Risk assessment and scoring help to prioritize patient care and clinical tasks to avert a poor outcome and reduce overutilization of services for low-risk patients. Andrew Beam, PhD, suggests that health algorithms (including risk assessments) exist "along a continuum between fully human-guided versus fully machine-guided data analysis."[70] We can add further granularity to the continuum by identifying four categories of risk assessment: human

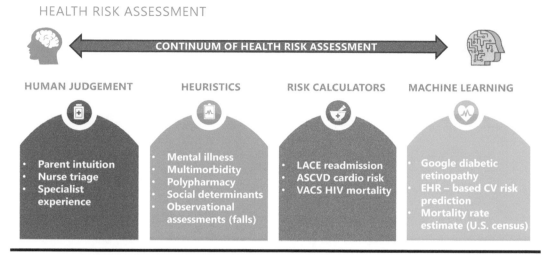

HEALTH RISK ASSESSMENT

Figure 13.1 Human–machine continuum of health risk assessment.

judgement, heuristics, risk calculators, and machine learning (Figure 13.1). Computer processing and machine learning do not inherently perform better than human-guided assessments, but computer analysis does allow us to incorporate vast quantities of health data to gain insights beyond the reach of human capabilities.

Human Judgement

The human judgement of a parent incorporates thousands of data points referencing a child's normal appearance and behavior, providing insight to supplement the training and experience of health professionals treating a sick child. The close interaction of nurses with their patients may uniquely qualify them to predict the likelihood of readmission. Although many computerized models claim to outperform human judgement, hybrid approaches that incorporate human assessments with computer models hold promise in the future.

Heuristics

Heuristics are relatively simple algorithms used to identify and weight conditions and traits known to increase the patient risk of a poor health outcome. Examples of heuristic models include observational assessments for fall

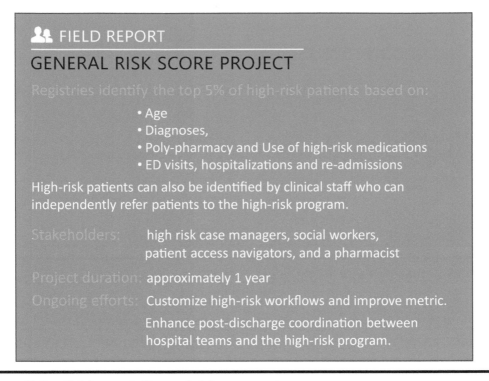

Figure 13.2   Field report: General risk score.

risk, multimorbidity (many concurrent diagnoses), and polypharmacy (many medications). Heuristics are relatively easy to develop, compute, and explain to humans, and can be very helpful for prioritizing care for patients with higher complexity or social needs. One example is a general risk scoring tool developed to support clinical outreach workflows for an ACO and managed care plans (Figure 13.2). Registries identify the patient cohort as well as chronic disease comorbidities. Additional factors include age, medication use, utilization (emergency and hospital visits), mental illness, and substance abuse. Based on this score, the top 5% of patients are automatically assigned to a high-risk program. The high-risk referral workflows combine the heuristic score and human judgement by allowing physicians and clinical staff to override the scoring and refer patients to the high-risk program directly. An advantage of this type of tool is that it may be refined over time as new data, such as social determinants of health, are added to the EHR.

Risk Calculators

Risk calculators use statistical regression analysis to compute the probability of an event such as admission, stroke, or death based on a weighting of risk factors. Examples of these scoring algorithms include arteriosclerotic cardiovascular disease (ASCVD) for likelihood of first heart attack or stroke; length of stay, acuity of admission, comorbidities, and emergency department visits (LACE) for unplanned readmission; and Veterans Aging Cohort Study (VACS) index risk of mortality for HIV patients. These coefficients for the risk terms are typically developed on a large cohort of patients (generally over 10,000). Based on the published findings, scoring tools can be deployed electronically via online calculators, apps, or built directly within the EHR system.

From the patient point of view, there are ethical questions about revealing health risk scores to patients. An obvious case would be a mortality risk score. More research is needed on the ethical use and best practices of risk scores in management of a clinical population and their impact on human behaviors and emotions.

CASE STUDY: IMPLEMENTATION OF HIV RISK CALCULATOR IN AN EHR

The purpose of this study was to translate a multidimensional mortality index described in the HIV literature into an operational metric within the EHR. The VACS index incorporates demographic information about age, gender, race, hepatitis C comorbidity, and laboratory data to predict all-cause mortality up to six years after antiretroviral therapy (ART) initiation.[71]

The VACS index calculations were embedded in a custom HIV registry in the EpicCare Ambulatory EHR system. Eleven metrics used rule functions to collect raw data from the patient record and store intermediate calculations for the final score. This design allows for the ongoing dynamic calculation of VACS scores in real time for all HIV patients in this EHR instance. Metric validation included manual chart review by a multidisciplinary informatics team, matching of results with an Internet-based VACS calculator, and a comparison of the resulting mean of VACS scores with the published mean of the North American AIDS Cohort Collaboration (NA-ACCORD). The mean VACS score across the cohort was 2 points lower than the published mean (19 versus 21). In light of the rigorous chart review and validation with the Internet calculator, we established that the scores were within the expected range of results. We could not make any

HIV REGISTRY REPORT WITH VACS MORTALITY INDEX

Name	VACS Mortality Risk%	HIV Viral Load	Last IP Admit DD/MM	Yearly Utilization in RVUs
Grover	66	10,500	05/10-05/26	37.50
Eleanor	41	200,652		0.75
Martha	32	Not Detected		0.20
George	30	Not Detected		1.50
John		Not Tested		0
Nick	20	Not Detected		12.80

Figure 13.3   HIV registry report with VACS mortality risk.

conclusions about the cause of the scoring difference between the local HIV cohort and NA-ACCORD cohort without further analysis.

The implementation of a risk algorithm for HIV mortality as a real-time operational metric within an EHR system demonstrates the feasibility and challenges inherent in the use of automatically generated risk scores. The VACS index is currently being used as a trigger for referral to case management and pharmacy services.

This study was approved by the university's institutional review board and funded by the California HIV/AIDS Research Program, award number: MH10-SD-640

Discussion Questions

Figure 13.3 shows a small set of data for test patients in an HIV registry. On each row, the patient name is followed by the VACS mortality risk score. The HIV viral load is a surrogate for disease severity. The last inpatient admission is in column 4, and the final column displays the patient utilization of clinic provider time (in relative value units, RVUs) over the past year.

1. Consider your personal reaction if you received a VACS score of 66% (like Grover in line 1). This means your personal risk of death is 66 percent within the next five years.
2. What if the risk of mortality was 80% within one year? How might that change clinical decision-making and lifestyle choices?

3. What are the potential ramifications of errors and/or misunderstanding of the subtleties of statistical analysis when these mortality risk data are shared?
4. What is your opinion about the sharing of this information with patients?
   a. Patients should always see all of the clinical information available, including mortality risk scores.
   b. Patients should never be exposed to mortality risk score data.
   c. Patients should be given the choice of knowing their score or not.
5. Based on this limited data set, does VACS risk of mortality appear to correlate well with utilization?

Machine Learning

When applied to risk scoring, machine learning is a computer science term that describes the ability to automatically improve performance based on analysis of previous predictions. It is growing in importance as a method to adapt to local conditions and improve algorithm performance over time. Unlike the LACE readmission risk score, which was developed using a cohort of 4,812 Canadian patients prior to 2008,[72] newer readmission risk models use data currently available within the EHR system to continually improve their own performance over time. A machine learning readmission model compares earlier predictions to data on actual readmissions within 30 days post-discharge. Based on this information, it automatically adjusts the model to improve accuracy. The application of machine learning to unstructured clinical notes also promises to unlock information that is currently inaccessible to heuristic algorithms that rely on structured data elements. There is great interest in the development and use of these models, and they are being deployed with increasing frequency.

Evaluating Risk Scores

A final caution about risk scores relates to the education of providers and patients in their use. People unfamiliar with the application of probabilistic methods may expect the computer to produce the techno-magical "right answer." Staff training should include the setting of reasonable expectations

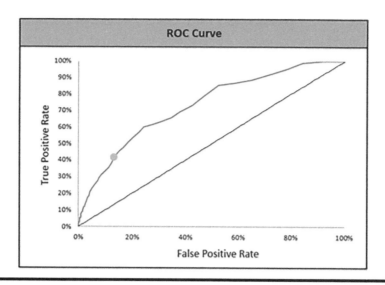

Figure 13.4 ROC curve for model performance.

for score accuracy, and follow-up analysis should evaluate the performance of the score in situ. Risk algorithms generate a likelihood score ranging from 0% risk (will never happen) to 100% (you can count on it). The threshold at which the user decides to take action establishes the sensitivity (true positive rate) and the specificity (true negative rate) of the algorithm. Think of it this way, if you had 100 patients and you know that 10 are going to be readmitted, then a group of 60 high-risk patients will be more likely to contain those 10 (true positives) than a group of 30. However, one would expect more false positives in the group of 60 than in the smaller group. The receiver operating characteristic curve, or ROC curve plots the trade-off between the true positive rate and the false positive rate (Figure 13.4). The diagonal line represents the random chance (50%) that a patient will fall into either group.

When presenting risk scoring performance to those unfamiliar with these statistics, it is helpful to state the results in terms of specific numbers of patients. The following example demonstrates an effective way to present the operating characteristics of a readmission risk score:

Risk threshold is 25% (scores >= 0.25 considered high-risk)
Positive predictive value (PPV) is 27.8%
367 patients predicted for readmission this month
Of those 102 actually were readmitted
We missed 144 false negatives
C stat 0.734 (0.5 is no better than chance, 1.0 is perfect accuracy)

Chapter 14

Analytics Dashboards

"There is no real magic to being a good leader. But at the end of every week, you have to spend your time around the things that are really important: setting priorities, measuring outcomes, and rewarding them."

—Jeffrey B. Immelt, American businessman[73]

Analytics dashboards are becoming the preferred method for effectively communicating success, failure, and current trends in the post-intervention context. Dashboards organize rich data streams to provide insights for mid-course corrections of systems and processes. Population health tools make measurement and reporting more effective, efficient, and reusable. Dashboard designs can be as simple as a table of information or may include advanced data visualizations to help steer and continuously assess the impact of quality interventions. Dashboards represent the post-intervention context of the technical foundation (Figure 14.1).

In this chapter, we have assembled examples of three dashboard domains to help contextualize their application: measure performance, technology performance, and quadruple aim (Figure 14.2). The first domain covers continuous performance measurement to inform quality score improvement using agile methods the require frequent reassessment and adaptation of plans. The technology performance domain includes key performance indicators for the technology itself. We will wrap up by exploring the integration of quadruple aim measures using innovative dashboard design.

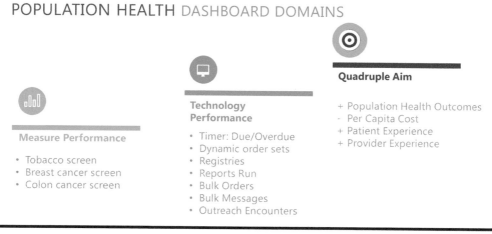

APPLIED POPULATION HEALTH
TECHNICAL FOUNDATION

Quality Measure Management System

EHR Population Health Toolset

Analytics Dashboards

PRE-INTERVENTION   **INTERVENTION**   **POST-INTERVENTION**

Figure 14.1   Technical foundation: Post-intervention context.

POPULATION HEALTH DASHBOARD DOMAINS

Quadruple Aim

Technology Performance

+ Population Health Outcomes
- Per Capita Cost
+ Patient Experience
+ Provider Experience

Measure Performance

- Timer: Due/Overdue
- Dynamic order sets
- Tobacco screen
- Breast cancer screen
- Colon cancer screen
- Registries
- Reports Run
- Bulk Orders
- Bulk Messages
- Outreach Encounters

Figure 14.2   Population health dashboard domains.

Measure Performance

Measure performance dashboards are the most common type used by health systems across the nation. When performance dashboards are deployed in an operational setting, they may be used as a motivational tool and facilitate care gap closure to drive performance improvement. These dashboards may be generated and/or displayed within an electronic health record (EHR) system or run on a business intelligence platform. The mock-up of a measure performance dashboard in Figure 14.3 includes columns of data for baseline and year-end targets, as well as the resulting scores. The right column includes a line graph of the performance over the measurement year. Color

MEASURE PERFORMANCE DASHBOARD

PRIME MEASURE	2018 TARGET	2018 SCORE	2019 TARGET	2019 SCORE	APRIL 2018 – MAR 2019 PERFORMANCE
Screening for Clinical Depression	45.00%	45.67%	55.00%	65.50%	
Sexual Orientation / Gender Identity Data Completeness	15.00%	23.14%	15.00%	55.64%	
Tobacco Assessment and Counseling	98.00%	97.88%	98.00%	97.94%	
Timely Transmission of Transition Record	85.00%	81.89%	89.00%	96.46%	
Advance Care Plan on File	49.00%	41.62%	55.00%	58.30%	

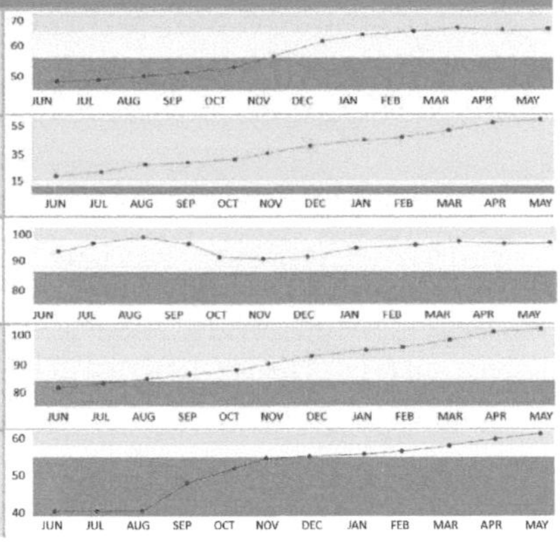

Figure 14.3   Measure performance dashboard.

coding includes red (target not met), yellow (external target met), and green (internal target met) and note that incorporation of shades that are inclusive of people with color blindness is important.

Interactive dashboard features allow users to dynamically filter, drill down, and provide additional details on demand through links and hover bubbles. A common drill-down hierarchy for hospital data includes business entity (by tax ID number), hospital location, service line, provider, and patient. An ambulatory drill-down includes business entity (by tax ID number), primary care or specialty, department, provider, and patient.

Provider Feedback

A provider panel dashboard is a hybrid tool for performance measurement and clinical decision support. This dashboard displays the harmonized operational metrics discussed in Chapter 4. On this dashboard, the provider can only see scores for their own patients. If a performance measure is below the goal, the provider can drill down to see which patients are failing the measure. Ideally, the dashboard will facilitate action within the EHR to close the gaps either through activity in an individual patient chart or through bulk activities or messaging.

Increasingly, organizations have linked some form of provider pay or incentive to this type of performance dashboard. Consequently, clinicians may be highly motivated to achieve the target scores. A dashboard quality assurance plan should anticipate and address any concerns voiced by clinicians regarding the accuracy and validity of the measures. The following three-part strategy will build confidence in the dashboards, which is necessary for them to be an effective tool:

1. Include clinicians as subject matter experts for quality measure validation. Clinician review should include value sets, measure logic, and chart review. Chart audits can be conducted more quickly if a report of patients includes key data used in measure calculations. Due to continuing challenges with interoperability, there is always a chance that the most detailed and rigorous measure calculations still won't identify all evidence of measure completion. Therefore, the measure code should provide clinicians the ability to attest to measure completion based on nonstandard data sources. In other words, for each measure, a clinician should be able to manually "pass" or "fail" an individual patient (adding documentation supporting the action).

2. Detailed information about the dashboard calculations should be readily accessible to viewers. Explain the measure inclusions, exclusions, and logic in clinical terms that accurately reflect the scoring algorithms. Emphasize that performance on a provider panel dashboard may not tie directly to the score of a particular quality program due to measure harmonization across programs, differences in denominators, measurement period, etc.

3. If a provider dashboard error is reported, work quickly to investigate the problem. If a coding error is discovered, assess whether the dashboard platform supports retroactive recalculation of scores as of a specified date. If this feature is not supported, a corrective plan must be developed to ensure that incentives are calculated and distributed fairly.

In some cases, responsibility for meeting a quality measure may be offloaded from the attending physician to a group of nurses within each clinic or a centralized population health team for the enterprise. These teams specialize in outreach workflows and closing care gaps per protocol. Performance dashboards should be made available to anyone responsible for closing the care gaps with the ability to target outreach for specific patients, providers, clinics, or topics.

CASE STUDY: OHSU AMBULATORY QUALITY REPORTING WHITE PAPER

Project Sponsor: Dr. Michael Lieberman
Project Lead: Adam Stone
Technical Lead: Mark Thomas
Project Analyst: Siran Abtin

The Oregon Health & Science University (OHSU) Ambulatory Quality Reporting Program developed a white paper to familiarize the reader with how clinical quality measures (CQMs) are calculated in OHSU's EpicCare Ambulatory system. The white paper aims to give providers enough detail to validate the measures and provide actionable information to improve care.

For each measure in the program, this document provides a descriptive definition followed by a technical definition of how patient populations are determined and measure outcomes are calculated based on data items identified in the patient's medical record.

Following is an example of the outcome measure for controlling high blood pressure.

NQF-0018	Controlling High Blood Pressure v. 2014
Measure Description	The percentage of patients 18 to 85 years of age who had a diagnosis of hypertension (HTN) and whose blood pressure (BP) was adequately controlled (<140/90) at the time of measurement.
Numerator Description	The number of patients in the denominator whose most recent BP is adequately controlled at the time of measurement. For a patient's BP to be controlled, both the systolic and diastolic BP are adequately controlled (systolic blood pressure < 140 mmHg and diastolic blood pressure < 90 mmHg).
Denominator Description	Patients 18 to 85 years of age at the beginning of the measurement period* who had at least one outpatient encounter with a diagnosis of HTN during the measurement period.
Exclusion Description	Patients with evidence of end-stage renal disease (ESRD), dialysis, or renal transplant before or during the measurement period. Also exclude patients with a diagnosis of pregnancy during the measurement period.*

*Measurement period start date = Measurement date – 365 days (rolling year)

PATIENT POPULATION

Identification of the patient population with hypertension diagnosis will be derived from the Epic Hypertension Registry, which includes the following:

■ Patient has at least one problem on the problem list with a diagnosis from ICD group HYPERTENSION in any status.
OR
Patient has at least one encounter diagnosis from ICD group HYPERTENSION within 365 days prior to measurement date.
OR
Patient has at least one billing diagnosis from ICD group HYPERTENSION within 365 days prior to measurement date.

AND

■ Patient is not deceased AND
■ Registry record is active AND
■ Patient has had an office visit in the last 365 days AND
■ Patient >= 18 and <= 85 years of age at the start of the measurement period

EXCLUSIONS

Pregnancy: exclude patients identified by

■ Active problem list diagnosis in ICD group PREGNANCY

OR

■ Encounter diagnosis in ICD group PREGNANCY within 365 days prior to measurement date

OR

■ Billing diagnosis in ICD group PREGNANCY within 365 days prior to measurement date.

End Stage Renal Disease (ESRD) or Chronic Kidney Disease: exclude patients identified by

■ Problem list diagnosis in ICD group CMS_EXCLUSIONS

OR

■ Encounter diagnosis in ICD group CMS_EXCLUSIONS within 365 days prior to measurement date

OR

■ Billing diagnosis in ICD group CMS_EXCLUSIONS within 365 days prior to measurement date

Exclude patients who ever had an encounter with an ESRD monthly outpatient service level of service (LOS) code, identified by:

■ Patient encounter with an LOS code in group ESRD MONTHLY OUTPATIENT SERVICES

Exclude patients who have ever had a completed procedure of dialysis education, vascular access for dialysis, kidney transplant, dialysis service, or other service related to dialysis, identified by:

■ Order with a result status of completed in group CMS_EXCLUSIONS

DATA ITEMS FOR MEASUREMENT

■ Systolic and diastolic blood pressures measured are the most recent blood pressures recorded in the medical record on the measurement date.

OUTCOME CALCULATION

IF patient is excluded by exclusion criteria, THEN "Excluded from Measurement" ELSE

IF systolic BP <140 AND diastolic BP <90 AND systolic BP taken date >= measurement period start date AND diastolic BP >= measurement period start date, THEN "Include in Numerator"
ELSE
"Do Not Include in Numerator"

CASE QUESTIONS

1. The white paper description of NQF-0018 Controlling High Blood Pressure lists a number of data items used in the measure calculation. Create a list of those data items you would abstract from the patient record for measure validation report.
2. Is a pregnant patient included in the measure denominator?
3. Assume the patient is in the denominator and has no exclusions. If the measurement period start date is 1/1/2018 and the last BP reading of 139/89 was taken on 12/3/2017, would this patient be numerator positive (in numerator = yes)?
4. What steps would you take to close the care gap for patients who are not in the numerator?

Troubleshooting

The use of performance dashboards for early identification of patients with care gaps is an effective approach to improving performance scores. What are the options when the dashboard indicates that a particular measure isn't performing at the expected level? What are the steps to triage whether the underperformance issues are related to a clinic, a provider, a missing data problem, or some other cause? The answer depends on what the intervention is.

When implementing a new outreach workflow via the web portal, there are additional details to measure. Is every clinic performing the patient outreach for outliers? If so, how frequently? Are there particular patients who are not being contacted? For patients lacking patient portal access, are calls being made? Are the calls effective? Are automated calls more effective than manual? How are patients with alternative linguistic preferences being serviced? Are those also being measured? All of these issues frequently contribute to suboptimal scores and can be reviewed on an ad hoc basis or established as supportive quality measurements for continuous monitoring.

Prediction

Continuous performance measurement enables the calculation of the probability of reaching a performance goal. In some cases, there may not be enough patients eligible for care gap closure to satisfy a measure. That number is limited by the number of untested or failing patients in the denominator pool. Here's an example of how to predict the likelihood of success:

Suppose that there were 2,000 patients eligible for an intervention, and in order to achieve the goal, 1,073 of them need to pass (become numerator positive). That is over 50% of available patients. If we begin efforts to close the gaps on these 2,000 patients and we find that we're only converting 1 in 3 patients when we need to convert 1 in 2 patients, we've established a poor likelihood of success. In this case the steering committee might decide to stop expending effort on this measure and reallocate resources to other measures where the likelihood of success is greater. Other options might include a detailed review of the measure code with chart review to ensure the numerator and denominator are being correctly assessed or a pivot to another supportive intervention to increase the conversion rate.

Technology Performance

As automation is increasingly being used to deliver interventions, the performance of the technology should be considered for inclusion in performance dashboards. The value of a technology investment can be evaluated by monitoring how many people are using it, monitoring the technology itself, or monitoring how well the technology is delivering results (efficacy).

Let's look at these methods in more detail.

Monitor Technology Use

An EHR query tool can provide aggregate information about a patient population that can't be deduced from reviewing one chart at a time. Because these types of tools have the potential to extract large amounts of protected health information, the implementation team engaged their compliance team and developed safeguards and strategies for use of the tool. One of

Session Count by User Type

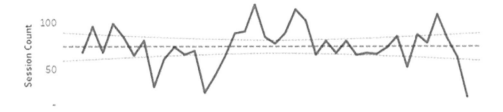

User Type

Attending Physician	
Resident	72
Pharmicist	51
Researcher	26
Analyst with Admin	23
Fellow	20
Registered Nurse	15
Manager	12
Anesthesiologist	8
Nurse Practitioner	8
UNKNOWN	7
Medical Student	5
Pharmacist	5
Analyst	4
Case Manager	3
Clinical User	2
Research (Research Templ..	2
Genetic Counselor	1
Infection Control	1
Nursing Student	1

instant | Last 3 quarters

Top Emp Types with session count

Attending Physician 1,105

Analyst with Admin 470

Pharmicist 358

Researcher 151

Resident 322

Fellow

Sessions Overtime

Figure 14.4   Usage dashboard for EHR query tool.

the security steps was to release access to the tools gradually by role. The attending physicians received access first, followed by pharmacists, and, gradually, more roles received access. To monitor progress on the uptake and use of the query tool, we used a dashboard of session count by user type, and tracked the sessions over time (Figure 14.4).

Monitor the Technology Platform

The STORE type registries as discussed in Chapter 5 are complicated sub-systems within the EHR and should be monitored. Figure 14.5 illustrates the

REGISTRY CENSUS OVER TIME

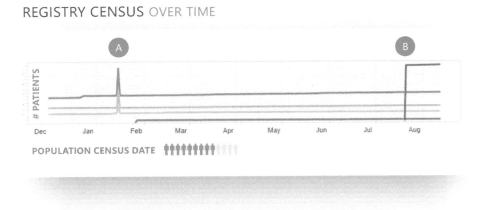

Figure 14.5   **Registry census over time.**

registry census over time, with each line representing a separate registry. Notice that at point A, the number of patients in every registry doubled. We discovered a processing error and corrected the anomaly. Point B shows the date on which a new registry was turned on. Viewing the registry census over time will alert support staff to processing issues and provide insight into registry growth for resource planning.

It is important to realize that the registry census does not show the true magnitude of changes. Terminology maintenance, which causes changes in diagnosis code mappings, can cause patients to be added to or dropped from a registry irrespective of any changes to their clinical history. Figure 14.6 shows registry census changes over time, with patients added to a single registry indicated by the top line, and patients removed from a registry represented by the bottom line. The sum of the additions and drops represents the true magnitude of change in a registry census.

Monitor Technology Efficacy

When population health tools are applied to close care gaps, we want to understand their effectiveness. For instance, consider the case of a bulk outreach message via patient portal to remind patients about influenza immunizations. We composed a message asking patients to call for an immunization appointment or to let us know if they had already received

REGISTRY CENSUS CHANGES INCLUDE ADDS AND DROPS

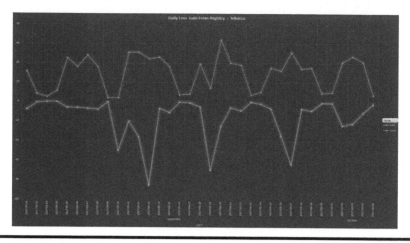

Figure 14.6   Registry census changes showing additions (top) and drops (bottom).

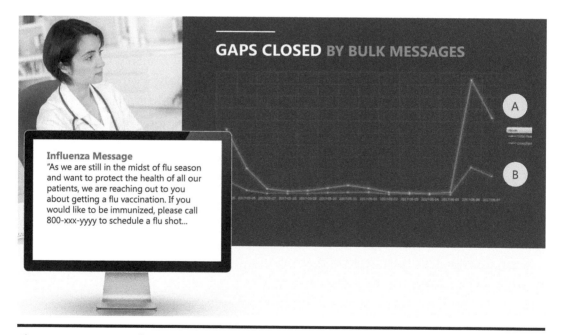

Figure 14.7   Gaps closed by bulk messages.

an immunization. We sent the bulk message to three cohorts of patients, distributing the outreach so that clinics wouldn't be overwhelmed with calls (Figure 14.7). Line A shows the number of messages read per day. You can see from the early downward slope that many patients read the reminder on the day sent, and over time, the number opening the messages dropped off. Line B shows the care gaps closed per day as a result of those messages. The data helps us predict the percentage of responses we are likely to get from this type of messaging in the future and to optimize our outreach plan in terms of timing, repetition, and size of the message groups.

Quadruple Aim Outcomes

The Value-based Measurement Framework (Chapter 2) illustrates how post-intervention outcomes reflect the Quadruple Aims. If we aim to simultane-ously achieve these outcomes, they must be regarded as a set, and viewed in relationship to one another. Otherwise, process optimization efforts may work at cross-purpose by improving quality while increasing overall cost, decreasing provider experience. A simple model for a Quadruple Aim Dashboard is shown in Figure 14.8.

Most of the time, however, health systems are not creating end-to-end measurements of populations and then evaluating whether cohorts have improvements in patient satisfaction, provider satisfaction, quality, and cost. As health systems become more directly accountable for the population-level costs and outcomes, they will increasingly seek to define population-level

Quadruple
Aims
Dashboard

Population Health Outcomes		
Adv Care Plan	Depression Remission	A1c In Control
↑ 58.03% [55.00%]	↓ 45.36% [50.00%]	↑ 84.08% [90.00%]
Per Capita Costs		
Cost/Visit	Collections/Visit	Physician RVU
↑ 4/10 sites at goal	7/10 sites at goal	10/10 sites at goal
Patient Experience		
CAHPS Recommend Provider	CAHPS Provider Communication	ED Provider Overall
6/10 sites at goal	4/10 sites at goal	2 of 2 sites at goal
Provider Experience		
Best Place to Work Survey	Physician Panel Size	% Physicians Over Empaneled
40%	1400	25%

Figure 14.8   Quadruple aims dashboard.

Table 14.1   Strategic Areas of Focus for Quadruple Aim Outcomes

Quadruple Aim	Strategic Areas of Focus
Population Health	1) Early identification and aversion of risk; 2) Improved chronic care management; 3) Promotion of health equity; 4) High reliability; 5) Improved outcomes
Cost Aversion	1) Identification and removal of waste; 2) Improved efficiency; 3) Reduction of unnecessary utilization
Patient Experience	1) Improved access; 2) Needs met
Provider Experience	1) Enabled decision support; 2) Team-based care delivery

quadruple aim metrics. For example, how are patient and provider satisfaction as related to a cohort of patients with heart failure? Have quality metrics such as number of patients on appropriate therapeutics or readmission rates improved? Has that improved the overall cost of providing care? Strategic areas of focus for Quadruple Aim outcomes are summarized in Table 14.1.

APPLIED POPULATION HEALTH TODAY AND TOMORROW

3

Chapter 15

Moving Into the Future With a Learning Health System

"We've been studying the intersection of innovation and implementation science where we apply the evidence chain, moving from local quality improvement all the way up to scale at the multiprovider consortium and national levels."

Lucy Savitz, PhD, MBA[46]

Health outcomes that matter to patients, providers, and payors include reduction of; new disease, health complications, emergency or hospital visits, and mortality. However, calculating whether outcomes have been achieved is not always practical in the operations setting at the local level of a single health system. Statistical computations that evaluate prevalence, incidence, and intervention effects are frequently more complex for a variety of reasons, including population movement, non-normally distributed populations, and lack of access to the right data. The populations being addressed are not static, but rather shift continuously as new patients join a practice and other patients move, change care providers, or pass away. Measuring the impact of quality interventions on a statistically small population that is continuously changing becomes challenging. Population selection may be biased and not representative of the broader community. Academic medical centers are often the tertiary and quaternary referral centers, thereby affecting incidence and prevalence computations. Finally, important data in terms of outcomes are frequently lacking such as readmission, surgical complications, and mortality due to siloed care fragmenting access to data. A solution to these challenges can be found in the learning health system approach in which researchers work side-by-side with clinical operations to collect and analyze observational data at the health system level and contribute curated data to research networks for study at higher levels of data aggregation.

Learning to Deliver Better Healthcare

As organizations move to improve the value of care delivery to their patients, increasingly health systems are seeking quantifiable evidence that technology investments and quality efforts are resulting in meaningful change. To better understand how to provide those answers, we contacted Dr. Savitz at Kaiser Permanente. She has dedicated her career to evaluating innovation in evidence-based health care delivery processes. About a decade ago, she was in a novel position as a researcher embedded with a clinical team led by Brent James, MD, a key innovator of learning health system science. In the beginning, Dr. Savitz's role on the quality teams was poorly understood, and occasionally she would hear comments from her operations counterparts like, "Oh, she's just a researcher." After a while, the teams came to value the rigorous outcomes evaluations, and the refrain changed to, "Where's Lucy? How do we know this works?" Here she describes the formation of a research collaborative that was used to evaluate the variations in total knee replacements across leading US health care systems.[74] Studies from this collaborative were later used to recommend and evaluate episodic (bundled) payments by Medicare for hip and knee replacements.

> Intermountain Healthcare, working with The Mayo Clinic and Dartmouth Health System, realized that their ability to perform conclusive studies on how best to transform care delivery and payment reform [was limited by the size of their patient populations and] needed to be amplified to inform the national debate. So, in late 2009 during health care reform, it joined with four delivery systems to create a research network called the High Value Health Care Collaborative. EHR data, claims, and other data were combined in a data trust that allowed us to study problems at scale, so when they came out with episodic bundle payment for hip and knee replacement, we were able to look across those organizations to evaluate the program.
>
> Lucy Savitz, PhD, MBA[46]

Population sizes are big challenges for performing observational research at the level of a single health enterprise. In order to generalize findings, researchers need data for a lot of patients, and sometimes within the health system, there just aren't the numbers required to conduct conclusive analyses in short order to support timely operational decision-making. The High Value Healthcare Collaborative's mission was, to improve healthcare value through data, evidence and collaboration using the following methods:

- Measure, innovate, test, and continuously improve value-based care
- Rapidly disseminate and facilitate adoption of proven high value care models across HVHC members and beyond
- Advocate for policy and payment models that support sustainable high value healthcare.[75]

Even when the data are sufficient, operational and quality departments generally don't consider research to be central to their role. However, with a relatively small incremental effort, population health teams can capture enough clean, formatted data from clinical processes to provide a solid baseline for future studies. This step ensures that the aggregated data retains its original meaning. The extra level of validation and curation at the operations level, often through the use of registries, creates data that are clean enough to drive clinical decision-making. If we can curate the "Little Data" at the enterprise level through population health applications and data governance, the aggregate data will be improved as well.

Creating a Learning Health System

How do we learn to deliver value in healthcare? A learning health system is "continuous improvement in effectiveness, efficiency, safety, and quality."[2] The Institute of Medicine (IOM) 2013 report, *Best Care at Lower Cost*, describes the learning health system as

> designed to generate and apply the best evidence for the collaborative healthcare choices of each patient and provider; to drive the process of discovery as a natural outgrowth of patient care; and to ensure innovation, quality, safety, and value in health care.[76]

The concept of a learning health system was first envisioned in the Institute of Medicine report, *Crossing the Quality Chasm* (2001); and later developed by the

IOM Roundtable on Value & Science-Driven Health Care in cooperation with the National Academy of Medicine (NAM formerly IOM) in 2006. The 15 volumes of the Learning Health System Series published by the National Academies Press are available at https://nam.edu. Outgrowth of the series includes the Learning Health Community, the Learning Health System Interest Group at Academy Health, and the AHRQ-PCORI–funded Learning Health System K12 Scholar program. More information may be found in Appendix H. The [learning health system] will [improve the health of individuals and populations] by generating information and knowledge from data captured and updated over time—as an ongoing and natural by-product of contributions by individuals, care delivery systems, public health programs, and clinical research.[77]

Learning health system concepts are in full alignment with the goals of value-based care. "By value, we mean the full value equation—the best outcomes, safety, and service for the best price."[78] With embedded research, a healthcare system is able to generate evidence using the data generated as a by-product of care delivery. Acknowledgement of the role of health systems in clinical operations research is fueling the expansion of the evidence base. Guise and Savitz[79] described how internal learning cycles work within the larger construct of the learning health system (Figure 15.1). Within each learning cycle, there are three phases: Knowledge to Performance (K2P), Performance to Data (P2D), and Data to Knowledge (D2K). Knowledge can be acquired and applied

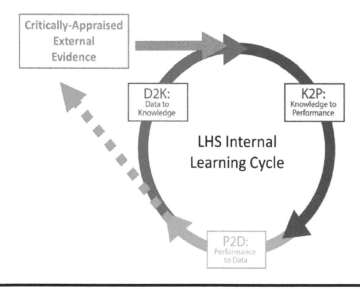

Figure 15.1   Learning health system internal learning cycle moving from quality improvement to scale.

locally, or the data can be critically appraised and become part of the external knowledge base. Learning cycles can be repeated at a local level, and the aggregation of data can continue up to the national or international level.

At Intermountain, Dr. Savitz solidified her understanding of the learning health system at the intersection of innovation and implementation science, particularly as applied to population health. She continued this work at Kaiser Permanente Center for Health Research, and formalized an Evidence-based Quality Improvement Process (EQuIP).[80] The EQuIP model uses an interactive, data-driven approach to show how we can use data science to identify opportunities to reduce unwarranted variation in practice and reduce low-value care. The model's applied learning experience, i.e. on-the-job operational training component, is extremely important. This is where frontline clinical teams acquire and apply the tools and concepts of rigorous quality improvement to implement change. Operations staff partner with researchers to incorporate clean data capture into their workflows. Without this training and partnership, requests for data analysis and embedded research support after the fact can be delayed or even rendered impossible. The researchers can use the EQuIP process to identify improvement opportunities, but empowered frontline staff are required to lead the change management efforts. McCannon and Berwick[81] pointed out that the real waste in healthcare occurs when we find something that works and we don't seek to scale, making such improvement ubiquitous. Scaling is a process by which best practices may be recognized or developed in a single clinic or specialty and then propagated deep and wide through the organization. Depth can be seen from top to bottom (executive, chief medical officer, physician, manager, nurse). Width can be seen across silos of work (call center, ambulatory, acute, procedural and skilled nursing). While particular measures may be relevant to one domain, such as transplant outcomes, the enterprise vision sees the organization as a complex adaptive system with opportunities to improve care delivery across the continuum. This importantly requires not only transparency and alignment but most importantly, a culture of learning at the highest levels. From the lens of the learning health system, the following systems will be necessary at the enterprise level to improve scale:

- **Communication:** Aligned, coordinated, and efficient patient notifications and outreach
- **Access to the right information:** Driven by actionable registries

- **Transparency:** Diverse and convergent sources of data truth via dashboards and ad hoc queries
- **Business intelligence:** Analytics that highlight improvements in delivery cost, outcomes, and patient safety

The learning health system provides a more sophisticated infrastructure to evaluate impact from simple institution-level regulatory reporting to more systematic process improvement and applied research. Scaling quality improvement is no easy task. Although standardization certainly helps in the process, the selection of core measures and aligned incentives (and hence prioritization) of those values are key. Centers for Medicare and Medicaid Services (CMS) has a role in establishing a small set of national quality markers for each care setting to provide focus on safety in acute settings (hospital and emergency), procedural, ambulatory, and long-term care, and professional organizations are leading efforts to standardize data sets for particular specialties and conditions.

Funding Research and Development

Dr. Savitz also stressed the importance of funding the research efforts, and one way to do that is through a negotiated financial investment in the learning health system portfolio by clinical operations departments. Funding supports researchers' time to work shoulder to shoulder with people in operations while listening to the problems that they are facing. This method leads to practical and testable research questions that can provide timely answers to refine clinical processes. Kaiser Permanente, Northwest made a three-year investment in 2018. In 2020, they will evaluate the impact of that investment to determine the next steps. Dr. Savitz offered the following closing advice:

> Think of the Learning Health System portfolio as a Research and Development investment. It builds your competitive advantage by figuring out how to excel in terms of providing state-of-the-art evidence-based care. It relates to design, discovery, efficiency and affordability. A big portion of what we do, especially in the population health space, is to identify and remove unwarranted, very low value care. Redeploying wasted resources is one source of value we bring to the team. Our ability to expand the research mission depends on the extent to which we can show those savings in a way that's believable to the Chief Financial Officer (CFO).
>
> Lucy Savitz, PhD, MBA[46]

Standardizing Financial Outcomes and Economic Impact

Convincing the CFO that R&D efforts are paying off requires analysis of financial outcomes. Risk sharing and capitated plans run by health systems have moved the financial analysis of healthcare closer to the clinical domain. Outcome domains can be standardized and then applied across various interventions and chronic disease domains. For instance, for the diabetic population, how have the implemented activities resulted in improvements related to the following?

- Generic utilization rate and costs
- Length of stay
- Admission per 1,000 stratified by risk
- Readmission per 1,000 stratified by risk
- Emergency room use per 1,000 stratified by risk
- Catastrophic outcomes such as amputation rate, blindness, end-stage renal disease, and bypass surgery
- Morbidity: acute myocardial infarction (MI), stroke, retinopathy, chronic kidney disease, and hospitalized infection rate

What is the potential economic impact considering patient, community, and health system perspectives? Although this may not be feasible to compute overall, it may be important for particular projects to highlight the total economic impact of the outcome to demonstrate the full benefit. For example, if home-based continuous glucose monitoring data were to be integrated into registries and care management resulted in 25% less admissions from type 1 diabetics age 18 and younger, this outcome could imply substantial reduction in missed school days, missed work by families, etc.

Progress to Date

> By the year 2020, ninety percent of clinical decisions will be supported accurate, timely, and up-to-date clinical information, and will reflect the best available evidence.
>
> —Goal of the Institute of Medicine Roundtable on Value & Science-Driven Health Care[2]

Without a doubt, measurable progress is being made. The 2018 CMS *National Impact Assessment of Quality Measures Report*[82] states:

▪ Patient impacts estimated from improved national measure rates indicated approximately:
  – 670,000 additional patients with controlled blood pressure (2006–2015)
  – 510,000 fewer patients with poor diabetes control (2006–2015)
  – 12,000 fewer deaths following hospitalization for a heart attack (2008–2015)
  – 70,000 fewer unplanned readmissions (2011–2015)
  – 840,000 fewer pressure ulcers among nursing home residents (2011–2015)
  – Nine million more patients reporting a highly favorable experience with their hospital (2008–2015)
▪ Costs avoided were estimated for a subset of key indicators, data permitting. The highest were associated with increased medication adherence ($4.2 billion to $26.9 billion), reduced pressure ulcers ($2.8 billion to $20.0 billion), and fewer patients with poor control of diabetes ($6.5 billion to $10.4 billion).

Investing in the health transformation to enable the learning health system is not an easy task for any organization to achieve. Questions remain about the benefits of new technology-enabled workflows. Only organizations that commit resources to evaluate R&D activities will be in a position to demonstrate value.

Today, we need new ways to quantify and publish the findings from experience in the learning health system so that they can be more broadly adopted. More than 20 years ago, Realistic Evaluation proposed an alternative to the randomized clinical trial that may be useful for evaluating context-specific interventions.[83] In a more recent publication, "Meta-Analysis by the Confidence Profile Method," a method was described that could be used to construct more appropriate designs for testing the complex interventions.[84] More recently, the Veterans' Administration has created two new approaches to evaluate clinical practice in the learning health system. Point-of-Care Research (POC-R) performs clinical trials with the daily structure of the healthcare system. Collaborative Research to Enhance and Advance Transformation and Excellence (CREATE) requires investigators to certify that health system partners engage in study design and commit to implementation of research findings.[85]

In summary, the future of the learning health system in the public sector will require continued reporting of observational data. Recent activity sparked in 2007 via Health Information Technology for Economic and Clinical Health (HITECH) launched our value-based journey and was followed in 2018 by high adoption of value-based payment methods through meaningful use, accountable care organization arrangements, and alternative payment models. However, the data collection requirements need to be standardized across the states so that EHR providers can anticipate the data needs and build virtuous cycles of curated data that can be easily accessed at the local system for iterative learning, as well as aggregated for public health and research services.

Discussion Questions

The Learning Health System cycles in Figure 15.1 capture observational data at the point of care (P2D), and use that to improve local knowledge of care delivery (D2K). If the performance data is critically appraised, it can add to the public knowledge base and scale across other organizations and geographical areas.

1. Describe some of the challenges and barriers that slow or prevent the incorporation of local performance data into the Critically-Appraised External Evidence Base?
2. What are the barriers that slow or prevent the application of Critically-Appraised External Evidence to performance improvement at the healthcare provider level?

Chapter 16

We've Come So Far . . .
Lessons Learned and
Call to Action

To remind ourselves how far we've come, it's useful to reflect on where we've been. In 2003–2004, HIV/AIDS care was largely funded by the U.S. Health Resources and Services Administration (HRSA) Ryan White program. The government stipulated that information from patient care be collected and shared to inform best practice. Every year, it would take *at least six weeks* to collect and curate the data and make sure everything was correct on paper. We performed chart reviews for approximately 3,000 patients to capture about 35 discrete data elements for each. Then we would type all this data into the Ryan White online system, where it was subsequently aggregated with data from other health systems and used for funding justification and research. It was frustrating that all these great data weren't helping the doctor or the patient directly because they weren't accessible within the electronic health record (EHR) to help drive care.

CASE STUDY: DISCOVERY OF
THE EHR AS A "THERAPEUTIC"

Fast forward about a decade. In addition to the HRSA reporting, our academic healthcare system submitted 10 HIV quality measures for the 2012–2013 Centers for Medicare and Medicaid Services (CMS) Delivery

System Reform Incentive Payment Medicaid (DSRIP) 1115 waiver program. An actionable registry for HIV was built in the EHR to provide decision support in the form of huddle reports, health maintenance alerts, and dynamic order sets. A sociotechnical approach enabled three key workflows: 1) encounter-based clinical decision support to close care gaps, 2) non–encounter-based targeted outreach, and 3) patient self-management through the EHR patient portal (offered in English and Spanish). Clinical teams used the EHR registry to leverage economies of scale, including bulk orders and messaging directly in the chart. A relentless plan, do, study, act (PDSA) cycle was used to drive performance gains. As a result, 9 of 10 final performance goals were achieved worth nearly $20 million.

Ultimately, we fell slightly short on one key outcome measure—suppression of HIV viral load to less than 200 copies/mL. Although baseline performance of 90.74% viral load suppression was well above the national rate for patients retained in care, the final reported outcome of 91.62% was under the performance target rate of 92.6 % HIV viral suppression for the DSRIP quality program. We were surprised at this outcome because of the apparent success of the multidisciplinary targeted outreach and intervention. When considering possible explanations for the failure to meet the goal, we realized that the rates of suppression were confounded by the increase in patients with uncontrolled HIV being brought back into care for viral load testing. The improvement in the measures to ensure timely office visits by patients and monitor viral loads every six months increased the likelihood that these patients would present with an unsuppressed viral load. Finding and re-engaging patients who fall out of care is an important outcome for the clinic, but finding and treating these patients in the last quarter of the measurement period negatively affected the clinic overall rate of viral suppression. Many of these patients had stopped taking medication and needed months to reach viral load suppression.

Another handicapping factor for failure to meet the HIV suppression goal was the Boolean (yes/no) design of the outcome measure. It was sensitive only to reduction of the HIV viral load to a fixed level (less than 200 copies/mL). The measure definition gave no credit for log reduction of an individual viral load from 1,000,000 copies/mL to 1,000 copies/mL. Viral load is the chief predictor of the risk of transmission of HIV-1, and transmission is known to be rare among persons with levels of less than 1,500 copies of HIV-1 RNA per milliliter.[86] Community viral load has been used at a public health level to estimate the success of test-and-treat initiatives aimed at reducing viral transmission.[87] To test our hypothesis, we compared the change in community viral load (at the clinic level) using the Centers for Disease Control (CDC) guidance on community viral load.[88] Results demonstrated a reduction in clinic HIV viral load by 44% (baseline 44,166,190 compared to final 29,852,201) suggestive of a population health impact. The log(10) reduction by 0.16 would predict a 0.392 decreased rate of transmission per 100 person years. We had discovered that applied population health methods could have a collective impact on the health status of an HIV population on the order of what might be expected from a new therapeutic regimen. However, in order to detect this change, we needed to apply a population measure of the mean or median. Figure 15.1 illustrates how high-reliability systems help ensure that each patient moves through the steps that would lead to a positive health outcome: 1) patient is in care; 2) patient receives evidence-based treatment; 3) patient achieves quantifiable goal. Boolean measures work well at the individual level when identifying care gaps in these steps. However, new measures of population median or mean, like the HIV community viral load, will be needed to understand if the cohort is better, worse or the same at a population level. The answer to that question should be accompanied by statistical analysis that quantifies

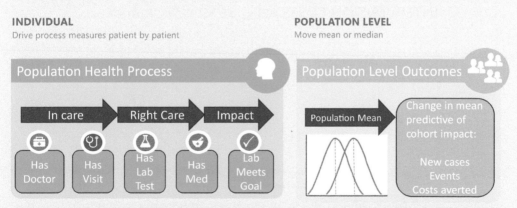

POPULATION MEASURES FOR POPULATION OUTCOMES

INDIVIDUAL
Drive process measures patient by patient

POPULATION LEVEL
Move mean or median

Population Health Process

Population Level Outcomes

In care → Right Care → Impact

Has Doctor · Has Visit · Has Lab Test · Has Med · Lab Meets Goal

Population Mean → Change in mean predictive of cohort impact:

New cases
Events
Costs averted

Figure 16.1   Process drives outcomes.

the role of random effects. Only then will we have a true picture of population outcomes.

CASE QUESTIONS

1. Name two factors that made it more challenging to meet the HIV viral load quality goal.
2. How does HIV viral load suppression affect value for the patient?
3. How does HIV viral load suppression affect value for the public health system?

How Good Is Good Enough?

The HIV case study illustrates how new measure types based on population means or medians may provide a more sensitive measure of clinical outcomes. There also exists an opportunity to become more practical when setting intervention targets. We have observed in our clinical practice that initial improvement can be brisk with the right intervention. Frequently, improving beyond the 75th percentile becomes incrementally more difficult to foster. Achievement at the rate of the 90th percentile becomes resource intense. Time and again, we see that the rate of intervention costs relative to performance is non-linear (Figure 15.2). As the financial burden to achieve high performance accelerates, we offer a word of caution. We suggest that

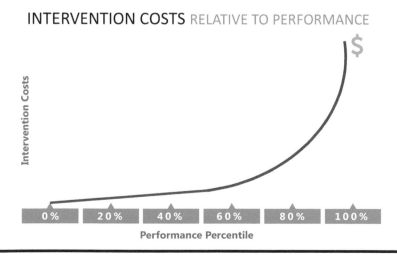

INTERVENTION COSTS RELATIVE TO PERFORMANCE

Intervention Costs

0% 20% 40% 60% 80% 100%

Performance Percentile

Figure 16.2   Intervention cost relative to performance score.

100% may not be the optimal target in the context of common ambulatory process measurement in light of the diminishing returns on quality improvement efforts and incomplete evidence on the clinical significance of incremental performance gains at the upper bounds of possible achievement.

Not all measures are the same. Process measures that are fully under the control of the delivery system and supported by automation such as post-discharge transmission of the discharge summary hold the potential to reach scores at or near 100%. When workflow design, training, and performance of standard work combine to consistently deliver the highest possible performance, we celebrate by admitting contributors to the "One Hundred Percent Club". High value measures to prevent or avoid patient harm and are also worthy of great effort, such as iatrogenic pneumothorax with central line placement. A "No Room for Error Club" provides recognition for teams that reduce complications or infections to zero. However, we acknowledge that as the financial burden of care continues to accelerate, high performance in one area may be offset in other areas. Consider the laudable direct impact of successful reduction in readmissions at a patient and population level. This improvement in outcomes satisfies the triple aim of improved clinical outcome, lower cost and higher patient satisfaction. Indirect impact could be that a hospital is, for instance, decreasing ward staffing to increase post-discharge access to registered nurses. If clinicians and staff are struggling under the increasing burden of quality reporting, this may be reflected in longer cycle times in clinic and high burnout and turnover rates. Organizations need to standardize and automate as much of the reliable care delivery as possible to counterbalance the impact on personnel time and expense.

Manage Complexity

A national quality program offers an incentive payment of nearly $300,000 in exchange for meeting or exceeding targets for managing elevated blood pressure without hypertension. The measure developed by the Agency for Healthcare Research and Quality (AHRQ) was complex with multiple interventions depending on the degree and history of the elevated readings. The required intervention arms included

- Monitor only
- DASH (Dietary Approaches to Stop Hypertension) diet with follow-up in one month
- Additional lab test or an electrocardiogram (a simplified interpretation)

The ambulatory cardiovascular workgroup struggled for months with the branching logic of the measure. As the intervention grew in complexity, the possibility of building the decision support in the EHR rapidly decreased. The workgroup decided that the DASH diet recommendation would be an excellent intervention for all persons with elevated blood pressure without known hypertension. From a clinical and operational perspective, this was "the right thing." Although this alone would not meet the measure requirements, we decided to move ahead with the first-line intervention for this population that presented with elevated blood pressure readings but were not on the hypertension registry (indicating a diagnosis of hypertension). Measure performance began to improve when we introduced clinical decision support to suggest an order for the DASH diet. Once the dietary intervention was operational, the team turned its attention to a more sophisticated decision support tool to apply additional interventions that somewhat paralleled the measure. Those included

- Repeat blood pressure measurements in the same encounter
- Follow-up blood pressure check appointments
- Lab or electrocardiogram (EKG) monitoring for repeat elevations without known hypertension

Design Systems for People

Reliable care does not happen randomly. It requires careful attention to human factors and usability in design so that the automation is powerful, cost-effective, and adequately redundant. With a growing number of quality performance measures, the optimal allocation of time and resources accounting for human factors such as cognitive load, interruptions, and visual complexity in the workload must be considered. More commonly, however, new measures create new workflows for a nurse or clinician that simply add to a long list of "to do's." One way to reduce the data entry burden on care providers is to enlist patients in entering their own information. Our experience with patient-entered depression screenings provided lessons in questionnaire design that may be generalized to other interventions.

At baseline, patients completed paper forms with the Patient Health Questionnaire (PHQ) along with other pre-visit questionnaires. Clinical staff manually entered the answers into the computer for clinical review. The data entry process for the PHQ varied across the organization because each department that needed this information had their own data collection methods in the EHR. To simplify the documentation, training, maintenance, and reporting of the PHQ results, we first had to standardize the collection of the PHQ. A common problem with healthcare data today is the lack of standards for data collection and storage even within a single institution. Data governance workflows and committees provide a place where issues of this nature can be resolved.

To improve efficiency, we wanted the patients to complete the data entry on their own. First, we had to ask a few questions:

■ Did patients have access to the patient web portal? Are patients using it?
■ Were they using pre-visit check-in on their mobile devices?
■ How should we handle patient completion of the suicidality question outside of the premises? What if the patient is Spanish speaking?
■ What if the patient lacks mobile access or has limited sight or literacy?
■ We had another set of questions regarding the presentation and clinical decision-making in response to the answers provided by the patient:
■ Where would a medical assistant or licensed vocational nurse find this information in the EHR office visit interface?
■ What would alert the physician to self-identified depression? Would the EHR require an acknowledgement and response to positive screenings?
■ How would critical responses be differentiated for easier identification?
■ What about follow-up? Once the patient was seen by the clinician, who would offer help and supportive services, counseling, and referrals?

The answers to these questions will vary depending on the local setting. However, these types of questions will help with the development of highly reliable systems that improve the efficiency, effectiveness, and experience of the patients and providers. A checklist of elements for workflow design in the clinical setting may help you through this process:

1. Data governance to establish consistent data collection and storage across the enterprise.
2. Development of documented standard clinical work processes.
3. Standardized clinical decision support to prompt for the completion of the right assessment(s). Dynamic assessments can streamline the data collection process by only asking screening questions that apply to a particular patient. For instance, everyone over 18 years without a current diagnosis of depression receives the short-form PHQ-2. Anyone

with an active diagnosis of depression receives the PHQ-9. Older patients may receive fall risk screenings, and various diagnoses or medications could trigger specialized assessments as appropriate.

4. Patient engagement is enhanced by both entering data into and reviewing their health record. Patient experience and trust are enhanced when they can verify that the previously entered information can be recalled from their record accurately.

5. Standardized order sets for positive screenings help reduce practice variation and increase the order efficiency for clinicians.

6. High-risk patients are identified by visual clues. Careful governance and monitoring of alerts will help mitigate the risk of alert fatigue, which renders providers less likely to respond to alerts.[89–91]

7. Continuous process measurement provides a feedback loop and accountability (by location, department, service line, provider, and care team).

Improve the Clinical Accuracy of Patient Groups

The inclusion rules for chronic care cohorts are highly complex and dynamic in clinically active EHRs. Diagnosis value sets designed for quality reporting programs may not be optimized for delivery of clinical care. By law, certified EHR systems must support ICD and SNOMED-CT diagnosis terminologies, and the terminology choice of for registry inclusion may significantly affect which patients are selected for a registry. The performance of these terminologies is inconsistent across the range of medical conditions, so we recommend careful evaluation for each registry.

ICD stands for International Classification of Diseases and comprises multiple versions, including ICD-9-CM and ICD-10-CM (Figure 16.3). The tenth revision, ICD-10-CM, was adopted in the United States in 2015, extending the length of the code from a maximum of five characters to seven characters. ICD diagnosis codes are a common choice for registry value sets because of their ubiquitous use throughout the U.S. medical system. Clinicians apply these codes in every encounter, and these codes are required to process medical claims in the government and private sectors. However, ICD is designed for billing, and in some cases, there are challenges in achieving high clinical accuracy in the patient groups defined by these codes. Errors of inclusion or exclusion may be due to codes that encompass conditions of differing severity or differences in the algorithms used to identify diagnosis groups.

The SNOMED (Systematized Nomenclature of Medicine) is reported to be used in over 50 countries, but a 2013 article in the ***Journal of Biomedical***

DIFFERENCES BETWEEN ICD-9-CM AND ICD-10-CM
DIAGNOSIS CODES FOR HEART FAILURE

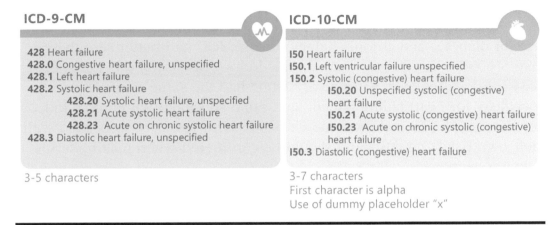

ICD-9-CM

428 Heart failure
428.0 Congestive heart failure, unspecified
428.1 Left heart failure
428.2 Systolic heart failure
    428.20 Systolic heart failure, unspecified
    428.21 Acute systolic heart failure
    428.23 Acute on chronic systolic heart failure
428.3 Diastolic heart failure, unspecified

3-5 characters

ICD-10-CM

I50 Heart failure
I50.1 Left ventricular failure unspecified
I50.2 Systolic (congestive) heart failure
    I50.20 Unspecified systolic (congestive) heart failure
    I50.21 Acute systolic (congestive) heart failure
    I50.23 Acute on chronic systolic (congestive) heart failure
I50.3 Diastolic (congestive) heart failure

3-7 characters
First character is alpha
Use of dummy placeholder "x"

Figure 16.3 Differences between ICD-9-CM and ICD-10-CM diagnosis codes.

SNOMED CT® DIAGNOSIS CONCEPT FOR HEART FAILURE

SNOMED CT ®
SEARCH | Heart Failure

Search Results

Heart Failure [84114007]

Parents(1)
Disorder of cardiac function [105981003]

Children (26)
Acute heart failure [56675007]
Cardiorenal syndrome [445236007]
Chronic heart failure [4844703]

Figure 16.4 Example of SNOMED-CT diagnosis concept for heart failure.

Informatics found that there is still much work ahead to bring SNOMED-CT into routine clinical use.[(92)] The SNOMED-CT concept hierarchies support retrieval of diagnosis data at various levels of granularity. Each concept has one or more parents in the polyhierarchical model and multiple children. One SNOMED concept may be mapped to just one or potentially thousands of ICD codes (Figure 16.4).

Each medical condition has its own unique hierarchies within the code sets, making it impossible to generalize value set performance across multiple conditions. A 2017 study of the electronic medical records of over 200,000 patients compared the sensitivity and specificity of national value sets for diabetes and chronic kidney disease. ICD had better sensitivity than SNOMED for diabetes and chronic kidney disease and better specificity for diabetes only. ICD and SNOMED had the same sensitivity and specificity for heart failure patient, and same specificity for chronic kidney disease.[50] The inclusion and exclusion error rates are associated with their own risks and costs and should be considered when making terminology selections.

The performance of SNOMED value sets can change over time even if the value set itself remains unchanged. Changes in a cohort census may not reflect the true magnitude of the change because patients added and excluded offset each other. Unexpected changes in cohort membership require clinical validation to determine if the change is good, bad, or irrelevant. A study of this phenomenon demonstrated that periodic EHR maintenance to apply terminology has caused unpredictable discontinuities in the size of chronic disease cohorts. In the conditions studied, the sensitivity and specificity of the SNOMED diabetes value set was statistically different before and after terminology maintenance. The changes were not significant for chronic kidney disease or heart failure. Based on these findings the recommendations for improving the accuracy of cohorts in national quality programs was proposed (Table 16.1).[50]

Table 16.1 Recommendations for Improving the Accuracy of Cohorts in National Quality Programs

	Observation	Recommendation	Goal
1	Current versions of national value sets for diagnosis cohorts were not designed for and may not be sufficiently accurate to drive clinical interventions, but may in fact be used for this unintended purpose.	The value set model should be expanded to a phenotype model that may include medications, labs, vitals, etc. in cohort selection.	National phenotypes will increase the efficiency of population health programs by sharing the burden for phenotype development for clinical interventions and quality reporting.

Table 16.1 (Continued)

	Observation	Recommendation	Goal
2	The Value Set Authority Center (VSAC) chronic disease value sets that are purportedly synonymous may have significant variation based on the choice of ICD or SNOMED terminology. There was little variation in the retrieval performance between ICD-9 and ICD-10 value sets in the conditions tested.	ICD should be the preferred diagnosis coding terminology for the retrieval of population health cohorts in national value sets. The hierarchical structure of the SNOMED concepts, coupled with the low interrater reliability for SNOMED coding, makes the retrieval of SNOMED cohorts more subject to unanticipated variability.	A clinically relevant and consistent set of national value sets and phenotype rules will improve the accuracy and consistency of reported quality measures. NOTE: This recommendation may not apply to EHR systems that apply diagnoses in native SNOMED-CT.
3	VSAC value sets are published without any quantitative measurement or rating of performance.	STARD (Standards for Reporting Diagnostic Accuracy) should inform the essential list of items to report in a study of population health value sets and phenotypes.	Reporting standards for population phenotype studies will facilitate comparisons between different approaches.
4	Use of existing standards such as LOINC and RXNORM are not fully implemented, and new standards such as visit types, common definitions of active patients, and outcomes such as hemorrhagic events are needed.	Quality programs should increase demands for the use of standard terminologies in quality reporting. Where national value sets are not yet mandated, the reporting of value sets used in report cohorts would provide a valuable raw data set with which to inform future phenotype research.	Health system interoperability and the foundations of the learning health system require the use of standardized terminologies.

Caught in the Middle

Although traditional fee-for-service and value-based capitated risk plans create entirely different economic drivers, most large health systems at the moment are caught in the middle between the two. If we put healthcare into the analogy of an Olympic competition, fee-for-service might be compared to figure skating, while value-based care delivery might be compared to ice hockey. The rules of the competition, the equipment, and teamwork needed to win are entirely different. Fee-for-service models incentivize complex high-cost care, and encourage capital investment in facilities, imaging, and laboratory infrastructure. Value-based models favor low-cost evidence-based care delivered systematically to targeted populations. Success in value based care models requires accurate measurement of care and outcomes, and can result in double to triple the costs in analytics infrastructure.

Call to Action

Population health has the promise to help address several challenges in the quadruple aims; however, to meet these more effectively, today's calls to action are:

- Lower the reporting burden of quality and data-driven systems
- Encourage organizations to build sustainable, high-reliability systems
- Develop strong, data-driven work teams for healthcare R&D composed of operations, computer analysts, financial analysts, informatics professionals, systems engineers, health and operations research, and patient advisors
- Focus activities on the quadruple aims, including measurement of the aims in each quality project
- Improve educational programs for applied clinical informatics

Chapter 17

Visioning Population Health of Tomorrow

Registries of the future will enable scalable delivery of precision medicine, personal digital health data, and integrated public datasets.

—*Amy M. Sitapati*

The future of population health will promote improved patient self-management, sophisticated decision support at the point of care, and exchange with state and national registries. Operational registries of the future will be the repository of curated little data for data governance, clinical decision-making, and process measurement. The operational registries will have stronger ties to external research registries where clinical data will be aggregated for big data analytics. A registry foundation will solve several long-term challenges: 1) organizing key data elements for clinical decision-making and segregating them from huge collections of heterogeneous health data; 2) enhancing clinical decision support for precision medicine inclusive of genomic data and balancing population-based standards with individual health risks; 3) applying predictive analytics that integrate multiple data contexts with dexterity to highlight decision trade-offs between cost, benefit, and timing; and 4) integrating state and national public health data inclusive of disparity perspectives into risk scoring algorithms.

As a result, health data will become more portable, meaningful, and valuable. The data will extend our ability to address the subtleties of preventive medicine to reduce the overall burden of chronic disease.

Population Health in the Patient Digital Health Era

"Wearable health monitors like the wrist-based ECG will warn heart patients of impending problems."

—Bill Gates[93]

Expansion of the digital health landscape has resulted in an explosion of data types that patients are using as part of their health experience. This includes biometrics such as pulse, electrocardiogram (EKG) readings, oxygen saturation, weight, blood pressure, and so on. But in addition to typical health biometrics, digital data from mobile applications, questionnaires, internal devices, and continuous monitoring are available to be harnessed. Patient-generated health data (PGHD) refers to data that have been "created, recorded, or gathered by or from patients (family members or other caregivers) to help address a health concern."[94] Population health will contribute to this domain by curating data into more digestible pieces. More specifically, the operational registries will merge, aggregate, risk-profile, and identify key outlier and critical values to assist a clinical team.

Precision Medicine for Individual Health Balanced With Population-Level Standards

One of the most difficult balances today in primary and secondary prevention is understanding trade-offs between national published standards and personalized precision optimization. For instance, a patient may be due for screening every decade using colonoscopy[95] Familial adenomatous polyposis increases that risk substantially (average age 39), and the attenuated version has a longer delay until onset (average by age 55). [96]

Consider the differing needs of two patients in the following hypothetical example:

> *Mary presents for colon cancer screening. Her screen for the APC and MUTYH genes are negative, but she shows a variant associated with a four-fold increase risk for colon cancer. Mary exercises, eats red meat, and has allergy to nonsteroidal anti-inflammatory drugs (NSAIDs).*
>
> *Mark carries the "KeepWELL" gene demonstrating five-fold reduction in all cancers.*

Whereas Mary is recommended to start colonoscopy at age 40, Mark is deferred to age 55. Population health of the future will pivot centralized approved U.S. Preventive Task Force recommendations alongside personalized estimates of risk, resulting in improved precision medicine.

Predictive Analytics With Dexterity Between Cost, Benefit, and Timing

Timing is everything. Population health of the future will help improve the management at a population level to balance trade-offs between cost, benefit, and timing. As part of an early population health experience, one organization was contemplating whether to routinize emergency room testing of HIV via screening on bloodwork. As part of that discussion, committees weighed the estimated $100,000 in cost expected to be incurred as part of the universal screening (at that time not individually billable) and considered whether this was more important than other population health prevention activities. The decision about which particular activity should be prioritized is not always straightforward. Improved access to prevalence, risk, and community-based benefit can be included in population health predictive analytics of the future. This should enable entities (patients), health systems and clinics (care delivery), insurers (payors), and public groups (local, state, and national) to better balance those tough decisions.

Aggregation and Risk Scoring of Data for State, National, and International Sharing Inclusive of Disparity Perspectives

> "[F]ocus on global inequality . . . we now have the ability to do so, the data required to assess and compare have become available for the first time in human history."
>
> —*Branko Milanovic*[97]

Although health organizations routinely submit data to public health entities, bidirectional data sharing with those same entities is still a dream. This dream will help to enable data sets to simultaneously serve public policy and science, and feed back into local healthcare systems to further define outcomes and improve individual care delivery. This effort will hinge on population health–related curated data sets and cohorting capabilities. Today, there are layers of challenges in securing patient identity and privacy. Tomorrow, when we have more sophisticated processes for privacy and protection, the means to incorporate diverse data into clinical decision-making and outcomes research may be possible. At that juncture, we will need algorithms that help to further refine the accuracy of our patient cohorts. From risk profiling (risk for disease), unmet diagnosis (probability of having disease), diagnosis (refined attribution), to disease severity ranking (seriousness of disease), stepwise improvements in our cohorting capabilities are sorely needed. How does one manage 1) gene sequence MAPK8IP1 bearing on increased risk for type 2 diabetes[98]; 2) compute whether the A1c at 6.8 was related to steroid-induced diabetes or type 2 diabetes; 3) accurately diagnose type 2 diabetes at 99.998%; and 4) rank diabetics into five categories of risk prioritizing outreach, testing, and follow-up? The local creation of better data sets will enhance the capabilities of "big data" analytics that are shared and centrally processed. Local, state, and national data can then be made available to the local health system to close the loop on patient status, activity, and outcomes.

How can a health system know whether "best ever surgery CPT xx123" is truly great without access to outcome data? Today, if patient "Jong" was given surgery CPTxx123, we would have no idea how the patient did unless "Jong" or his family called to provide that information. Furthermore, the outcome is not documented in a standardized way. We cannot assess value when we do not know the outcome. Step one in determining outcomes is to know whether the patient is living. Integrated secure health exchange with public data sources can provide promise in this domain. What if "Jong" was hospitalized at outside facility "YouNeverHeardOf" and had 25-day follow-up procedural (CPT) information that the patient suffered an acute myocardial infarction? Was CPTxx123 associated with the acute event? What if CPTxx123 is actually harmful? Or is the harm relevant to a particular subpopulation?

Disparities exist, but how do you see them? Without vision, how can health equality happen? Within our current systems it is often difficult to discern whether difference in health outcomes are statistically and/or clinically significant. Larger data sets that have uniform and reliable health information related to race, ethnicity, age, language, gender identity, sexual orientation, and geospatial data will help to identify those differences. Without communication back to the care delivery site, how will that information be processed to make a difference?

Improved Access to the Right Clinical Expertise

One of the most exciting prospects about the population health of the future is going to enable scalability of our providers. Currently, a specialist will manage a cohort of challenging patients, such as an endocrinologist matched to 300 patients with type 1 and 2 poorly controlled diabetes. The future of population health will enable improvements in primary, secondary, and tertiary wellness and disease management. As a result, an endocrinologist sitting in Vail, Colorado, may someday be able to manage 30,000 lives (100 times the current rate). This specialist will serve to define primary, secondary, and tertiary prevention that is shared with the primary care provider. Additionally, subspecialty expertise can be directed based on improved accuracy of the genomic, phenotypic, and patient-reported data to the right provider. Patients with exotic variants can be profiled using machine learning algorithms to help prioritize access to quaternary expertise.

Pushing the Envelope on the Subtleties of Prevention

> *"If we could look even further out—let's say the next 20 years from now— I would hope to see technologies that center almost entirely on well-being."*[93]

The continuum of wellness in a future state will not just identify patients with disease such that diagnosis, engagement, testing, and therapeutic optimization are addressed. Future wellness will look to the left on the continuum of wellness to illness, and identify opportunities to change patient risks and avert future illness. In order to better explain the vision, take a look at the care offered through the lens of "Virtual Care: Cardiologist of the Future" (Figure 17.1).[99]

At a patient level, imagine "Jack," age 39, who has noted an increase in stress due to late hours resulting in increased sympathetic tone (basal cortisol as well as peak epinephrine surge) propagating the risk for hypertension and arrhythmia. Dr. Pop Tech sitting in the virtual cardiology control tower noted a few outliers in the "young and healthy" primary prevention group of his panel. Specifically, "Jack" has the top 1% of unhealthy cortisol surges over the past month. Additional device data and other mobile health information (m-health) include patient symptoms (headache, poor

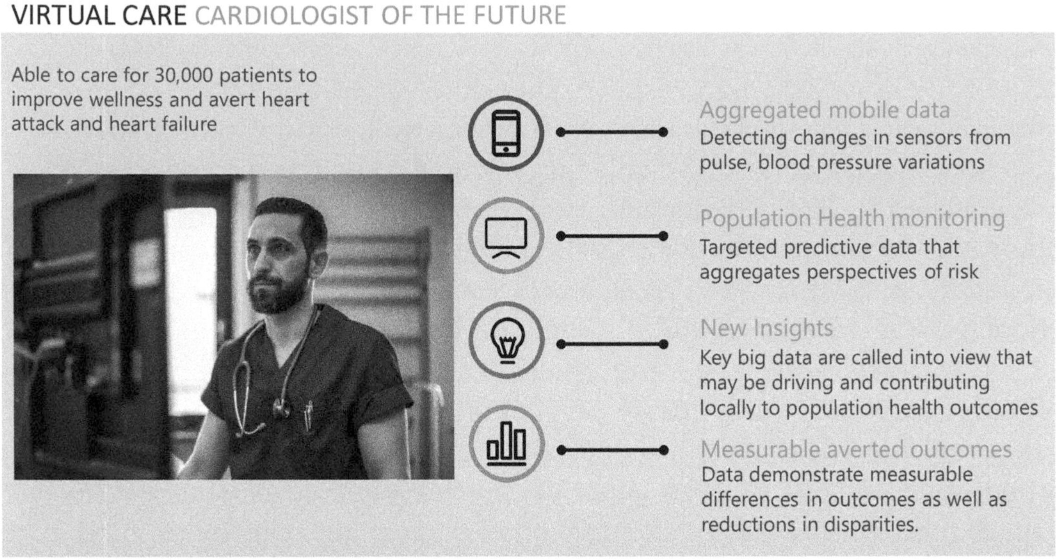

VIRTUAL CARE CARDIOLOGIST OF THE FUTURE

Able to care for 30,000 patients to improve wellness and avert heart attack and heart failure

Aggregated mobile data
Detecting changes in sensors from pulse, blood pressure variations

Population Health monitoring
Targeted predictive data that aggregates perspectives of risk

New Insights
Key big data are called into view that may be driving and contributing locally to population health outcomes

Measurable averted outcomes
Data demonstrate measurable differences in outcomes as well as reductions in disparities.

Figure 17.1   Virtual Care: Cardiologist of the Future.

sleep, and anxiety), combined with digital health readings such as pulse (average rate is up 15 points), systolic blood pressure (showing increased variability of the 350 measurements with more than 10 readings per day at rest with systolic blood pressure 145 to 155), and on the wearable EKG increased variability (average two premature ventricular contractions per minute). The Pop Health cardio calculator has notified Dr. Pop Tech that this year Jack has a 30% risk of developing essential hypertension, a 7% risk for myocardial infarction, and a 3% risk for arrhythmia. From the Pop Health Cardio Control Tower, patient navigator William securely texts Jack to set up a virtual appointment. If Jack follows the recommended exercise, walking, and 15-pound weight loss program, his risk for hypertension should be cut in half. William will continue to track, coach, and interact with Jack for 90 days with a light-touch model. Can this intervention avert chronic essential hypertension? In addition to reducing risk for chronic disease, compliance with this program is estimated to save $3,000 per patient per year.

As a result, population health of the future will redefine wellness for large populations to include a continuum of wellness to various severities of disease and control, resulting in improvements in the ability to achieve goal-targeted therapy and improve health outcomes (Figure 17.2).

REDEFINING WELLNESS FOR LARGE POPULATIONS

Figure 17.2   Redefining wellness for large populations.

Epilogue

We know that the care of tomorrow starts today with the work that you are doing. We hope that this book has armed you with the knowledge and understanding to make a difference in the lives of our families, friends, and community. Together, we are but one world. With your hands and minds, we hope to more effectively make it healthier for us all. If there is one thing that we have both learned in our population health journey, it is that the road is meant to be shared. Collaboration and exchange of ideas are fundamentally how we will move population health to be truly awesome. Laser-like accuracy of decision support married with multifaceted diverse data has taken the efficiency of a fly wheel, and bam(!)—population health informatics will become the virtual "penicillin" of the future.

Dr. Barbara Berkovich and Dr. Amy M. Sitapati

Funding and Support

1. Delivery System Reform Incentive Pool (DSRIP) for Category 5 HIV transitions 7/1/2012–12/31/2013
   Role: Principal Investigator/Physician Lead
   Major Goals: To improve quality outcomes for patients receiving HIV primary care through a patient-centered medical home model of care delivery.
2. California HIV/AIDS Research Program: MH10-UCSD-640 12/01/2010–11/30/2014

ANCHOR: A Novel Care Home Optimizing Retention
Role: Principal Investigator
Major Goals: This project will strive to improve the construction of a model HIV primary care medical home.
The ANCHOR project [A Novel Medical Home Optimizing Retention] was approved by the University of California San Diego Human Research Program, #121595X.

References

1. Bodenheimer T, Sinsky C. From triple to quadruple aim: Care of the patient requires care of the provider. *The Annals of Family Medicine.* 2014;12(6):573–6.
2. National Academy of Engineering. *Engineering a Learning Healthcare System: A Look at the Future.* Workshop Summary: National Academies Press; 2011.
3. Bill Chappell CD. *The Two-Way: Breaking News from NPR [Internet] 2018.* Available from: www.npr.org/sections/thetwo-way/2018/01/30/581804474/amazon-berkshire-hathaway-and-jpmorgan-chase-launch-new-healthcare-company.
4. Berwick DM, Nolan TW, Whittington J. The triple aim: Care, health, and cost. *Health Aff (Millwood).* 2008;27(3):759–69.
5. Office of the actuary national health statistics group national health expenditures as a share of gross domestic product, 1987–2016 Centers for Medicare & Medicaid Services; 2018.
6. FitzGerald B. *A Look at Trends in Population Health.* HIMSS 17: HIMSS Analytics; 2017.
7. James BC, Poulsen GP. The case for capitation. *Harvard Business Review.* 2016;94(7–8):102–11.
8. James J. Health policy brief: Pay-for-performance. *Health Affairs.* 2012;11:2043–50.
9. Mcleod A, Keefe A, Kemp, A. *CMS Approves California's Medi-Cal 2020.* Demonstration Waiver: California Hospital Association; 2016. updated January 4, 2016. Available from: www.calhospital.org.
10. California Association of Public Hospitals and Health Systems CHCSNI. *California's Public Health Care Systems' Journey to Value-Based Care.* 2019.
11. Porter ME. What is value in health care? *New England Journal of Medicine.* 2010;363(26):2477–81.
12. Jason Arora IS, Jean S, Shan W, Stephanie W. *What Matters Most: Patient Outcomes and the Transformation of Health Care.* Cambridge, MA: ICHOM International Consortium for Health Outcomes Measurement; 2014. Available from: https://ichom.org/files/books/ICHOM_Book.pdf.
13. DeVore S, Champion RW. Driving population health through accountable care organizations. *Health Affairs.* 2011;30(1):41–50.

14. Centers for Medicare & Medicaid Service. *Accountable Care Organizations (ACOs)*. Baltimore, MD: U.S. Centers for Medicare & Medicaid Services; 2018. Available from: www.cms.gov/Medicare/Medicare-Fee-for-Service-Payment/ACO/index.html.

15. Crimmins MM, Lowe TJ, Barrington M, Kaylor C, Phipps T, Le-Roy C, et al. QUEST®: A data-driven collaboration to improve quality, efficiency, safety, and transparency in acute care. *The Joint Commission Journal on Quality and Patient Safety*. 2016;42(6):247–53.

16. Donabedian A. The quality of care: How can it be assessed? *JAMA*. 1988;260(12):1743–8.

17. Centers for Medicare & Medicaid Services. 2019 Merit-based Incentive Payment System (MIPS): Quality performance category fact sheet. In: *Department of Health and Human Services*, editor; 2019.

18. Fremont A, Kim A, Bailey K, Rees Hanley H, Thorne C, Dudl R, et al. One in five fewer heart attacks: Impact, savings, and sustainability in San Diego County collaborative. *Health Affairs*. 2018;37(9):1457–65.

19. Matthew DB. Report to congress on the administration, cost, and impact of the Quality Improvement Organization (QIO) program for medicare beneficiaries for fiscal year 2017. In: *Services DoHaH*, editor. Washington, DC: Center for Medicare & Medicaid Services (CMS); 2018. p. 18.

20. Centers for Disease Control and Prevention. Million hearts: Meaningful progress 2012–2016. In: *Department of Health and Human Services*, editor; 2018.

21. Fryar CD, Ostchega Y, Hales CM, Zhang G, Kruszon-Moran D. Hypertension prevalence and control among adults: United States, 2015–2016. *NCHS Data Brief*. 2017(289):1–8.

22. National Center for Health Statistics (U.S.). Health, United States, 2017: With special feature on mortality. In: *Department of Health and Human Services*, editor. Hyattsville, MD: Centers for Disease Control and Prevention; 2018.

23. Papanicolas I, Woskie LR, Jha AK. Health care spending in the united states and other high-income countries. Jama. 2018;319(10):1024–39.

24. Crits-Christoph P, Gallop R, Noll E, Rothbard A, Diehl CK, Connolly Gibbons MB, et al. Impact of a medical home model on costs and utilization among comorbid HIV-positive medicaid patients. *American Journal of Managed Care*. 2018;24(8):368–75.

25. Thompson S. Experiences with pay-for-performance and value-based care programs. In: *Personal Interview with Barbara Berkovich*. January 25, editor; 2019.

26. Center for Medicare & Medicaid Services (CMS). *Measures Management System: Structural Measures CMS.gov2018*. Available from: www.cms.gov/Medicare/Quality-Initiatives-Patient-Assessment-Instruments/MMS/Downloads/Structural-Measures.pdf.

27. Bodenheimer T, Ghorob A, Willard-Grace R, Grumbach K. The 10 building blocks of high-performing primary care. *The Annals of Family Medicine*. 2014;12(2):166–71.

28. Sitapati A, Longhurst, C. Analytics and Population Health. In: *The CMIO Survival Guide: A Handbook for Chief Medical Information Officers and*

Those Who Hire Them. 2nd ed. Rydell RL, editor. Healthcare Information & Management Systems Society; 2018.

29. Lighter D. *Advanced Performance Improvement in Health Care: Principles and Methods*. Jones & Bartlett Learning; 2010.

30. Chen EH, Bodenheimer T. Improving population health through team-based panel management: Comment on "Electronic medical record reminders and panel management to improve primary care of elderly patients". *Archives of Internal Medicine*. 2011;171(17):1558–9.

31. Edwards ST, Rubenstein LV, Meredith LS, Hackbarth NS, Stockdale SE, Cordasco KM, et al. editors. *Who Is Responsible for What Tasks Within Primary Care: Perceived Task Allocation Among Primary Care Providers and Interdisciplinary Team Members Healthcare*: Elsevier; 2015.

32. Rothenberger DA. Physician burnout and well-being: A systematic review and framework for action. *Diseases of the Colon & Rectum*. 2017;60(6):567–76.

33. Epstein RM, Privitera MR. Doing something about physician burnout. *The Lancet*. 2016;388(10057):2216–17.

34. Porter ME, Michael Porter EOT, Teisberg EO. *Redefining Health Care: Creating Value-based Competition on Results*. Harvard Business School Press; 2006.

35. ICHOM. *Why Standardized Outcomes?* Boston, MA; 2019 [International Consortium for Health Outcomes Measurement, Inc. US]. Available from: www.ichom.org/healthcare-standardization.

36. Douglas PO, Benjamin JO, Navarro SM. *Standardizing Social Determinants of Health Assessments 2019*; updated March 18, 2019. Available from: www.healthaffairs.org/do/10.1377/hblog20190311.823116/full/.

37. Burchard EG, Ziv E, Coyle N, Gomez SL, Tang H, Karter AJ, et al. The importance of race and ethnic background in biomedical research and clinical practice. *New England Journal of Medicine*. 2003;348(12):1170–5.

38. National Institutes of Health Department of Health and Human Services. *CDCREC Race & Ethnicity Code Set Roll-Up Codes*. U.S. National Library of Medicine Value Set Authority Center; 2017.

39. Carter-Pokras O, Baquet C. What is a" health disparity"? *Public Health Reports*. 2002;117(5):426.

40. Polit DF, Yang F. *Measurement and the Measurement of Change: A Primer for the Health Professions*. Wolters Kluwer; 2016.

41. Sitapati AM, Limneos J, Bonet-Vázquez M, Mar-Tang M, Qin H, Mathews WC. Retention: Building a patient-centered medical home in HIV primary care through PUFF (Patients Unable to Follow-up Found). *Journal of Health Care for the Poor and Underserved*. 2012;23(3):81–95.

42. National Institute of Drug Abuse (NIDA). Cascade of care model recommended for opioid crisis. In: *(U.S.). NIoH*, editor. Rockville, MD: NIDA; 2019.

43. The National Quality Forum (NQF). *Guidance for Measure Harmonization: A Consensus Report*. Washington, DC: NQF; 2010.

44. Davis K, Schoen C, Guterman S, Shih T, Schoenbaum SC, Weinbaum I. Slowing the growth of US health care expenditures: What are the options. *The Commonwealth Fund*. 2007;47:1–34.

45. Drolet BC, Johnson KB. Categorizing the world of registries. *Journal of Biomedical Informatics.* 2008;41(6):1009–20.

46. Savitz L. Personal Interview with Dr. Lucy Savitz, Director at Kaiser Permanente Center for Health Research, Northwest and Hawaii. Berkovich, B, Sitapati, AM. updated December 18, 2018.

47. Panzer RJ, Gitomer RS, Greene WH, Webster PR, Landry KR, Riccobono CA. Increasing demands for quality measurement. *Jama.* 2013;310(18):1971–80.

48. Mayo Clinic. Type 2 Diabetes Mayo Clinic: Mayo Foundation for Medical Education and Research (MFMER); 2019. Available from: www.mayoclinic.org/diseases-conditions/type-2-diabetes/diagnosis-treatment/drc-20351199.

49. National Institutes of Health: National Cancer Institute. Cancer Stat Facts: Pancreatic Cancer Bethesda, MD: Surveillance Research Program (SRP) in NCI's Division of Cancer Control and Population Sciences (DCCPS); 2019 Available from: https://seer.cancer.gov/statfacts/html/pancreas.html.

50. Berkovich BA. *Impact of Terminology Mapping on Population Health Cohorts—IMPaCt*, PhD dissertation; 2017.

51. Plana JC, Galderisi M, Barac A, Ewer MS, Ky B, Scherrer-Crosbie M, et al. Expert consensus for multimodality imaging evaluation of adult patients during and after cancer therapy: A report from the American society of echocardiography and the European association of cardiovascular imaging. *European Heart Journal—Cardiovascular Imaging.* 2014;15(10):1063–93.

52. da Graca B, Filardo G, Nicewander D. Consequences for healthcare quality and research of the exclusion of records from the death master file. *Circulation: Cardiovascular Quality and Outcomes.* 2013;6(1):124–8.

53. Jones B, Vawdrey DK. Measuring mortality information in clinical data warehouses. *AMIA Summits on Translational Science Proceedings.* 2015;2015:450.

54. Gliklich RE, Dreyer NA, Leavy MB. *Registries for Evaluating Patient Outcomes: A User's Guide.* April 2014 ed. Rockville, MD: Agency for Healthcare Research and Quality; 2014.

55. Sitapati A, Berkovich, B. *Presentation: Use of a Local Learning Healthcare System to Improve the Health of Patient and Community.* American Medical Informatics Association iHealth 2016; 2016.

56. Gliklich RE, Leavy MB, Karl J, Campion DM, Levy D, Berliner E. A framework for creating standardized outcome measures for patient registries. *Journal of Comparative Effectiveness Research.* 2014;3(5):473–80.

57. Wikipedia.org. *Routine Health Outcomes Measurement 2019.* updated February 20, 2019. Available from: https://en.wikipedia.org/wiki/Routine_health_outcomes_measurement.

58. Leavy MB, Schur C, Kassamali FQ, Johnson ME, Sabharwal R, Wallace P, et al. Development of Harmonized Outcome Measures for Use in Patient Registries and Clinical Practice: Methods and Lessons Learned. Final Report. In: *U.S. Department of Health and Human Services,* editor. Rockville, MD: AHRQ; 2019.

59. Gottlieb L, Tobey R, Cantor J, Hessler D, Adler NE. Integrating social and medical data to improve population health: opportunities and barriers. *Health Affairs.* 2016;35(11):2116–23.

60. Center for Medicare & Medicaid Services (CMS); 2018. *Medicare Shared Savings Program Quality Measure Benchmarks for the 2019 Performance Year.* Retrieved from https://www.cms.gov/Medicare/Medicare-Fee-for-Service-Payment/sharedsavingsprogram/Downloads/2019-quality-benchmarks-guidance.pdf

61. Greenberg PE, Fournier AA, Sisitsky T, Pike CT, Kessler RC. The economic burden of adults with major depressive disorder in the United States (2005 and 2010). *The Journal of Clinical Psychiatry.* 2015;76(2):155–62.

62. Pretnik R, Smart S. *Quality Management 2019: The Search for a One-Stop Shop.* KLAS Research. Available from klasrearch.com; 2019.

63. Google. *Search Results: Healthcare Quality Measure Management System.* [Google® search results]. In press; 2019.

64. Change Healthcare. *Quality Measure Insights Change Healthcare 2019.* Available from: www.changehealthcare.com/solutions/quality-measure-insights.

65. Sarah H (editor). *What Clinical Quality Measures Mean to Healthcare Providers.* Danvers, MA: Extelligent Healthcare Media. Available from: https://ehrintelligence.com/features/what-clinical-quality-measures-mean-to-healthcare-providers.

66. Center for Medicare & Medicaid Services (CMS). *A Brief Overview of Qualified Clinical Data Registries (QCDRs)* 2018. Available from: www.cms.gov/Medicare/Quality-Initiatives-Patient-Assessment-Instruments/MMS/Downloads/A-Brief-Overview-of-Qualified-Clinical-Data-Registries.pdf.

67. Dean ML. *Lean Healthcare Deployment and Sustainability.* McGraw-Hill Education; 2013.

68. Osheroff J, Teich J, Levick D, Saldana L, Velasco F, Sittig D, et al. *Improving outcomes with clinical decision support: An implementer's guide.* HIMSS Publishing; 2012.

69. Bisantz AM, Singh R, Singh G, Naughton BJ. What happens to orders written for older primary care patients? *Family Medicine.* 2012;44(4):252–8.

70. Beam AL, Kohane IS. Big data and machine learning in health care. *Jama.* 2018;319(13):1317–8.

71. Justice AC, Modur S, Tate JP, Althoff KN, Jacobson LP, Gebo K, et al. Predictive accuracy of the Veterans Aging Cohort Study (VACS) index for mortality with HIV infection: A North American cross cohort analysis. *Journal of Acquired Immune Deficiency Syndromes (1999).* 2013;62(2):149.

72. van Walraven C, Dhalla IA, Bell C, Etchells E, Stiell IG, Zarnke K, et al. Derivation and validation of an index to predict early death or unplanned readmission after discharge from hospital to the community. *CMAJ.* 2010;182(6):551–7.

73. Jeffrey R. *Immelt Quotation on Leadership.* updated June 16, 2019. Available from: www.brainyquote.com/quotes/jeffrey_r_immelt_643681.

74. Tomek, IM, Sabel, AL, Froimson, MI, Muschler, G, Jevsevar, DS, Koenig, et al. A collaborative of leading health systems finds wide variations in total knee replacement delivery and takes steps to improve value. *Health Affairs.* 2012;31(6):1329–38.

75. Savitz, LA, Weiss, LT. A data driven approach to achieving high value health-care. *EGEMS (Wash DC)*. 2017;5(3):1. Published 2017 Dec 15. doi:10.5334/egems.241

76. Institute of Medicine. *Best Care at Lower Cost: The Path to Continuously Learning Health Care in America*. Washington, DC: National Academies Press; 2013.

77. Learning Health Community. *Core Values Underlying a National-Scale Person-Centered Continuous Learning Health System (LHS)*. 2012. Retrieved from http://www.learninghealth.org/corevalues.

78. Stead W, Starmer J. *Leadership Commitments to Improve Value in Health Care, Toward Common Ground: Workshop Summary*. Washington, DC: The National Academies Press; 2008.

79. Guise J-M, Savitz LA, Friedman CP. Mind the gap: Putting evidence into practice in the era of learning health systems. *Journal of General Internal Medicine*. 2018;33(12):2237–9. Retrieved from https://doi.org/10.1007/s11606-018-4633-1

80. Benuzillo, J, LA Savitz. "EQUIP, An Evidence-based Quality Improvement Process: Improving the Speed to Insight," *BMJ Open Quality*, 2018; 7(Suppl 1) A5-A6.

81. McCannon, C. J., Berwick, D. M., & Massoud, M. R. (2007). The science of large-scale change in global health. *Jama*, 298(16), 1937–1939.

82. National Impact Assessment of the Centers for Medicare & Medicaid Services (CMS). *Quality Measures Report*. Baltimore, MD. updated February 28, 2018. Available from: www.cms.gov/Medicare/Quality-Initiatives-Patient-Assessment-Instruments/QualityMeasures/National-Impact-Assessment-of-the-Centers-for-Medicare-and-Medicaid-Services-CMS-Quality-Measures-Reports.html.

83. Pawson R, Tilley N, Tilley N. *Realistic Evaluation*. Sage; 1997.

84. Eddy DM, Hasselblad V, Shachter R. *Meta-Analysis by the Confidence Profile Method*. London: Academic Press London; 1992.

85. Kupersmith J. New Approaches to Learning in the Learning Healthcare System. *Health Affairs Blog [Internet]*; 2013. updated April 15, 2019.

86. Quinn TC, Wawer MJ, Sewankambo N, Serwadda D, Li C, Wabwire-Mangen F, et al. Viral load and heterosexual transmission of human immunodeficiency virus type 1. *New England Journal of Medicine*. 2000;342(13):921–9.

87. Das M, Chu PL, Santos G-M, Scheer S, Vittinghoff E, McFarland W, et al. Decreases in community viral load are accompanied by reductions in new HIV infections in San Francisco. *PLoS ONE*. 2010;5(6):e11068.

88. Centers for Disease Control and Prevention. *Guidance on Community Viral Load: A Family of Measures, Definitions, and Method for Calculation*. Atlanta, GA: CDC Stacks Public Health Publications; 2011. Available from: https://stacks.cdc.gov/view/cdc/28147.

89. Carspecken CW, Sharek PJ, Longhurst C, Pageler NM. A clinical case of electronic health record drug alert fatigue: Consequences for patient outcome. *Pediatrics*. 2013;131(6):e1970-e3.

90. Kane-Gill SL, O'Connor MF, Rothschild JM, Selby NM, McLean B, Bonafide CP, et al. Technologic distractions (Part 1): Summary of approaches to manage alert quantity with intent to reduce alert fatigue and suggestions for alert fatigue metrics. *Critical Care Medicine*. 2017;45(9):1481–8.

91. Wright A, Aaron S, Seger DL, Gordon LS, David DS, Bates W. Reduced effectiveness of interruptive drug—drug interaction alerts after conversion to a commercial electronic health record. *Journal of General Internal Medicine*. 2018;33.

92. Lee D, Cornet R, Lau F, De Keizer N. A survey of SNOMED CT implementations. *Journal of Biomedical Informatics*. 2013;46(1):87–96.

93. Gates B. How we'll invent the future. *MIT Technology Review*. 2019;122(2):10.

94. HealthIT.gov. *What are Patient-Generated Health Data?* Washington, DC: Office of the National Coordinator for Health Information Technology (ONC); 2018. updated January 19, 2018. Available from: www.healthit.gov/topic/scientific-initiatives/patient-generated-health-data.

95. U.S. Preventive Services Task Force. *Final Recommendation Statement: Colorectal Cancer: Screening*. updated May 2019. Available from: www.uspreventiveservicestaskforce.org/Page/Document/RecommendationStatementFinal/colorectal-cancer-screening2.

96. National Institutes of Health. *Familial Adenomatous Polyposis*. Bethesda, MD: National Library of Medicine; 2019. updated October 2013. Available from: https://ghr.nlm.nih.gov/condition/familial-adenomatous-polyposis#diagnosis.

97. Milanovic B. *Global Inequality: A New Approach for the Age of Globalization*. Harvard University Press; 2016.

98. National Institutes of Health. *MAPK8IP1 gene*. Bethesda, MD; 2019. updated July 16, 2019. Available from: https://ghr.nlm.nih.gov/gene/MAPK8IP1.

99. Bhavnani SP, Sitapati AM. Virtual care 2.0—A vision for the future of data-driven technology-enabled healthcare. *Current Treatment Options in Cardiovascular Medicine*. 2019;21(5):21.

100. Wysowski DK, Nourjah P, Swartz L. Bleeding complications with warfarin use: A prevalent adverse effect resulting in regulatory action. *JAMA Internal Medicine*. 2007;167(13):1414–19.

101. Agency for Healthcare Research and Quality. *Defining Categorization Needs for Race and Ethnicity Data*. Rockville, MD. updated May 2018. Available from: www.ahrq.gov/research/findings/final-reports/iomracereport/reldata3.html.

Answer Key

Chapter 3

Case Study Provider Engagement at OCHIN
Answers will vary. Following is an example of a completed communication plan.

Purpose	Participants	Format	Frequency
Upcoming EHR changes Hot topics Clinical programs Quality campaigns	This is typically for middle managers from the EHR (IT) and operations teams.	One-hour webinar	Twice-monthly or monthly. May choose to align with EHR change release schedule.
Mitigation strategies for provider burnout OpenNotes	Special ad hoc teams. Important to pair clinical/technical team members.	In-person or remote collaboration	Weekly
Ad hoc longitudinal issues Specific topics: OB history data collection Streamlined contraception ordering	Data-driven value improvement workgroups	One-hour virtual meeting	Every two weeks
Executive oversight	Executive committee	In-person	Quarterly

(continued)

Purpose	Participants	Format	Frequency
Clinical oversight Regulatory reporting Local priorities	Steering committee	Thirty-minute to one-hour virtual meeting	Weekly
Dissemination of best practices, networking	Open invitation	One-day conference	Yearly

Chapter 4

Case Study: Doing the Right Thing with Medication Monitoring

1. How would you resolve the potential conflict in timing of the lab tests for patients with diabetes and on statins?

   The bulk orders and messages for patients with diabetes should be processed on the same schedule as for those on statins. Ideally, all topics should be processed on the same schedule so that if individuals are members of multiple cohorts, all of the lab orders and messages are delivered on the same day.

2. What are the possible patient benefits of using applied population health methods monitoring warfarin? (Hint: Search for warfarin.)

   Warfarin has risk of bleeding (hemorrhage)
   "Use of warfarin has increased, and bleeding from warfarin use is a prevalent reaction and an important cause of mortality. Consequently, a "black box" warning about warfarin's bleeding risk was added to the U.S. product labeling in 2006."[100]

3. In your personal experience, are compliance rates for medication monitoring routinely measured by health systems?

   Answers will vary.
   Medication safety has traditionally focused on the drugs themselves and prescribing behaviors. The Food and Drug Administration (FDA) has primary responsibility for ensuring the safety and effectiveness of pharmaceutical products. It also tracks adverse events and

*medication error reports in the FDA Adverse Event Reporting System
(FAERS). Black box warnings for serious or life-threatening risks
are frequently embedded in clinical decision support for medication
ordering.*

*Health systems have not routinely adopted measurement systems for
ensuring that patients receive systematic medication monitoring while
undergoing treatments with known health risks. That may be changing
as opioids are an example of a medication class recently subject to close
monitoring.*

Chapter 5

Case Study: Use of Social Security Decedent Data in an EHR Registry

1. What types of validation would you perform to ensure that truly alive
   patients weren't marked as deceased?

   There is no visit history in the EHR after date of death.

2. Although California does allow the use of a limited set of death data
   from the Vital Statistics Office, the patient Social Security number is not
   included. How would you perform patient matching without a Social
   Security number?

   *There are special algorithms with varying degrees of accuracy, but in
   general, match on multiple data elements like name, gender, and date
   of birth. Because the likelihood of error is higher, the reported death
   status and date could be stored in a separate field to be used as a filter
   for population health outreach and quality reporting.*

3. What steps would promote the routine update of electronic health
   records based on public vital statistics?

   *A national patient identifier, a single system with a categorical reason
   of death (accident, heart failure, stroke, suicide, etc.), and a cloud-based
   national interface for approved health providers.*

Chapter 8

Case Study: Tactical Planning for Quality Programs

CALIFORNIA PRIME-YEAR 4 BASELINE & GOALS REPORT

MEASURE	NAME	DENOM	NUMERATOR	BASE RATE	PATIENTS TO GOAL	GOAL	AT RISK $
Project 1.1 Integration of Physical Health and Behavioral Health							
1.1.1	Alcohol and Drug Misuse Screening	30,000	300	1.00%	2,700	10.00%	300,000
1.1.5	Screening for Clinical Depression and follow-up	20,000	8,000	40.00%	1,000	45.00%	300,000
1.1.6	Tobacco Use Assessment and Counseling	30,000	29,100	97.00%	300	98.00%	300,000
Project 1.2 Ambulatory Care Redesign: Primary Care							
1.2.1	Alcohol and Drug Misuse Screening	30,000	300	1.00%	2700	10.00%	300,000
1.2.4	Diabetes Poor Control (HbA1c > 9)	3,500	600	17.14%	75	<15.00%	300,000
1.2.5	Controlling Blood Pressure	10,000	7200	72.00%	-200	70.00%	300,000
1.2.7	Ischemic Vascular Disease Patients on Aspirin or other Antithrombotic	3,000	2610	87.00%	60	89.00%	300,000

1. Based on the criteria presented, assess the level of difficulty for the following measures and explain your rationale. Assume the screenings are simple questionnaires.

    1.1.1, 1.2.1 Alcohol and Drug Misuse Screening [*easy screening test*]
    1.1.5 Screening for Clinical Depression and follow-up
    [*moderate because of follow-up requirement*]
    1.1.6 Tobacco Use Assessment and Counseling
    [*moderate because of counseling requirement*]
    1.2.4 Diabetes Poor Control (A1c >9) [*difficult clinical outcome*]
    1.2.5 Controlling Blood Pressure [*difficult clinical outcome*]
    1.2.7 Ischemic Vascular Disease Patients on Aspirin or Other Antithrombotic [*difficult process outcome*]

2. Based on Figure 8.7, what other data might you consider for prioritizing efforts?

* *Patients to goal or conversions per day or per week.*
* *Measures with higher-than-average incentive payments.*

    Note that 1.1.1 and 1.2.1 Alcohol and drug misuse screening are the same, meaning that the incentive is double ($600,000 total)

3. Considering the incentive dollars at stake, how much would you be able to spend on each measure to achieve the goal?

This is an open discussion question with many right answers. The simple answer is $300,000 per measure, except Alcohol and Drug Misuse Screening is $600,000. The total incentive dollars for this subset of measures is $2,100,000. Organizational goals and program leadership will determine if the goal is to induce change in clinical practice at no additional cost to the organization (altruistic). In this case, 1.2.5 Controlling Blood Pressure is already passing at baseline, so $300,000 for that measure could be reallocated to other measures. But if the goal is to earn incentives for the organization (profit), then each measure should stand on its own value, and once earned, should be set aside, and work done on the failing measures to maximize the total incentive return at the smallest possible investment. Automation tends to have higher up-front costs but lower operation costs. Is the time horizon for the return in one year or multiple years?

4. Which measure would you work on first? Why?

Answers may vary. Common choices may include:

1. *Alcohol and Drug Misuse Screening (1.1.1, 1.2.1) generates double other measures*
2. *Work the hard measures first. 1.2.7 Ischemic Vascular Disease is difficult, but has only 60 patients to goal*
3. *Consider the ratio of the "patients left to goal" ÷ "numerator negative patients."*

   In measure 1.2.7, that would be 60 ÷ (3000 − 2610) = 0.15 or 15%
   That is a relatively low rate and would imply a likely successful outcome

4. Work the easy measures first to generate project momentum.

Chapter 9

Case Study: Automated Clinical Documentation Project

1. It's quite easy in hindsight to recognize a failure. How might you have defined success for this project in a way that is measurable and time-bound?

Possible answers:
One hundred hours of obstetrician chart documentation per year.
Tool is used 100 times within one year.

2. Review Figure 9.2. In which quadrant would you place the clinical documentation project (A, B, C, or D)?

   D—High complexity and low volume

3. For project prioritization purposes, which quadrant of the project complexity versus patient volume matrix would be most favorable for a population health project?

   A—Low complexity and high volume

Case Study: Registry Project Request

Complete the SBAR, Intervention and Justification Checklists in Appendix F for the scenario. Answers will vary, but should contain content similar to that shown below.

SBAR

Situation: What is the justification for this new metric and/or registry?	Background: What relevant factors or challenges led up to this request?
Homeless patients are high utilizers of emergency and inpatient services. This is problematic for the patient and represents a disproportionate share of the expenditures for the ACO.	**The ACO is losing money on homeless, high utilizing patients. It is believed that closer coordination with local housing services will reduce overutilization patterns.**
Assessment: How will this metric and/or registry improve the current situation and quality performance?	Recommendation:
Goal is to reduce emergency and hospital utilization for this group by 30% within the first year of the program.	**Create a registry of Housing Insecurity to track referral to housing services and placement in housing.**
	Registry to track rolling 365 day history of emergency and inpatient admissions, billed charges, and housing status over this period (including periods of homelessness and temporary housing)

1) Justification checklist	
Quality Measure(s): *What measure(s) are you planning to change with this intervention?*	**Average Utilization Costs per patient accrued for a period of 365 days prior to project completion, and prospectively on a go-forward basis. The rolling metric is activated when a homeless patient is admitted as an emergency or inpatient case.**
Rationale *What are the clinical, quality, and/or financial grounds and supporting evidence for the intervention? Please attach any guidelines, studies, etc.*	**Follow national trend of providing housing interventions for homeless patients.** https://www.healthcaredive.com/news/ hospitals-tackling-homelessness-to-bring-down- costs/510631/
Baseline Data: *Describe your plans for baseline data*	**Data on ACO acute care services for persons with homeless status is being analyzed**
Measure Target: *What is the definition of success in terms of the quality measure(s)?*	**Reduce emergency and hospital utilization for this group by 30% within the first year of the program**

2) Intervention Checklist		Enter a filter condition (or N/A) on each line
The Who (Denominator) Define the selection criteria for the cohort of patients to be included in this intervention	Registry Inclusion	**Homeless, Admissions**
	Inpatient	**Yes**
	Ambulatory	**N/A**
	Primary Care	**ACO payor plan**
	Age Start	**18**
	Age End	**100**
	Gender	**All**
	Social Determinants	**Homeless + acute services**
	Diagnoses	**N/A**
	Lab Values	**N/A**
	Medication	**N/A**
	Exclusions	**N/A**

The What (Numerator) What value in the patient chart with indicate that the measure is complete	Lab Order	N/A
	Referral Order	**Referral to Housing Program**
	Medication Management	N/A
	Outreach	N/A
	Questionnaire	N/A
	Assessment	N/A
	Immunization	N/A
	Examination	N/A
	Chart Documentation	N/A
	Other	N/Agno
The When (Timing) If the intervention to be repeated, what is the schedule or trigger for repeating?		**Housing status every 90 day**
How (EHR tools) Which EHR tools will be required to move the measure?	Intervention scheduler	**Housing status every 90 day**
	Intervention order	N/A
	Dynamic order set	N/A
	Bulk order	N/A
	Bulk message	N/A
	Risk score	N/A
	Report	**Housing Insecurity ACO patients**
	Alert	N/A
	Work queue	**Housing program**
	Other	N/A
By Whom: Will this create new work? For whom? Does it automate an existing task?	MD	N/A
	PharmD	N/A
	Registered Nurse	N/A
	Lic.Vocational Nurse	N/A
	Front Office	N/A
	Scheduler	N/A
	Care Manager	**ACO Housing specialist**
	Patient	N/A
	Automation	N/A
	Other	N/A

Chapter 12

Use Case Questions

1. Table 12.2 estimates that 81% of patients will pass the lab test measure if every eligible person received an order for test and blood draw. If the clinics hired phlebotomists so that each person who had an order also

received a blood draw during their appointment, what would be the estimated measure rate?

The rate would improve to 90% because only numerator failures would be 10% due to CMP result not in the computer.

2. This simplified case study lists five reasons that patients didn't pass the numerator conditions. Name some other reasons that might prevent patients from completing their scheduled care.

Possible answers include patient refusal, programming error in the measure calculation, patient was laid off and lost insurance mid-year, patient switched to another doctor without notifying the clinic, patient passed away.

Chapter 13

Risk adjustment questions:

1. What does it mean if a patient's RAF score is 0.6?

a. It is projected that the patient's care would cost 60% *less* than the average beneficiary for their enrollment type
b. It is projected that the patient's care would cost 60% *more* than the average beneficiary for their enrollment type
c. It is projected that the patient's care would cost 40% *less* than the average beneficiary for their enrollment type
d. It is projected that the patient's care would cost 40% *more* than the average beneficiary for their enrollment type
Answer: C

2. Does the RAF score accurately reflect the relative amount of clinician time required for each patient visit?

No. The RAF score represents the relative amount of spend. The spend is affected by the number of visits, hospitalizations, procedures, etc.
A RAF score does not imply that a patient of RAF score 0.5 will require half the appointment time of a patient with a RAF score of 1.0. The score

was not designed for that purpose and should not be used to determine the appropriate appointment length for a patient.
The RAF score is also based on linear models of spend for a given condition; it does not accurately reflect the impact of complex comorbidities on patient utilization.

3. Does the RAF score accurately reflect the relative spend for the adult population age 18 to 64 at a single hospital?

No. Although the score does account for the demographic and diagnosis components contributing to utilization, the Medicare HCC model was not designed for this age group. Local treatment practices, diagnosis coding, and cost factors may affect the relative spend. The RAF scores may be a starting point from which to evaluate the relative spend at the local level, but it would probably be more effective to compute the spend directly.

Case Study: Implementation of HIV Risk Calculator in an EHR

1. Consider your personal reaction if you received the VACS score of 66% (like Grover in line 1). This means your personal risk of death is 66% within the next five years.

   Answers will vary by individual. It is likely that due to the length of time (five years) and risk that is not much higher than chance (66%), this will not affect behavior.

2. What if the risk of mortality was 80% within one year? How might that change clinical decision-making and lifestyle choices?

   Answers will vary by individual. It is more likely that patients would take action based on this information.

3. What are the potential ramifications of errors and/or misunderstanding of the subtleties of statistical analysis when this mortality risk data are shared?

   Errors in implementation of risk scores are not uncommon. The more complicated the scoring algorithm, the higher the risk of error. Another effect of computational complexity is that patients (and providers) may consider this a highly scientific black box and not question the methodology or explore the implications in depth. New medications and treatment protocols that were not available in the study population may render this scoring methodology obsolete within a specific local cohort.

4. What is your opinion about the sharing of this information with patients?

a. Patients should always see all of the clinical information available, including mortality risk scores.
b. Patients should never be exposed to mortality risk score data.
c. Patients should be given the choice of knowing their score or not. Answer C would leave this decision up to the patient.

5. Based on this limited data set, does the VACS risk of mortality appear to correlate well with utilization?

No, this limited data does not show a strong correlation between mortality risk and utilization. This is an anecdotal finding, and would need further research to state conclusively.

Exercises: Risk stratification

What does it mean if a patient's RAF score is 0.6? **Correct Answer: C**

a. It is projected that the patient's care would cost 60% less than the average beneficiary for their enrollment type
b. It is projected that the patient's care would cost 60% more than the average beneficiary for their enrollment type
c. **It is projected that the patient's care would cost 40% less than the average beneficiary for their enrollment type**
d. It is projected that the patient's care would cost 40% more than the average beneficiary for their enrollment type

Chapter 14

Case Study: OHSU Ambulatory Quality Reporting White Paper

Case Questions:

1. The white paper description of NQF-0018 Controlling High Blood Pressure lists a number of data items used in the measure calculation. Create a list of those data items you would abstract from the patient record for measure validation report.

A report with the following information will be helpful both during the measure validation and post-submission as an audit report. Chart review will confirm that patients failing the numerator do not meet the criteria.

Patient ID

Problem list diagnosis that matches ICD-9 group HYPERTENSION

Encounter diagnosis and date that matches ICD-9 group HYPERTENSION

Billing diagnosis and date matches ICD-9 group HYPERTENSION

Patient status (alive or deceased)

Patient is active in hypertension (Y/N)

Date of last office visit within 365 days

Patients age as of start of the measurement period

In denominator (1 = yes, 0 = no)

_____

Problem list diagnosis that matches ICD-9 group PREGNANCY

Encounter diagnosis and date that matches ICD-9 group PREGNANCY

Billing diagnosis and date matches ICD-9 group PREGNANCY

Problem list diagnosis that matches in group CMS_EXCLUSIONS

Encounter diagnosis and date that matches in group CMS_EXCLUSIONS

Billing diagnosis and date matches in group CMS_EXCLUSIONS

Patient encounter date and level of service code, where level of service code is in group ESRD MONTHLY OUTPATIENT SERVICES

Patient order ID, order description, and order completion date where completed order is in group CMS_EXCLUSIONS

Patient excluded (1=yes, 0=no)

_____

Most recent systolic blood pressure and date (as of measurement date)

Most recent diastolic blood pressure and date (as of measurement date)

In numerator (1 = yes, 0=no)

2. Is a pregnant patient included in the measure denominator?

   No. Exclusions are factors supported by the clinical evidence that should remove a patient from measure population (denominator).

3. Assume the patient is in the denominator and has no exclusions. If the measurement period start date is 1/1/2018 and the last blood pressure

reading of 139/89 was taken on 12/3/2017, would this patient be numerator positive (in numerator = yes)?

No. The blood pressure measurement needs to be taken on or after the measurement period start date.

4. What steps would you take to close the care gap for patients who are not in the numerator?

The patients need to have another blood pressure reading that falls below 140/90. If they haven't recently had the blood pressure checked in the office, they may just need a nurse visit. If blood pressure continues to be over the target, they should be referred to their PCP or a pharmacist to explore ways to reduce their blood pressure. Any other answer that moves patients toward the goal would be correct.

Chapter 15

1. Describe some of the challenges and barriers that slow or prevent the incorporation of local performance data into the Critically-Appraised External Evidence Base?

Answers may include: Issues with data interoperability; HIPAA and consenting to share personal health information; Heterogeneity of EHR systems and processes.

2. What are the barriers that slow or prevent the application of Critically-Appraised External Evidence to performance improvement at the healthcare provider level?

Answers may include: expense and difficulty in changing and managing clinical processes; resistance to change; provider burnout with an increasing burden of documentation of the deliver of evidence-based care; challenges identifying the right patients for inclusion in a new intervention protocol.

Chapter 16

Case study questions

1. Name two factors that made it more challenging to meet the HIV viral load quality goal.

   Possible answers:
   - *Successful outreach to re-engage patients who had fallen out of care added patients to the measure denominator who had high HIV viral load. Because it takes months of treatment for these patients to reach the suppression goal, any patients introduced to care during the third quarter of the measurement period (a good thing) counted against the viral load suppression metric (reflecting a timing issue, not a quality of care issue).*
   - *Measure design was not sensitive to the reduction in viral load across the cohort.*
   - *The measure goal was based on a fixed percentage improvement over baseline. Because this was a well-performing clinic, the goal was set unusually high.*
   - *This clinical outcome goal had a high inherent difficulty because patient compliance and efficacy of the antiretroviral therapeutics were outside the control of the provider and health system.*

2. How does HIV viral load suppression affect value for the patient?

   It helps keep patients in a healthy state, free of complications. It protects their partners from infection with HIV, and it prevents mothers from passing the infection to their babies.

3. How does HIV viral load suppression affect value for the public health system?

   The Pennsylvania Chronic Care Initiative (CCI) found a total cost savings of $214.10 per patient per month. Costs of higher outpatient utilization were more than offset by lower inpatient utilization. Reduction in HIV transmission reduces the overall incidence and prevalence and the associated cost of treating the disease.

Appendix A. Implementation of CDC Race and Ethnicity Codes (CDCREC)

The multiplicity of race and ethnicity code sets is problematic for the collection of health data in the electronic health record (EHR). A comprehensive review of the literature and recommendations by the Agency for Healthcare Research and Quality (AHRQ) provide this guidance:

> *Given variations in locally relevant populations, no single national set of additional ethnicity categories is best for all entities that collect these data. Collection of data in the OMB [Office of Management and Budget] race and Hispanic ethnicity categories, supplemented by more granular ethnicity data, is recommended, with tailoring of the latter through locally relevant categories chosen from a standardized national set.*[101]

Based on this recommendation, we suggest two Centers for Disease Control (CDC) sources of standardized CDCREC codes from which you can fashion a locally appropriate value set. Following that is the description of the authors' methods for converting to the new data collection standard in an existing EHR.

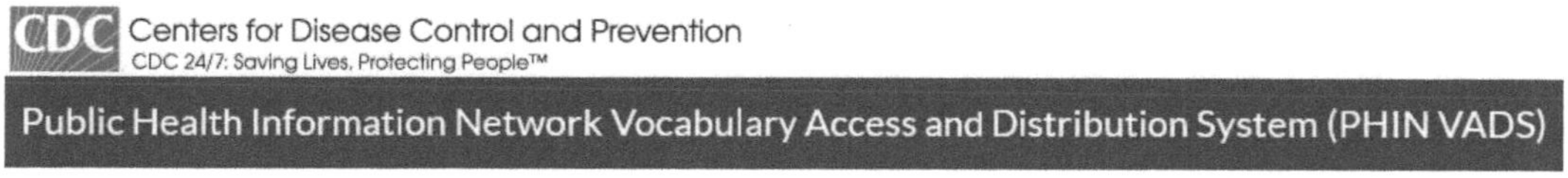

CDC Centers for Disease Control and Prevention
CDC 24/7: Saving Lives, Protecting People™

Public Health Information Network Vocabulary Access and Distribution System (PHIN VADS)

Figure A.1   CDCREC website header.

Source: www.cdc.gov/phin/resources/vocabulary/documents/CDC-Race-Ethnicity-Background-and-Purpose.pdf.

Centers for Disease Control and Prevention
CDC 24/7: Saving Lives, Protecting People™

National Center for Health Statistics

Figure A.2   HL7/CDC Race and Ethnicity code set header.

Source: https://www.cdc.gov/nchs/data/dvs/Race_Ethnicity_CodeSet.pdf.

The CDC Public Health Information Network Vocabulary Access and Distribution System (PHIN VADS) maintains the lists of race and ethnicity codes in the CDCREC standard (www.cdc.gov/phin/resources/vocabulary/documents/CDC-Race-Ethnicity-Background-and-Purpose.pdf).

The CDC National Center for Health Statistics Division of Vital Statistics provides the HL7/CDC Race and Ethnicity code set as well as the crossmapping to hierarchical codes used by the department of Health and Human Services for standard certifi cates and reports. (www.cdc.gov/nchs/ data/dvs/ Race_Ethnicity_CodeSet.pdf).

The authors adapted these two standards to a new Race/Ethnicity data collection interface in an existing EHR. A project of approximately six months in duration resulted in implementation of a new data element in the EHR called "Ethnic Background." The effort required the education and approval of the registration staff and communication with the reporting team and researchers about the change. The medical center implemented a subset of the CDCREC standard with 127 detail race and ethnicities.

The principles that guided this conversion:

1. The existing race and ethnicity data interfaces with external systems must not be changed. There would be no way to ensure that any new mapping would be received correctly at all external interface destinations.
2. Because the finer statistical distinctions between detailed ethnicity and detailed race are lost on the general public, all detailed race and ethnicity codes are collected in a single new data element called Ethnic Background. We require all race and ethnicity items to be selected from lists to maintain the data integrity. This approach follows the recommendation of the EHR vendor.
3. Human factors considerations required the use of synonyms for related terms and common misspellings. For example, Afghanistan and Afgan were assigned as synonyms for the Afghan ethnicity. Consequently, if Afgan is entered (without the h), the data is stored as Afghan.

4. The CDCREC code (e.g., 2028–9) was entered as the short name for each list item. The hierarchical race and ethnicity codes were mapped as synonyms where a clear mapping existed. If there was no equivalent on the list, the synonym of "custom" was applied so that we could easily find these items in a search. Examples of custom ethnic backgrounds included Kumeyaay, a local Native American tribe, and Canadian.

5. No existing race and ethnicity information was lost in the data conversion to the new standard.

A data conversion effort remapped approximately 20,000 Level 2 races (e.g., Chinese, Cambodian, Filipino) from the Race data element to the new "Ethnic Background" data element (Table A.1). The field previously called "Ethnicity" is now called "Hispanic?," because the only ethnicities collected in that data element are Hispanic. The underlying data did not change in the Level 1 Ethnicity field.

Table A.1 Mapping of Legacy Races to CDCREC

Prior Race	Current Level 1 Race (rolled up)	Mapped Level 2 Ethnic Background
White	White	N/A
Black	Black or African American	N/A
Native American/ Eskimo	American Indian or Alaska Native	N/A
Asian	Asian	N/A
Pacific Islander	Native Hawaiian or Other Pacific Islander	Other Pacific Islander
Asian Indian	Asian	Asian Indian
Cambodian	Asian	Cambodian
Chinese	Asian	Chinese
Filipino	Asian	Filipino
Guamanian	Native Hawaiian or Other Pacific Islander	Guamanian
Hawaiian	Native Hawaiian or Other Pacific Islander	N/A
Japanese	Asian	Japanese
Korean	Asian	Korean
Laotian	Asian	Laotian
Middle Eastern	White	Middle Eastern
Other SE Asian	Asian	Other SE Asian
Samoan	Native Hawaiian or Other Pacific Islander	Samoan
Vietnamese	Asian	Vietnamese

The new "Ethnic Background" data element supports the CDC Race and Ethnicity standards and currently has 127 combined Level 2 Races and Level 2 Ethnicities (e.g., Central American, Costa Rican, Guatemalan, South American) (Table A.2). We found that many of the 914 Level 2 races in the

Table A.2   Mapping of Ethnic Background to CDCREC and CMS Codes and Synonyms

Ethnic Background	CDC REC	CMS Roll-up Codes and Synonyms
Afghan	2126–1	R5.02.008~Afghanistan~Afgan
African	2060–2	R3.03~Black~Nigritian
African American	2058–6	R3.02~Negro~Black
Agua caliente Cahuilla	1045–4	R1.01.013.001~Native American~Indian
American Indian or Alaska Native	1002–5	R1
Arab	2129–5	R5.03
Argentinian	2166–7	E1.04.001~Argentina
Armenian	2109–7	R5.01.001~Armenia
Asian	2028–9	R2
Asian Indian	2029–7	R2.01~India
Assyrian	2119–6	R5.02.001~Syria~Asturian
Australian	Australian	Custom~Australia
Bahamian	2067–7	R3.04~Bahamas
Bangladeshi	2030–5	R2.02~Bangladesh
Barbadian	2068–5	R3.05~Barbados~Barbadan
Bhutanese	2031–3	R2.03~Bhutan
Black	2056–0	R3.01~Negro~African American
Bolivian	2167–5	E1.04.002~Bolivia
Botswanan	2061–0	R3.03.001~Botswana
Burmese	2032–1	R2.04~Myanmar~Burma
California tribes	Indian	Custom~Native American~Indian
Cambodian	2033–9	R2.05~Cambodia~Kampuchean
Canadian	Canadian	Custom~Canada
Central American	2155–0	E1.03
Chamorro	2088–3	R4.02.003~Chamorro
Cherokee	Cherokee	Custom
Chicano	Chicano	Custom
Chilean	2168–3	E1.04.003~Chile

Table A.2 **(Continued)**

Ethnic Background	CDC REC	CMS Roll-up Codes and Synonyms
Chinese	2034–7	R2.06~China
Colombian	2169–1	E1.04.004~Columbia
Costa Rican	2156–8	E1.03.001~Costa Rica
Croatian	Croatian	Custom
Cuban	2182–4	E1.07~Cuban
Cupeno	1211–2	R1.01.049~Native American~Indian
Dominica islander	2070–1	R3.07~Dominica Island
Dominican	2069–3	R3.06~Dominican Republic
Ecuadorian	2170–9	E1.04.005~Equador
Egyptian	2120–4	R5.02.002~Egypt
English	2110–5	R5.01.002~British~UK
Ethiopian	2062–8	R3.03.002~Ethiopia
European	2108–9	R5.01~Europe
Fijian	2101–4	R4.03.001~Figi
Filipino	2036–2	R2.08~Philipino~Fillipino
French	2111–3	R5.01.003~France
German	2112–1	R5.01.004~Germany
Guamanian	2087–5	R4.02.002~Guam
Guatemalan	2157–6	E1.03.002~Guatemala
Haitian	2071–9	R3.08~Haiti
Hispanic or Latino	2135–2	E1~Spanish~Latina
Hmong	2037–0	R2.09
Honduran	2158–4	E1.03.003~Honduras
Indonesian	2038–8	R2.10~Indonesia
Iranian	2121–2	R5.02.003~Iran~Persia
Iraqi	2122–0	R5.02.004~Iraq
Irish	2113–9	R5.01.005~Ireland
Israeli	2127–9	R5.02.009~Israel
Italian	2114–7	R5.01.006~Italy
Iwo Jiman	2048–7	R2.20~Iwo Jima
Jamaican	2072–7	R3.09~Jamaica
Japanese	2039–6	R2.11~Japan
Korean	2040–4	R2.12~Korea
Kumeyaay	Indian	Custom~Native American~Indian
Kurdish	Kurdish	Custom~Kurdistan~Kurd

(Continued)

Table A.2   Mapping of Ethnic Background to CDCREC and CMS Codes and Synonyms (Continued)

Ethnic Background	CDC REC	CMS Roll-up Codes and Synonyms
Laotian	2041–2	R2.13~Laos
Latin American	2178–2	E1.05~LATIN, LATINO
Lebanese	2123–8	R5.02.005~Lebanon
Liberian	2063–6	R3.03.003~Liberia
Luiseno	1331–8	R1.01.081~Native American~Indian
Madagascar	2052–9	R2.24
Malaysian	2042–0	R2.14~Malaysia
Maldivian	2049–5	R2.21~Maldives
Mariana islander	2089–1	R4.02.004~Mariana Islands
Marshallese	2090–9	R4.02.005~Marshall Islands
Melanesian	2100–6	R4.03~Oceania
Mexican	2148–5	E1.02~Mexicano~Chicano
Mexican American	2149–3	E1.02.001
Micronesian	2085–9	R4.02~Oceania
Middle Eastern or North African	2118–8	R5.02
Mongolian	Mongolian	Custom~Mongolia
Namibian	2064–4	R3.03.004~Namibia
Native American/Eskimo	1002–5	R1~Indian~Alsaka Native
Native Hawaiian	2079–2	R4.01.001~Hawaii~Hawaiian Islands
Native Hawaiian or other pacific islander	2076–8	R4~Hawaii
Nepalese	2050–3	R2.22~Nepal
New Hebrides	2104–8	R4.03.004
New Zealander	Kiwi	Custom~New Zealand~Kiwi
Nicaraguan	2159–2	E1.03.004~Nicaragua
Nigerian	2065–1	R3.03.005~Niger~Nigeria
Not Hispanic or Latino	2186–5	E2
Okinawan	2043–8	R2.15~Okinawa
Other Pacific Islander	2500–7	R4.04~Oceania
Other Race	2131–1	R9
Other Southeast Asian	2028–9	R2.25
Pakistani	2044–6	R2.16~Pakistan
Palauan	2091–7	R4.02.006~Palau
Palestinian	2124–6	R5.02.006~Palestine~West Bank Gaza Strip
Panamanian	2160–0	E1.03.005~Panama

Table A.2 (Continued)

Ethnic Background	CDC REC	CMS Roll-up Codes and Synonyms
Papua New Guinean	2102–2	R4.03.002~Papua New Guinea~Papa New Ginny
Paraguayan	2171–7	E1.04.006~Paraguay
Peruvian	2172–5	E1.04.007~Peru
Polish	2115–4	R5.01.007~Poland
Polynesian	2078–4	R4.01~Polynesia
Portugal	Portugal	Custom~Portuguese
Puerto Rican	2180–8	E1.06~Puerto Rico
Russian	Russian	Custom~Russia~Soviet Union
Saipanese	2095–8	R4.02.010~Saipan
Salvadoran	2161–8	E1.03.006~El Salvador
Samoan	2080–0	R4.01.002~Samoa
Scottish	2116–2	R5.01.008~Scotland
Singaporean	2051–1	R2.23~Singapore
Solomon Islander	2103–0	R4.03.003~Soloman Islands
South American	2165–9	E1.04
Spaniard	2137–8	E1.01~Spanish~Spain
Sri Lankan	2045–3	R2.17~Sri Lanka
Syrian	2125–3	R5.02.007~Syria
Tahitian	2081–8	R4.01.003~Tahiti
Taiwanese	2035–4	R2.07~Taiwan
Thai	2046–1	R2.18~Thailand
Tobagoan	2073–5	R3.10~Tobago
Tongan	2082–6	R4.01.004~Tonga
Trinidadian	2074–3	R3.11~Trinidad
Turkish	Turkish	Custom~Turkey
Unknown Ethnicity	Unk Ethn	Custom~Unknown (Patient cannot or refuses to declare ethnicity)
Unknown Race	Unk Race	Custom~Unknown (Patient cannot or refuses to declare race)
Uruguayan	2173–3	E1.04.008~Uruguay
Venezuelan	2174–1	E1.04.009~Venezuela
Vietnamese	2047–9	R2.19~Vietnam~Viet
Welsh	Welsh	Custom~British~Wales
West Indian	2075–0	R3.12~West Indies
White	2106–3	R5~Caucasian
Zairean	2066–9	R3.03.006~Zaire

CDC standard were specific indigenous tribes that were not prevalent in our area. We did find the need to add ethnicity types so that more patients in our health system could identify with an item on the list. Although the addition of small ethnic groups to the list increased the cultural competency and inclusion of our health system, the low number of patients in these cohorts rendered them statistically insignificant without further data aggregation with other health systems.

Appendix B. Population Health White Paper

This white paper is a template for the creation of a population health electronic health record (EHR) team in information services. Brackets denote names that should be replaced to reflect the local situation.

Aligning People, Technology, and Quality Performance to Improve the Health Delivery of Populations

[Health Delivery System] needs to implement a population health program to meet its strategic vision for value-based care. *[Population Health Vendor]* offers a comprehensive approach to drive accountable, high-quality, coordinated, and safe care to patients. Improved population health systems will ensure that patients have memorable positive experiences and that the organization meets contractual quality and incentive targets.

Vision is to deliver outstanding population health through innovative use of the EHR

Mission is to create a healthier population through:

Actionable patient registries

Operational reporting for patient care and coordination

Tools that help patients and providers achieve health goals

Population-based performance measurement and quality improvement

Population Health Framework

Figure B.1 Population Health Framework.

Resource Request

People

- Establishment of the population health team does the following:
  - Allows *[Health Delivery System]* to develop standard processes, approaches, prioritization methodologies, and efficiencies for population health
  - Allows *[Health Delivery System]* to mature its existing build into the full population health framework including:
    - Primary care
    - HIV
    - Diabetes
    - Cardiovascular
    - Chronic kidney disease (CKD) registries
  - Establishes resources to address new registry requests, including but not limited to:
    - Anticoagulation
    - Acute kidney injury
    - Anesthesia
    - Burn
    - Hepatitis C
    - Managed care

- – Future capabilities would support new strategic initiatives such as:
  - Accountable care organization (ACO)
  - Population health for community affiliates
  - Contract negotiations
- Dedicated team includes the chief medical information officer for population health (60% time), application analyst, and reporting analyst
  - – Utilize trained individuals who were supporting HIV and primary care initiatives.
- Governance:
  - – Population Health Governance committee will be formed to set priorities and promote adherence to best practice.
- Leadership: The population health medical director would oversee the activities of the population health application analyst and population health reporting analyst. There would be a matrix relationship for technological alignment to the clinical systems and enterprise reporting teams.

Technology

- To be provided by *[Population Health Vendor]* including support for:
  - – Medicare Shared Savings Program (MSSP) clinician and executive dashboards
  - – Hierarchical condition category/risk adjustment factor (HCC/RAF) scoring for Medicare reimbursements
  - – Clinical decision support
  - – Quality reporting
- See attached materials for product and service specifications
- Purchasing the five-month *[Population Health Vendor]* implementation support package ensures focused install and optimization of all facets of the framework.

Population Health Framework

- *[Population Health Vendor]* offers a comprehensive approach to integrate applications for the workforce using a more cost-effective model to improve care delivery.

Early Successes

- Over the past several years, *[Health Delivery System]* has developed electronic medical record (EMR) tools to support population-based care delivery, such as:
  - *[add as appropriate—examples include]*
  - Actionable health registries within the EMR
  - Operational reporting for patient care and coordination
  - Bulk orders/communication messages for overdue labs/radiology exams
  - Decision support tools
  - Rigorous quality improvement activities
- To date, *[Health Delivery System]* population health milestones include:
  - *[add as appropriate—examples include]*
  - Bulk orders/communication messages to patients overdue for lab and radiology exams
  - Deployment of provider dashboards to manage care gaps

The Population Health Pillars of Value

Patient Experience	Clinical Excellence	Performance Management	Growth
Encourage patients to actively participate in care using the patient portal.	Drive nationally recognized, high-quality, and safe care.	Develop systems to support improved organizational accountability (by provider, team, department, service line).	Improve efficiencies to drive down costs so that more care can be provided. Expand capabilities to share and coordinate care.
Measure change in number of users (growth), volume, and patient satisfaction.	Measure increases in quality improvement in terms of number of lives affected, financial gain, or decreased adverse outcomes.	Measure, standardize benchmarks, and compare performance using dashboards and utilization metrics.	Develop capabilities to better understand quality/cost trade-offs. Increase capabilities to respond to employer/health plan care coordination and data sharing.

Timeline

- Project kickoff: Secure team
  - Medical director
  - Application analyst
  - Reporting analyst
- Two months after kickoff: Onsite support
- Seven months after kickoff: Quality program relaunch

Appendix C. Job Descriptions for Population Health Team Members

The resource request in the Population Health White Paper (Appendix B) includes a chief medical information officer: population health (60%), one application analyst, and one reporting analyst. We realize that the size and composition of the team will vary, but at minimum, a dedicated population health team will require a strong clinical leader and strong analysts for the front-end user interface of the electronic medical record (EMR), as well as for the data mart and analytics back-end. Based on experience, the most effective team composition includes a minimum of three team members. For administrative management, the analysts typically are embedded with the electronic health record (EHR) quality reporting team or the ambulatory team. In either case, population health links these two teams together through clinical decision support and quality measurement, so there is a need to foster collaboration between the two teams.

Sample job descriptions for these roles are offered next.

Chief Medical Information Officer for Population Health
EMR Application Analyst (intermediate or advanced)
Reporting Analyst (intermediate or advanced)

As the population health infrastructure grows, additional staff may be justified.

Population Health Lead Application Analyst (advanced)
Enterprise Population Health Architect

Please note: Attached job descriptions reference Healthy Planet, the collection of Epic population health tools. Organizations not using the Epic system will need to substitute the technical requirements and certifications.

Job Description: Chief Medical Information Officer for Population Health

Responsibilities

The chief medical informatics officer (CMIO) directs the information technology to meet the vision of integrated clinical, quality, patient safety, and research missions. The CMIO provides vision and direction related to enterprise population health, identifying opportunities to enhance the safety, efficiency, and effectiveness of care delivery. Responsible for identification of opportunities to enhance population health priorities and ensure effective change management. Provides leadership to develop, coordinate, implement, and improve informatic systems to provide remarkable customer care. In collaboration with division leaders, the incumbent plays a key role in advancing, implementing, and improving organizational initiatives and strategies and participates in leadership committees. The CMIO is responsible for supporting the development, implementation, and optimization of Epic. Promotes an environment conducive to staff and physician satisfaction and retention while assuring a respectful and sensitive diverse work environment. Communicates the value of the EMR and associated changes to the physician/provider community. Champions workflow redesign as needed.

Leadership Accountabilities

- This member of senior leadership is accountable for leading population health initiatives aligned with organizational mission, vision, and goals.
- Leads nontechnical faculty, administrative leadership, and staff and serves as liaison between faculty leaders and clinical systems.
- In partnership with the CMIO-Inpatient, collaborates with inpatient and ambulatory leadership to achieve the goals stated in the strategic plan.
- Participates in the development and execution of the clinical improvement and development strategies, including clinical efforts for improved customer outcomes, reduced variations in care, and enhanced physician and patient engagement.

- Oversees the use of the EHR and other clinical informatics systems, including analytics tools, to support quality and performance improvement initiatives.
- Serves as liaison to the clinical staff, medical executive committees, clinical departments, and other constituents to use informatics to promote the clinical agenda.
- Improves clinician adoption, acceptance, and use of information technology while enhancing physician satisfaction with the clinical information system.
- Manages the expectations of clinical information system end users.
- Monitors EMR system interoperability features to ensure that the organization is meeting criteria ahead of deadlines.
- Serves as a member of information technology committees.
- Participates in ongoing clinical/customer care activities as requested by the chief medical officer (CMO).
- Actively participates in Epic conferences.

Education

- Graduate of an accredited medical school or osteopathic school required.
- Graduate of accredited residency required in area of specialty.

Experience

- Three to five years of clinical informatics experience, preferably with Epic EMR.
- Board certified in chosen field (family medicine, general surgery, etc.).
- Physician leadership experience desired (ex-department chair, physician champion).

Knowledge, Skills, and Abilities

- Demonstrated leadership and management skills.
- Strong communication, interpersonal, and conflict resolution skills.
- Strong analytical and problem-solving skills.
- Ability to work effectively and build consensus among individuals with diverse interests.

Licensure/Certification(s)/Registration

- Current medical doctor state license.
- Current medical staff credentials and privileges for hospital and clinics.
- Board certification in informatics is desirable.

Adapted from online job posting, North Memorial Health (2019). Chief Medical Informatics Officer. Retrieved from www.indeed.com July 31, 2019.

Job Description: Healthy Planet Application Analyst

Payroll category: Clinical Applications Professional 4

Responsibilities

The Healthy Planet applications analyst will be responsible for implementing Epic Healthy Planet tools that focus on improving quality scores (i.e., Healthcare Effectiveness Data and Information Set HEDIS), lowering cost of care, and improving patient satisfaction scores at the organization for specific patient populations (i.e., at-risk arrangements with payors).

She or he will be an integral part of the population health team supporting enterprise population health workflows. This analyst will deploy and support a number of Epic Healthy Planet tools, including Chronic Disease Registries, Patient Outreach, Patient Goals, Registry-based Navigator Support, Best Practice Advisory, Longitudinal Plan of Care, and Workbench Reports.

Responsibilities will include requirements analysis and collaborative design of population health tools, dashboards, operational reports, and training materials. Support the project development lifecycle of design, build, test, training, deployment, evaluation, and on-going support of systems used in the delivery of population health. Additional responsibilities will include data quality validation of quality scores, process metrics, utilization metrics, cost metrics, and other metrics to be defined.

Qualifications

Required

- Bachelor's degree in healthcare administration, public health, mathematics, healthcare informatics, or computer science or equivalent experience.
- Epic Ambulatory certification or Healthy Planet certification.

- Experience with Epic EMR build and configuration.
- Experience working with multiple clinical information systems or system implementation teams for complex projects and/or application development.
- Knowledge of clinical practices and principles.
- Experience with methods and tools for systems development lifecycle as related to clinical informatics.
- Experience with designing and monitoring technology-enabled organizational change.
- Experience with quality improvement principles, practices, and tools into system design.
- Experience with coordinating system development and implementation with relevant clinical operations initiatives and informatics projects.
- Experience with advanced application of adult learning principles and clinical system design standards.
- Experience with organizational strategies, business operations, and end-user requirements to develop system design and training projects.
- Proficient in office automation software (word processing, spreadsheets, visual presentation, etc.) and strong presentation skills.
- Experience with project management, information systems trends, and professional practice standards.

Preferred

- Experience working in an academic institution or large integrated health system.
- Epic Ambulatory, Healthy Planet, Reporting Workbench, and/or Radar certifications.
- Experience with population health management programs and/or accountable care organizations (ACOs).

Job Description: EMR Reporting Analyst

Payroll Category: Clinical Applications Professional Advanced

Responsibilities

The EMR reporting analyst will actively contribute to an innovative team dedicated to establishing a new foundation for advancing clinical delivery and quality outcomes. Incumbent will gain knowledge of the Epic EMR software, as well as medical center operations and workflow, and will work closely with the project team's senior application analysts and clinical leaders to translate business needs into EMR functionality.

The incumbent displays critical thinking, analytical, organization and documentation expertise, and acquires Epic system certifications and reporting tools expertise in order to present creative design solutions that meet the customer needs. Business intelligence (BI) and reporting content development will range from creating dashboards, Crystal reports, BusinessObjects Universes, to SQL queries and data extracts. Participates in all aspects of the requirements, design, development, testing, and deployment of BI and reporting content for the network's EMR application, Connect. The EMR reporting analyst works collaboratively with business and clinical stakeholders, application analysts, the program management organization (PMO), and technical support teams in order to design, develop, and support BI and reporting content that leads to actionable intelligence. Designs and develops reporting dashboards, Crystal reports, BusinessObjects Universes, and data extracts for team based on industry best practices

- Collaboration with EMR application analysts, Clarity database administrators (DBAs), and the reporting server administrator to ensure BI and reporting content is developed accurately and deployed effectively.
- Designs and develops database tables, views, functions, and stored procedures in Microsoft SQL Server.
- Reviews Epic release notes and updates to reporting content during Epic upgrades.
- Consultation with business and clinical stakeholders to extract and document requirements and validate reporting content.
- Data analysis to support organization and client improvement.
- Data accuracy within the EMR data stores, identification and reporting of data issues, working with appropriate IT staff, and reporting stakeholders toward resolution.
- Evaluates and implements new BI content from Epic.
- Provides production support of BI and reporting content.
- Performs other duties as assigned.

Education

Bachelor's degree in healthcare information technology, computer science, or related area.

Experience

- Four years in healthcare, IT or financial sectors.
- Three years in reporting, database, or software development.
- Intermediate-level capabilities with Microsoft Access and Microsoft SQL Server and related technologies.
- Knowledge and intermediate-level experience working with Transact SQL, Crystal Reports 11, online analytical processing (OLAP) structures, and/or other related technologies.
- Excellent project management skills.
- Knowledge and experience of database management technologies.
- Extensive experience and working knowledge of all Microsoft Office products.
- Ability to work in a group setting and group projects.
- Excellent verbal and written communication skills, presentation and report writing.
- Excellent interpersonal skills and ability to manage multiple projects independently, setting priorities to meet deadlines.

Licenses and Certifications

Clarity Ambulatory Data Model certification or proficiency. EpicCare Healthy Planet certification is preferred.

Job Description: Population Health Lead Application Analyst

Payroll Category: Clinical Applications Professional Advanced

Courtesy of Ryan Peck, MHA, CPHIMS
Senior Manager, Epic Population Health & Government Programs
University of California Davis Health

Brief Description

The population health lead application analyst supports the ambulatory clinics' increasing demand for Healthy Planet reporting tools for patients with chronic diseases and conditions. Works closely with others on the application team to coordinate all system issues that arise during the use of the application(s) by the ambulatory clinics. Knowledgeable about the procedures, workflows, and business operations within the end-user organizations. The analyst has in-depth knowledge of the EpicCare Ambulatory system with a focus in population health management and administration and serves as a bridge between the end users, vendors, and other information system (IS) support teams. Position will support the ambulatory clinics leadership and reporting team along with the health system population health management solution. The focus of this position will be on implementing Epic Healthy Planet tools for improving quality scores (i.e., HEDIS), lowering cost of care, and improving patient satisfaction scores at the organization for specific patient populations (i.e., at-risk arrangements with payors).

This role involves complex projects and demands independent decision-making, project management skills, and superior customer service interactions with a wide range of constituents. The analyst will partner with health system faculty and staff to develop and implement Epic Healthy Planet (population health) workflows. Responsibilities will include the collaborative design of population health tools, dashboards, reporting workbench reports, and clinical documentation requirements in the Epic EMR environment; manage design, testing, deployment, and ongoing support of Epic systems used in the delivery of population health tools. Additional responsibilities will include data quality validation of the population health Epic dashboards that may include quality scores, process metrics, utilization metrics, cost metrics, and other metrics to be defined.

The analyst will be a leader on the team by partnering daily to monitor responsibilities, tasks, and other duties assigned to the team. Analyst will be available to answer any support/project questions, assist in troubleshooting, and give guidance on projects and general next steps, as well as provide detailed status to the team manager. The analyst will help oversee the team's daily responsibilities to ensure tasks are completed on time and will escalate to manager as necessary.

Incumbent provides advanced-level software support to health system staff and faculty in the assigned department and clinics, implementing and supporting specialized, complex distributed clinical information systems and multiple complex ancillary/patient care systems. Aligns assigned departmental technical solutions with Health System Information Technology Division goals, guidelines, and directives. Incumbent has the responsibility for supporting large, complex, and/or unique projects that affect multiple departments and will include product analysis and assessment, recommendation, implementation, testing, and roll-out of new technologies in a cross-matrixed environment.

For EMR operational projects, this position performs analysis, build, and testing for assigned projects. This may include system changes across multiple environments. Coordinate communication, testing, and updating any changes to support documentation for assigned operational EMR changes.

ESSENTIAL FUNCTIONS

Function A Title: Leadership Percent of Time: 30%
  Duties:

Provides leadership and technical direction to team members and end users to ensure proper implementation of the application in a timely fashion.

Directs, educates, and mentors project and operation team analysts in clinical workflow, technical design, support, and build of applications. Serves as resource to staff and project team to resolve unusual problems/situations.

Independently requests and manages work performed by clinical stake holders and outside departments to perform analysis and design activities required to fulfill project objectives. Tracks resource progress toward meeting project deadlines and fulfilling stated requirements.

Develops standardized processes and design build style guides for gathering clinical content from health system stakeholders.

Mentors new staff or assigned resources in analysis processes to work with clinical stakeholders using standardized communication and style guides.

Accurately estimates the effort required for completion of projects and the impact of requested changes to scheduled tasks and milestones.

Monitors outcomes of project activities and provides periodic reports of project outcomes, issues, and cross-team impacts.

Mentors the user community and team members on the use of clinical information systems.

May recommend to program team changes in methods, processes, hardware/software to provide a better product for end users.

Function B Title: System Analysis   Percent of Time: 50%
Duties:

Designs, tests, implements, and evaluates clinical systems for the organization to ensure successful implementation of the products, a highly
productive work force, and the delivery of quality patient care.

Designs, develops, and implements system functionality to meet strategic
needs of the organization and complex cross-departmental needs based
on the organization's overall guiding principles.

Utilizes appropriate planned change management models (problem solv-
ing, diffusion, social interaction, other), principles, and techniques in
system planning, development, implementation, and evaluation.

Analyzes current documentation and data flows in departments and works
with management and staff to redesign workflow as necessary; designs
system to reflect appropriate workflow and scope of practice of users.

Develops clinical system functionality and tools to meet organizational and
clinical department needs in collaboration with end-user departments.

Participates in the application training program, including retraining as
updates and modifications occur.

Incorporates information system standards and operational standardization
in accordance with administrative/operational strategies.

Demonstrates integrated information system functionality to a variety of
audiences, including physicians, providers, and leadership.

Prioritizes user requests for enhancements to Epic EMR system.

Provides after-hours on-call production environment support for multiple
Epic EMR clinical modules, including modules not certified in. Ability
to leverage documentation, testing, experience, previous training, and
other resources to provide timely technical support to clinical end users
when required.

Function C Title: Project Management   Percent of Time: 20%
Duties:

Participates in the planning, development, implementation, and evaluation of information systems that support clinical practice and clinical
decision-making in support of the overall organizational strategy for
clinical information systems.

Performs needs assessment (identification of functional and system requirements) for complex workflows that cross multiple departments.

Integrates standardized clinical nomenclatures, naming and numbering conventions, and/or security classifications into clinical applications, using recommendations developed in collaboration with other healthcare disciplines.

Participates in the development and integration of clinical practice guidelines, clinical pathways, evidence-based rules, standards of care, and research protocols into relevant clinical systems.

Coordinates and evaluates the development and integration of standardized charting tools and user preference lists into clinical applications.

Participates in measurement, monitoring, and evaluation of overall project and process outcomes.

Provides project planning and incorporates clinical information needs and process improvements into clinical applications.

Modifies project management based on trends in healthcare delivery and the impact of informatics through involvement in professional organizations and networking with other best practice healthcare organizations.

Consults and works closely with other members of the program team, IT staff, and stakeholders to ensure development and implementation of functionality that will best meet the needs of UCDHS.

Develops and analyzes indicators for ncw and existing functionally to ensure optimal user effectiveness and efficiency.

Monitors and evaluates new functionality for potential implementation as application updates.

Leads project and related meetings and works cooperatively with management and staff to coordinate with the overall program.

Develops system fallback processes and procedures in collaboration with IT and other affected departments.

Assists with development of cost–benefit analysis.

Prepares polished, grammatically correct emails, memos, and documents as required, including requests for proposals (RFPs) and management reports.

Role model for professional telephone skills and conversational style. Mentors staff in verbal communication skills.

Leads, schedules, and coordinates project meetings with other IS staff and clinical end users.

Skills, Knowledge, and Abilities

List in descending order of importance the skills, knowledge, and abilities necessary for successful performance of the essential functions of this position.

Required:

- Bachelor's degree in healthcare administration, public health, mathematics, healthcare informatics, or computer science or equivalent experience.
- Epic Ambulatory certification or Healthy Planet certification is required.
- Experience with Epic EMR build and configuration.
- Experience working with multiple clinical information systems or system implementation teams for complex projects and/or application development.
- Demonstrated comprehensive knowledge of clinical practices and principles.
- Experience with methods and tools for systems development lifecycle as related to clinical informatics.
- Demonstrated ability to gather information from multiple sources and analyze applicability and appropriateness and develop an efficient workflow and subsequent computerized process.
- Experience with designing and monitoring technology-enabled organizational change.
- Experience with quality improvement principles, practices, and tools into system design.
- Experience with coordinating system development and implementation with relevant clinical operations initiatives and informatics projects.
- Experience with advanced application of adult learning principles and clinical system design standards.
- Experience with organizational strategies, business operations, and end-user requirements to develop system design and training projects.
- Excellent interpersonal, communication, leadership, and change management skills to establish and maintain positive and productive working relationships.
- Proficient in office automation software (word processing, spreadsheets, visual presentation, etc.) and strong presentation skills.
- Experience working in an academic institution or large integrated health system.
- Experience with project management, information systems trends, and professional practice standards.

Preferred

- Epic Healthy Planet, Reporting Workbench, and/or Radar certification is preferred.
- Experience with population health management programs and/or ACOs is preferred.

Job Description: Enterprise Population Health Architect

Payroll Category: Clinical Applications Professional Advanced

Description

Population health registries and data models are the cornerstone for delivering the right care to the right patient at the right time. Not only do they serve as a cohorting tool, they aggregate payors and outcomes to help better appreciate the value-based impact. Registries are an engine that drives healthcare. The interconnected processes and complex rules require expertise to manage. These tools identify patients who will receive interventions clinically from ordering providers, including new labs, procedures, medication, and follow-up.

The rules and accuracy are critical for that to function accurately. In order to serve in this role, the enterprise population health architect needs to understand Epic Healthy Planet and data architecture, highly accurate groups, rule-based decision support tools, health maintenance, bulk outreach and communication, and robust understanding of the reporting workbench. The individual must have the ability to visualize cross-enterprise solutions that can be repurposed into multiple workflows.

This position will involve design, building, testing, and implementation of registries and data models within the clinical application system. Provides support to clinical users through knowledge of clinical processes, documentation needs, workflows, and clinical practice standards when adapting software to meet their needs. Works with clinicians to prepare detailed specifications encompassing clinical processes, information flow, risk, and impact analysis. May provide customer service, troubleshooting, and maintenance. As a technical leader in population health, applies advanced professional concepts and extensive industry knowledge to lead and/or work on medium to large projects of broad scope and complexity. May be recognized expert of an area of focus of business in clinical applications.

Minimum Qualifications

Bachelor's degree in healthcare information technology, computer science, or related area and/or equivalent combination of experience/training.

A minimum of five or more years of relevant professional-level experience working with clinical application systems.

Must obtain EpicCare Healthy Planet certification within four months of initial hire.

Must maintain current certification for primary EMR module(s) as a condition of employment.

Experience and proven success in IS implementation, development, and support within a large-scale healthcare organization.

Preferred Qualifications

EpicCare Ambulatory certification or EpicCare Healthy Planet certification

Demonstrated experience as a major participant in a clinical system implementation.

Appendix D. DIY System for Quality Measure Management

Disclaimer:
Measures may be used for noncommercial implementation and/or reporting of performance data. Contact the measure steward if you wish to use the measure details for another purpose. The authors and publisher are not responsible for the application or outcomes of quality measures.

The Do-It-Yourself (DIY) Measure Management system runs off a database that contains structured information about quality programs, quality measures, and measure details. This guide provides details for the four-step process described in Chapter 8 (Figure 8.2). Go to www. AppliedPopulationHealth.com for copies of the DIY Measure Management Dictionary and the DIY Measure Management Sample Tables. Sample data was extracted from https://www.cms.gov/Medicare/ Medicare-Fee-for-Service-Payment/sharedsavingsprogram/ program-guidance-and-specifications.
Remember: Measure specifications from the program website should serve as the source of truth.

Quality Program Table

Every quality program should be tracked in a common application.

The quality program table organizes program documentation, submission history, deadlines, key contacts, and potential financial impact. The creation and maintenance of this table would likely be the responsibility of the director of quality reporting or designee, as this information would be required for any submission. The advantages of having a common table for all quality programs include a curated master list of current reporting requirements, a single source of truth for program participation status, and a directory for internal program sponsors and managers. Suggested minimum data elements for the quality program table are listed in Table D.1. The combined key of business entity (KEY1_BUS_ENTITY), program (KEY2_PGM_ABBR), and report period (KEY3_PGM_RPT_PERIOD) is associated with a unique set of measure specifications. Any time the measure specification document changes, a new record should be added to this table.

The Medicare Shared Savings Program accountable care organization (MSSP ACO) program is a de facto national standard for healthcare quality that includes preventive and chronic care in the ambulatory (office visit) setting.

Table D.1 TBL_QUALITY_PGM

Name	Description
KEY1_BUS_ENTITY	Submitting business entity—for upside/downside payments
KEY2_PGM_ABBR	Program name in abbreviated format
KEY3_PGM_RPT_PERIOD	Reporting period associated with applicable measure specification
PGM_STATUS	Active, past, future, not reporting
PERIOD_START	Calendar date of first day of measurement period
PERIOD_END	Calendar date of last day of measurement period
SUBMIT_DEADLINE	Quality report submission deadline
SUBMIT_YR	Number of years participating in program
INCENT_FIRST_PAY	Date award or penalty applied. If there's a recurring payment/penalty schedule, this is the first date.
INCENT_RECUR_PER_YR	Options: 1 for one-time payment; 2 for semi-annual payment; 4 for quarterly payments; 12 for monthly payments
MAX_UPSIDE_DOLLARS	Maximum 12-month upside potential for quality incentive payments
MAX_DOWNSIDE_ DOLLARS	Maximum 12-month downside potential for quality penalties
PAYOR	Name of payor associated with this quality program
PLAN	Name of insurance plan
PGM_NAME	Full name of quality program
TOT_MEASURES	Total count of measures
URL_PGM	Hyperlink to program website
URL_MEASURE_SPEC	Hyperlink to measure specification (one row per specification version)
URL_TARGETS	Hyperlink to benchmark targets for the entire program

Quality Measure Table

The measure specification documents identified in the quality program table contain the official rules for each program. Always look to the primary source document for the creation of the quality measure table. The table may contain measures that the organization is considering, is reporting, or has reported in past reporting periods, as well as internal quality measures that are not reported outside the organization.

To provide insight into the management of measure development, workflow design, and prioritization, three lookup tables will be added to the measure table. These will ensure consistency in coding the intervention domain, scope of practice, and measure difficulty.

The suggested minimum data elements for the quality measure table are listed in Table D.2. The combined key of program, report period, and measure number is unique for each row. Multiple versions of the same measure may be utilized so that benchmarks and incentives/penalties may be applied that are specific to each measurement period to account for variances within measures from year to year. The minimum suggested columns for the quality measure table include program abbreviation, reporting period, measure number, measure name, and submission method. Ensure as well that the specification details and versioning are also kept in the metadata for that particular measure. We have manually summarized the measure information from the 2018 and 2019 specifications in the quality measure table template.

Table D.2   TBL_QUALITY_MEASURE

Name	Description
KEY1_BUS_ENTITY	Submitting business entity—for upside/downside payments
KEY2_PGM_ABBR	Program name in abbreviated format
KEY3_PGM_RPT_PERIOD	Reporting period associated with applicable measure specification
KEY4_MEAS_NUM	Program-assigned measure number (may have synonyms)
MEAS_NAME	Program-assigned measure name
MEAS_GROUP_NUM	Quality program group (example: MSSP group 1)
MEAS_GROUP_NAME	Quality program group name (example: MSSP Patient/ Caregiver Experience)
PAY_FOR	Values are "Reporting" or "Performance." Pay for reporting measure means submission is required, but there is no defined threshold of performance. Pay for performance has a minimum or scaled payment based on the measure value.

(Continued)

Table D.2   (Continued) TBL_QUALITY_MEASURE

Name	Description
EXTERNAL_GOAL	Performance rate set by the quality program for the maximum financial incentive payment. If met, measure status is GREEN.
INTERNAL_GOAL	The internal target typically is more difficult to achieve than the external goal and provides a safety zone for achieving the external target. If met, measure status is YELLOW.
MEAS_UPSIDE	Maximum 12-month upside potential for quality payments in dollars.
MEAS_DOWNSIDE	Maximum 12-month downside potential for quality penalties, that is, the amount the submitting organization will pay back (in dollars) if it fails to meet the external goal.
SUBMIT_METHOD	Submission method options: claims, survey, web interface.
INTERVENTION_DOMAIN	Value from lookup table TBL_INTERVENTION_DOMAIN indicating the type of primary intervention data.
SCOPE_OF_PRACTICE	Value from lookup table TBL_SCOPE_OF_PRACTICE indicating the lowest cost/training-level role that can perform primary intervention of this measure.
DIFFICULTY	Value from lookup table TBL_DIFFICULTY indicating the inherent difficulty of the measure.
NQF_ID	National Quality Forum ID (if endorsed).
URL_MEASURE_SPEC	Hyperlink to measure specification.

Table D.3   TBL_SCOPE_OF_PRACTICE

Name	Description
Role_ID	Table key
Role_Abbr	Short-form professional designation or job title
Role_Name	Long-form professional designation or job title
Role_Desc	List of things this role can do
Role_Comment	General comments about this role—for future use

Table D.4   TBL_INTERVENTION_DOMAIN

Name	Description
Intervention_ID	Table key.
Intervention	Intervention domain indicates the type of data being measured (e.g., labs, medications, referrals, etc.). Each domain has one row.

Table D.5   TBL_DIFFICULTY

Name	Description
DIFFICULTY_ID	Table key
DIFFICULTY	Category of the inherent difficulty of a measure based on objectives
DIFF_DESC	Description of the measures that would fall in the category
DIFF_EXAMP	Examples of measures within this category

Table D.6   MSSP ACO 2019 Measures by Group

		Submission Method
Patient/Caregiver Experience		
ACO-01	Getting Timely Care, Appointments, and Information	CAHPS Survey
ACO-02	How Well Your Providers Communicate	CAHPS Survey
ACO-03	Patient's Rating of Provider	CAHPS Survey
ACO-04	Access to Specialists	CAHPS Survey
ACO-05	Health Promotion and Education	CAHPS Survey
ACO-06	Shared Decision-Making	CAHPS Survey
ACO-07	Health Status/Functional Status	CAHPS Survey
ACO-34	Stewardship of Patient Resources	CAHPS Survey
ACO-45	Courteous and Helpful Office Staff	CAHPS Survey
ACO-46	Care Coordination	CAHPS Survey
Care Coordination/Patient Safety		
ACO-08	Risk Standardized, All Condition Readmissions	Claims
ACO-13	Falls: Screening for Future Fall Risk	Web Interface
ACO-38	Unplanned Admissions for Patients with Multiple Chronic Conditions	Claims
ACO-43	Ambulatory Sensitive Condition Acute Composite (AHRQ Prevention Quality Indicator [PQI] #91)	Claims
Preventive Health		
ACO-14	Influenza Immunization	Web Interface
ACO-17	Tobacco Use Assessment and Cessation Intervention	Web Interface
ACO-18	Depression Screening and Follow-up	Web Interface
ACO-19	Colorectal Cancer Screening	Web Interface
ACO-20	Breast Cancer Screening (Mammography)	Web Interface
ACO-42	Statin Therapy for Prevention and Treatment of Cardiovascular Disease	Web Interface

(Continued)

Table D.6 (Continued) ACO 2019 Measures by Group

At-Risk		
ACO-27	Diabetes Mellitus: Hemoglobin A1c Poor Control	Web Interface
ACO-28	Controlling High Blood Pressure (Hypertension)	Web Interface
ACO-40	Depression: Remission at 12 Months	Web Interface
Informational		
ACO-35	Skilled Nursing Facility 30-Day All-Cause Readmission Measures (SNFRM)	Claims
ACO-36	All-Cause Unplanned Admissions for Patients with Diabetes	Claims
ACO-37	All-Cause Unplanned Admissions for Patients with Heart Failure	Claims
ACO-44	Use of Imaging Studies for Low Back Pain	Claims

Import Additional Measure Details From CMS

Additional measure details for the DIY Quality Measure Management system can be imported from the CMS Measure Inventory Tool (CMIT), which can be found online at https://cmit.cms.gov/. The expanded quality measure table includes additional columns for population age, conditions, subconditions, measure type, and care. *Measure details from CMIT.cms.gov are specific to CMS measures only and should be reviewed periodically for updates.*

In the event that a required measure specification has not been included from the central sponsor such as CMS, the National Quality Forum (NQF) Quality Positioning System (QPS) tool provides another option for aggregated measure details and can be online (www.qualityforum.org/QPS/). The NQF is a nonprofit organization that brings together stakeholders to develop, review, and endorse quality measures. Many value-based programs utilize NQF-endorsed measures, however, making the QPS tool an attractive option. However, use caution with these publicly available tools, as measure specifications may somewhat vary between QPS and the sponsor program website. Furthermore, the QPS tool is limited to measures that have been endorsed by the NQF and may not include all of the measures in a particular quality program. *The measure specification document from each program should be maintained as the source of truth.*

Appendix E. Ambulatory Care Health Screening Order Protocol

Policy/Procedure Title

Ambulatory Care—Ambulatory Care Screening Order Protocol

RELATED TO:	[ ] ADMINISTRATIVE [X] CLINICAL
[ ] Medical Center Policy (MCP) [ ] The Joint Commission (TJC) [X] Centers for Medicare and Medicaid Services (CMS) [X] Internal Patient Care Standards [X] Board of Registered Nursing [X] Pharmacy Services [X] Infection Control [ ] Other —	**Effective Date: 11/20/2012** **Latest Revision Date: 03/14/2018** **Latest Review Date: 3/14/2018**
	Unit/Department of Origin: Ambulatory Care
	Approvals: **Medical Group Quality** **Committee—04/17/2018**

Ambulatory Care Screening Order Protocol (ACSOP)

I. Policy:

All patients receiving ambulatory care will be eligible for receiving appropriate health screening and monitoring tests. Standards for appropriate health screening and monitoring tests have been defined by the U.S. Preventive Services Task Force (USPSTF) and interpreted by the state of California Integrated Healthcare Association Systems (IHA) Value-Based Pay for Performance (VBP4P), Physician Quality Reporting System (PQRS), the Public

Hospital Redesign and Incentives in Medi-Cal (PRIME), the Quality Incentive Program (QIP), the Medicare Shared Savings Programs (MSSP), and Medicare Advantage Stars Programs. The programs mentioned here have devised quality measures that aim to abide by the USPSTF recommendations on screening and monitoring.

The priorities of the health screening and monitoring are to enhance the population quality of care while honoring personalized, appropriate routine screening. Health screening and monitoring of tests are configured within the electronic health record to reflect national standards related to the types of tests, frequency of testing, and exclusions from testing. Frequently, the health maintenance topic in the electronic health record has also been configured to support personalized health, enabling clinicians to define patients who would not benefit from screening or require higher frequency of monitoring.

Additional chronic disease monitoring tests were added to support the care of individuals living with chronic kidney disease and hypothyroidism on replacement therapy. Additional metabolic tests are added to the protocol to support the ongoing care of the patient per usual clinical care guidelines to prevent missed monitoring opportunities.

This Ambulatory Screening Order Protocol (ASOP) has been developed to improve the efficiency and effectiveness of routine care delivery reflecting national standards. Patients eligible for health screening and monitoring tests will have appropriate tests ordered according to national standards. The Health Maintenance Screening Protocol Order (HMSOP) is activated by completion of a signed order in the electronic medical record by a licensed physician or advanced practice provider (APP), which includes a pharmacist, advanced practice nurse practitioner (NP), and physician assistant (PA). The patient-specific HMSOP will expire in five years. The active order enables tests to be ordered under protocol by registered nurses (RNs). This procedure provides the authorized criteria for ordering the health screening and monitoring tests per the physician-signed HMSOP.

In addition to outreach orders, the clinical team, including RNs, licensed vocational nurses (LVNs), medical assistants (MAs), and health assistants (HAs), may contact patients via various communication methods, as outlined next, regarding health screening and monitoring tests that are due.

Forms of communication that are used to remind and engage patients may include but are not limited to:

■ Electronic health record (EHR) patient portal messages
■ Automated phone calls

- Staff-generated phone calls
- Letters
- Educational videos

II. Scope:

All patients receiving ambulatory care at *[insert health system name]* are eligible for the ASOP.

III. Definitions:

Alert—A type of decision support within the electronic medical record that automatically monitors a patient's records and highlights specific areas of risk or opportunity based on best practice. "Best practice" is a method or technique that has consistently shown results superior to those achieved by other means and is used as a benchmark.

EHR—A computerized medical record that is a local stand-alone health information system that allows storage, retrieval, and modification of patient care records.

Protocol Topic—A topic within the EHR that tracks screening and monitoring tests at a patient level. It indicates the status of specific protocol activities (e.g., completed, due soon, and overdue). In addition, the topic is modifiable to include edits to the frequency (timing) as well as modifications to the indication (such as exclusions based on past surgical or medical history).

MSSP—A national quality program that provides physician practices with incentives and payments based on performance.

Persistent Medications—The percentage of patients 18 years of age and older who received at least 180 treatment days of ambulatory medication therapy for a select therapeutic agent during the measurement year and at least one therapeutic monitoring event for the therapeutic agent in the measurement year.

Healthcare Effectiveness Data and Information Set (HEDIS)—Tool used by America's health plans to measure performance on important dimensions of care and service.

PQRS—A national quality program that provides physician practices with financial incentives based on performance.

PRIME—A California statewide quality program that is part of the CMS Medicaid Waiver program aiming to enhance value-based care.

QIP—A California statewide quality program that is part of CMS Medicaid aiming to enhance value-based care.

USPSTF—The national task force that defines standards related to health screening.

VBP4P—A California statewide quality program that rewards hospitals, physician practices, and other providers with both financial and nonfinancial incentives to improve the quality and efficiency of healthcare.

IV. Procedure:

A. **The (ASOP)** must first be activated by the completion of a signed order in the EHR by a licensed physician or APP, which includes pharmacist, advanced practice NP, or PA. This signed order is valid for five years.

B. **Electronic Patient Call Lists:** EHR decision support will generate call lists on a regular basis and provide them to the clinic managers as secure reports. The patient call list will include patients eligible for health screening and monitoring tests. The clinical team (e.g., RN, LVN, MA, and HA) can call patients based on the list to communicate the tests that are due.

C. **Registry-Based Patient Lists:** may also be generated within the EHR to identify those patients who are eligible for health screening and monitoring test(s), including provider- and practice-level information.

D. **Decision Support Tools:** may also be employed within the EHR to help alert the clinical team and patients when health maintenance screening tests are due. The decision support tools include health protocol alerts (visible to patients and providers) and dynamic order sets that include only protocol topics due at the time of order.

E. **Performance Quality Reporting:** Many of the health screening and monitoring tests are also reported within the EHR for continuous performance monitoring dashboards. This practice enables providers to drill into the records of individual patients who are overdue for a screening to efficiently resolve the identified care gap.

F. **Actions by Clinical Team for Ordering Health Screening and Monitoring Tests:** When a patient is identified as having a health screening test(s) due soon or overdue, the **RN** will order the appropriate test(s), including 1) patient-specific individual orders, 2) patient-specific dynamic order sets (see item D), and 3) at a population level (i.e., multiple patients simultaneously) using bulk orders.

The screening and monitoring tests listed next are based on HEDIS specifications and other quality programs, including PRIME, QIP,

VBP4P, and the MSSP ACO. The measure-related care gaps are embedded within the bulk order queries, which are updated as needed. Refer to the following table.

Health screening and monitoring tests include the following:

Topic	Test Ordered	Frequency
Category: Wellness		
- Breast Screening	Screening Bilateral Mammogram	Annual
- Colon Screening	Fecal Immunochemical Test (FIT)	Annual
- Osteoporosis Screening	Routine Screening DEXA Scan	Once
- Tobacco Screening and Cessation Counseling	Referral to No BUTTS; EMMI Tobacco Video	Annual
- Gonorrhea and Chlamydia Screening (add age)	Urine GC/Chlamydia PCR Test linked to pregnancy order as appropriate	Annual and ad hoc with any pregnancy test
- Depression Screening	PHQ2 Test Screening	Annual
- Hepatitis C Screening	Anti-HCV and reflexive HCV PCR as appropriate for abnormal screen	Once for individuals born between 1945 and 1965
- Influenza Immunization	Flu Vaccine	Annual
- Pneumonia Immunization	Prevnar and Pneumovax	A series at 0 and 6 months
- Human Papillomavirus Immunization	Human Papillomavirus 9-Valent Administration	A three-dose series at 0, 2, and 6 months ages 9 through 26
- Tetanus Diphtheria Pertussis Immunization	TDap/TD	11 years and older once and ad hoc, TD every 10 years
- Elevated BMI	Above 25 without follow-up plan. Use of high BMI dynamic order set that includes consult to nutrition.	Every 6 months and ad hoc
Diabetic Patients		
- Hb A1C	Hemoglobin A1C (A1C)	Twice per year
- Microalbumin	Urine Microalbumin/Creatinine Ratio Panel	Annual
- Eye screening	Ophthalmology Referral for Diabetic Retina Screening	Annual
- Monofilament foot test	Diabetic Foot Exam (monofilament)	Annual

(Continued)

(Continued)

Topic	Test Ordered	Frequency
- Blood Pressure Screening and Control	N/A	Annual
- Lipid Screening	Lipid Panel	Annual
- Comprehensive Metabolic Screen	Comprehensive Metabolic Panel (CMP)	Twice per year
- Diabetic Education/ Referrals	Diabetic Education Pharm D Clinic Endocrinology	Annual
Cardiovascular Care		
- Assess Statin Use in Cardiovascular Disease (CVD)	N/A	Annual
- Cholesterol Screening	Lipid Panel	Annual
- Assess Aspirin, Antiplatelet, and Anticoagulant Use in Ischemic Vascular Disease (IVD)	N/A	Every 6 Months
Hypertension		
- Blood Pressure Measurement and Control	Blood Pressure Monitoring with Recorded BP in a Face-to-Face Visit	Annual
- Comprehensive Metabolic Screen	CMP	Annual
Laboratory Monitoring for Safety of Persistent Medications		
- Digoxin	Digoxin level, CMP	Annual
- Angiotensin-Converting Enzyme Inhibitor and Angiotensin II Inhibitor	CMP	Annual
- Loop, Potassium-Sparing, and Thiazide Diuretics	CMP	Annual
- Statin Therapy	CMP, Fasting Lipid	Once per year
- Thyroid Replacement Therapy	Thyroid-Stimulating Hormone (TSH)	Once per year
Screening for Contraindication of Anticoagulants		
- Review Allergies, Including Aspirin	N/A	Arrived ambulatory encounters
- Document Adverse Drug Reaction, Including Hemorrhage to Anticoagulants, in "Allergy" Section	N/A	Arrived ambulatory encounters

Topic	Test Ordered	Frequency
Chronic Kidney Disease		
- Stage 3 and Higher Chronic Kidney Disease	U/A, Complete Blood Count (CBC) with Differential, CMP	Twice per year and ad hoc
Depression Follow-up		
- Reassess Depression Using the PHQ-9	PHQ-9 Test Follow-up	Every 6 months

G. **Actions by the Clinical Team for Messaging Patients about Health Screening and Monitoring Tests:** When a patient is identified as having a health screening test(s) due, the clinical team, including the RN, LVN, MA, HA, pharmacist, care coordinator, or social worker (SW), may provide communication about appropriate health screening and monitoring test(s) that are due. Bulk messages for the screening and monitoring tests listed next are based on HEDIS specifications and other quality programs. The measures are embedded within the bulk order queries, which are updated as needed. Refer to the following table.

Messaging for health screening and monitoring tests include the following:

Category of Screening and Monitoring Tests	Preferred Types of Communication	Frequency Running Report and Communicating with Patients
Wellness Active Patients		
- SOGI Review/Completion Incomplete	Automated phone call Bulk message (patient portal)	Every 6 months and ad hoc
- Breast Screening	Automated phone call Bulk message (patient portal)	Annual and ad hoc
- Colon Screening	Automated phone call Bulk message (patient portal)	Annual and ad hoc
- Cervical Cancer Screening	Automated phone call Bulk message (patient portal)	Annual and ad hoc
- Osteoporosis Screening	Automated phone call Bulk message (patient portal)	Annual and ad hoc
- Tobacco Screening and Cessation Counseling	Automated phone call Bulk message (patient portal)	Annual and ad hoc
- Gonorrhea and Chlamydia Screening	Automated phone call Bulk message (patient portal)	Annual and ad hoc

(Continued)

(Continued)

Category of Screening and Monitoring Tests	Preferred Types of Communication	Frequency Running Report and Communicating with Patients
- Depression Screening	Automated phone call (patient portal) survey	Annual and ad hoc
- Hepatitis C Screening	Automated phone call Bulk message (patient portal)	Annual and ad hoc
- Behavioral Health Screening Incomplete	Automated phone call Bulk message (patient portal)	Annual and ad hoc for screening
- Advance Directive Incomplete Patients over 65	Automated phone call Bulk message (patient portal)	Annual and ad hoc
- Influenza Immunization	Automated phone call Bulk message (patient portal)	Annual and ad hoc
- Pneumonia Immunization	Automated phone call Bulk message (patient portal)	Annual and ad hoc
- Human Papillomavirus Immunization	Automated phone call Bulk message (patient portal)	Annual and ad hoc
- Tetanus Diphtheria Pertussis Immunization	Automated phone call Bulk message (patient portal)	Annual and ad hoc
Diabetic Patients		
- A1c	Automated phone call Bulk message (patient portal)	Twice per year and ad hoc
- Microalbumin	Automated phone call Bulk message (patient portal)	Annual and ad hoc
- Eye screening	Automated phone call Bulk message (patient portal)	Annual and ad hoc
- Monofilament foot test	Automated phone call Bulk message (patient portal)	Annual and ad hoc
- Blood Pressure Screening and Control	Automated phone call Bulk message (patient portal)	Annual and ad hoc
- Lipid Screening	Automated phone call Bulk message (patient portal)	Annual and ad hoc
- CMP	Automated phone call Bulk message (patient portal)	Twice per year and ad hoc
Cardiovascular Care		
- Cholesterol Screening	Automated phone call Bulk message (patient portal)	Annual and ad hoc
Hypertension		
- Blood Pressure Measurement and Control	Automated phone call Bulk message (patient portal)	Annual and ad hoc

Category of Screening and Monitoring Tests	Preferred Types of Communication	Frequency Running Report and Communicating with Patients
- Pre-Hypertension Without Counseling and/or Follow-Up	Automated phone call Bulk message (patient portal)	Annual and ad hoc
Laboratory Monitoring for Safety of Persistent Medications		
- Digoxin	Automated phone call Bulk message (patient portal)	Annual and ad hoc
- Angiotensin-Converting Enzyme Inhibitor and Angiotensin II inhibitor	Automated phone call Bulk message (patient portal)	Annual and ad hoc
- Loop, Potassium-Sparing, and Thiazide Diuretics	Automated phone call Bulk message (patient portal)	Annual and ad hoc
- Statin Therapy	Automated phone call Bulk Message (patient portal)	Annual, and ad hoc
- Thyroid Replacement Therapy	Automated phone call Bulk message (patient portal)	Annual and ad hoc
Screening for Contraindication of Anticoagulants		
- Review allergies (to aspirin)	N/A	Arrived ambulatory encounters
- Review adverse medication history including hemorrhage on anticoagulants	N/A	Arrived ambulatory encounters
Screening for Contra-indication of Anticoagulants		
- Stage 3 and Higher Chronic Kidney Disease	Automated phone call Bulk message (patient portal)	Twice per year and ad hoc

H. Results Management of Health Screening and Monitoring Tests: All results will be routed electronically through the EHR to the patient's primary care provider (PCP) who will be responsible for reviewing the result(s) and providing appropriate counseling and/or treatment to the patient. If the patient's PCP is outside of *[insert health system name]*, then they will be routed to the patient's ambulatory specialty provider under whom the RN reports. RNs will follow their scope of practice to educate the patient and escalate information to the PCP as noted in the Ambulatory Care Scope of Practice Reference Guide v01/04/16.

An abnormal screening outreach program will be conducted for fecal occult blood testing (FIT). Patients with a new abnormal screening test will be sent a follow-up bulk communication that requests that the patient either follow up with their primary care clinician or complete a colonoscopy.

V. Requirements for Use of Ambulatory Screening Order Protocol

A. Education, Training, and Experience:
1. Any RN hired in an ambulatory clinic or population health role who meets the education and competency requirements of this protocol is allowed to order health screening and monitoring tests.
2. The clinical team can message clients regarding tests that are due.
3. The clinical team will be trained by:
   a. Completing a 30-minute PowerPoint in-service of the ASOP.
   b. Verbalizing and demonstrating the competency elements of the ASOP.
   c. Initial and ongoing annual evaluations by direct observation from an RN who has completed the competency protocol requirement and deemed competent by a licensed provider (e.g. MD, NP).

B. Competency Elements of the ASOP:
1. Verbalizes key elements of the ASOP, including a provider-signed order in the EMR.
2. Demonstrates how to view best practice alerts in Epic.
3. Verbalizes specific tests that can be ordered under the ASOP.
4. Identifies which patient populations are appropriate to screen using the ASOP.
5. Demonstrates how to generate a screening report in the EHR and order tests from ASOP provider–signed orders.
6. Verbalizes method of communication to patient regarding the screening orders.
7. Demonstrates knowledge of the automated calling system for notification of patient regarding health screening and monitoring tests.
8. Demonstrates knowledge of EHR patient portal for notifying and reminding patients of health screening tests.
9. Demonstrates how to cancel erroneous bulk orders.

C. The Clinical Team Must Demonstrate Competency through:

1. Direct observation utilizing the ASOP competency tool. The observation may be conducted by a clinic nurse manager or RN who has completed the competency protocol requirement and deemed competent by a licensed provider (e.g., MD, NP).
2. The competency assessment will be maintained in the departmental human resource files.

D. Ongoing Evaluation:

Ongoing evaluation will be performed through the annual performance appraisal process, as well as through monitoring of the patient call list and health screening and monitoring tests ordered.

VI. Cancelling Erroneous Bulk Orders

A. If a user following the protocol knowingly places bulk orders or communication in error at the time of the order involving fewer than 100 patients, the user should notify the authorizing physician and cancel the bulk order.

B. If a user following the protocol places bulk orders or communication and identifies an error more than 24 hours following the bulk order or communication OR if the bulk activity involves more than 100 patients, the **Population Health Team** through the **UCSD help desk** should be notified for analysis, communication plan, and management. The goal of notifying the population health team is to identify methods to minimize patient impact, as well as to prevent future errors.

References

HEDIS: www.cms.gov/Medicare/Quality-Initiatives-Patient-Assessment-Instruments/QualityInitiativesGenInfo/Downloads/2017_QRS-Measure_Technical_Specifications.pdf

State of California Integrated Healthcare Association (IHA) Value Based Pay for Performance (VBP4P) Manual—Measurement Year MY 2016 P4P Manual (updated on December 1, 2016)

www.iha.org/sites/default/files/resources/my_2016_value_based_p4p_manual_1.pdf

USPTF Recommendations: www.uspreventiveservicestaskforce.org/BrowseRec/Search

PRIME Specifications: www.dhcs.ca.gov/provgovpart/Pages/PRIME.aspx

Appendix F. Population Health Project Request

Requestor Name:	E-mail Address: Phone:	Request Date:
Name of Request: (Brief Title)		Metric/s Impacted:
CLINICAL LEAD SPONSOR: (Name/Title, Group or Committee)		
Specific Request Brief Description:		
SITUATION, BACKGROUND, ASSESSMENT, RECOMMENDATION (SBAR)		
Situation:	*Background:*	
Assessment:	*Recommendation: P.*	
Date Required/Reason:		
SIGNATURES (Required)		
Requestor: _____ Title: _____ Date: _____ _____		
Approval by Sponsoring Committee Representative		
Name: _____ _____ Title: _____ Date: _____ _____		

Population Health Intervention Checklists (One for Each Intervention)

Justification Checklist

Quality Measure(s):	
Rationale	
Baseline Data:	
Measure Target:	

Intervention Checklist

1	**The Who** (Denominator) Define the selection criteria for the cohort of patients to be included in this intervention	Registry Inclusion Inpatient Ambulatory Primary Care Age Start Age End Gender Social Determinants Diagnoses Lab Values Medication Exclusions	
2	**The What** (Numerator) What value in the patient chart will indicate that the measure is complete?	Lab Order Procedure Order Medication Management Outreach Questionnaire Assessment Immunization Examination Chart Documentation Other	
3	**The When** (Timing) If the intervention is to be repeated, what is the schedule or trigger for repeating?		

| 4 | **How** (EHR tools)
Which EHR tools will be
required to move the
measure? | Intervention scheduler
Intervention order
Dynamic order set
Bulk order
Bulk message
Risk score
Report alert
Work queue Other | |
| 5 | **By Whom:**
Will this create new work?
  For whom?
Does it automate an
  existing task? | MD
PharmD
Registered Nurse
Licensed Vocational Nurse
Front Office
Scheduler
Care Manager
Patient
Automation
Other | |

Project Management Checklist

Primary stakeholders:	
Established level of consensus?	
Impact on patient experience?	
Impact on provider/caregiver experience?	
Financial cost?	
Financial benefit?	

Design Checklist for the Intervention Scheduler

This worksheet helps collect the information required to configure the intervention scheduler. Examples of the type of information to enter are included in brackets.

Name of Intervention:	[*Depression Screening*]
How name should appear to clinician:	[*PHQ2 depression screen (18 yr or older)*]
Name to appear to patient:	[*Depression screening (18 yr or older)*]
Inclusion Criteria: Registry Inclusion Inpatient Ambulatory Primary Care Age Start Age End Gender (M, F, X) Social Determinants Diagnoses Lab Values Medication	
Diagnosis Inclusion:	[no]
Exclusion Criteria:	[Patient is on Depression Registry]
	[Or Depression Diagnosis]
Hospice	[N/A]
Allergy	[N/A]
Medications:	[N/A]
Completion Criteria (what has to be done?):	[Complete PHQ2 questionnaire or flowsheet]
Completion Order:	[no]
Flowsheet:	[yes]
Questionnaire	[yes]
Education	[no]
Phone call	[no]
What is the timing? How frequently must it be completed?	[yearly]
Visit Workflow:	[MA/LVN rooming workflow- Intake questionnaire]

Name of Intervention:	[*Depression Screening*]
Patient-entered data:	[Patient portal questionnaire]
Overrides:	
HMM already done (override)	[Yes]
Do next time	[Yes]
Being done somewhere else	[No]

Appendix G. Registry Best Practices

Glossary of Registry Terms

Wellness registries and the active patient registry function as a patient index segmented by age. They hold key demographic, payor, and acuity index values. The wellness and subordinate registries are intended to drive clinical outreach and interventions, so only active patients are included based on encounter history. Patients must meet the following criteria in addition to the age criteria in order to belong to an active patient registry:

- Patient is not deceased
- Patient is not a test patient
- Patient does not have limited life expectancy
- Patient has had a person-to-person encounter at our facility in the last 1,095 days (3 years)

The *primary care registry* is used to track and deliver wellness interventions for quality performance measures that only apply to primary care. Inclusion in the patient panel registry is dependent on a primary care provider (PCP) associated with a department included in the primary care department value set.

Chronic care registries are used for patient engagement and outreach interventions for chronic care management of specific disease states. These may be used by primary care (diabetes) or by specialty (HIV clinic) or by both (cardiovascular). These registries typically have a mix of patient encounter history, process metrics, and data used to assess clinical outcomes.

Payor-based registries capture a cohort of patients who are subscribed to or eligible for payor-based benefits.

Metadata is used for internal documentation of registry build much as inline comments might be used for SQL code. The practice of documenting within the operational system ensures that documentation on inclusion rules and metrics is always available and current.

Registry update schedules determine the timeliness of the registry metrics. The common practice is to have individual records update in real time with a full refresh every two to four weeks. See guidance from registry support personnel to find the best schedule for your organization based on your requirements and system performance.

Diagnosis Value Sets

Value set ownership within an electronic health record (EHR) or registry system should be established through naming conventions and metadata. *There is no universal best method for building value sets because the sensitivity and specificity of a code set vary by disease prevalence and coding practices at the local EHR level.* As compared with SNOMED value sets, ICD often enables more discrete control over the inclusion/exclusion of specific terms. However, the organization must commit resources to maintain the groups with a periodic review. Diagnosis groups for ICD9-CM and ICD10-CM perform similarly.

It is *not* recommended to use SNOMED groups for diagnosis value sets because of the unpredictable impact of terminology updates to SNOMED mappings. If you choose to use SNOMED groups, ensure that registry administrators are included in planning and testing for the twice-yearly diagnosis terminology updates. Because terminologies and mappings evolve over time, registry inclusion groups should be revalidated yearly.

Registry Testing Environment

New inclusion rules and changes to existing rules must be validated in a nonproduction environment that has a production-size data set. Use a testing environment that is refreshed quarterly or yearly from production data. The inclusion rule test will typically not complete within a daily refresh cycle. You may need to work with technical advisors to evaluate the impact of inclusion rule changes on the database size and database journaling effect. This is to prevent the accidental creation of long-running registry jobs that include more records than expected.

Required Reports

Registries are data aggregation tools that have no analyst- or user-facing display on their own.

To facilitate testing and validation, each registry will have an analyst-facing "Administration" report displaying critical information, as shown here.

Default Columns	
Demographic Information	Patient medical record number
	Patient name
	Patient age
	Patient sex
Registry Inclusion Criteria	Create a column to show what data triggered inclusion in the registry (for example, problem list and encounter diagnoses)
Empanelment (Cohort Definition)	Current primary and/or specialty care provider
Key Registry Metrics	Add a couple of important registry metrics such as last lab value and date important to registry intervention
Encounter History	Last encounter date
	Last office visit date
	Last visit provider
	Last inpatient admission date
	Number of encounters
Patient Portal Status	Portal status

Appendix H. Resources

Centers for Medicare and Medicaid Services (CMS)

Report to Congress: Identification of Quality Measurement Priorities—
Strategic Plan, Initiatives, and Activities, March 2019
www.cms.gov/Medicare/Quality-Initiatives-Patient-Assessment-Instruments/
QualityMeasures/Downloads/CMS-RTC-Quality-Measurement-March-1–
2019_508.pdf
Meaningful Measures Alignment with 2018 Impact Assessment Key
Indicators (Crosswalk)
www.cms.gov/Medicare/Quality-Initiatives-Patient-Assessment-Instruments/
QualityInitiativesGenInfo/Downloads/Meaningful-Measures-Alignment-
with-2018-Impact-Assessment-Key-Indicators.pdf
Meaningful Measures Tools
www.cms.gov/Medicare/Quality-Initiatives-Patient-Assessment-Instruments/
QualityInitiativesGenInfo/MMF/Sharcable-Tools.html
Office of Minority Health Resources for Health Care Professionals and
Researchers
https://www.cms.gov/About-CMS/Agency-Information/OMH/resource-
center/hcps-and-researchers/index.html
The Data Tools accessible via this page include:
Mapping Medicare Disparities Tool
Sexual and Gender minority (SGM) Clearinghouse
Compendium of Resources for Standardized Demographic and Language
Data Collection

Outcomes

International Consortium for Health Outcomes Measurement, Inc.
www.ichom.org/resource-library/
Articles, Case Studies, Videos, Data Dictionary, Implementation Materials,
Medical Condition Flyers, Reference Guides, Newsletters, FAQ, Protocols,
Books

IHI Institute for Healthcare Improvement

www.ihi.org

For more than 25 years, the Institute for Healthcare Improvement (IHI) has used improvement science to advance and sustain better outcomes in health and healthcare across the world. IHI accelerates learning and the systematic improvement of care; develops solutions to previously intractable challenges; and mobilizes health systems, communities, regions, and nations to reduce harm and death.

Public Data Sets

Data.gov

Data.gov is the repository for federal, state, local and tribal government information that is available to the public. Health data is just one of a number of topic sections for open data managed and hosted by the U.S. General Services Administration.

CAHPS Data for Research

www.ahrq.gov/cahps/cahps-database/index.html

Researchers may gain authorized access to de-identified data files from the CAHPS Database to help answer important health services research questions related to patient experience of care as measured by CAHPS surveys.

SEER-CAHPS

https://healthcaredelivery.cancer.gov/seer-cahps/overview/

The data set is a resource for quality of cancer care research based on a linkage between the NCI's Surveillance, Epidemiology and End Results (SEER) cancer registry data and the Centers for Medicare & Medicaid Services' (CMS) Medicare Consumer Assessment of Healthcare Providers and Systems (CAHPS) patient surveys.

National Center for Health Statistics

www.cdc.gov/nchs/ahcd/about_ahcd.htm

National Hospital Ambulatory Medical Care Survey (NHAMCS)

National Ambulatory Medical Care Survey (NAMCS)

Electronic Clinical Quality Improvement (eCQI)

eCQI Resource Center

https://ecqi.healthit.gov/ecqms#quicktabs-tabs_ecqm3

Electronic clinical quality improvement (eCQO) is the use of health information technology, the functionality, and data in an EHR and/or other health information technology, along with clinical best practices, to support, leverage, and advance quality improvement initiatives.

HIT Enabled Clinical Quality Improvement (eCQI) Toolkit

https://mpqhf.com/corporate/wp-content/uploads/2016/05/1-DPHHS-HTS-eCQI-Toolkit-Verion-4.pdf)

Mountain-Pacific Quality Health: Health Technology Services and Montana DPHHS

Offers a toolkit that combines aspects of the Agile/Scrum delivery cycle (created for the IT industry) with the PDSA quality improvement methodology. The goal of this combined approach is to help produce valuable quality results in a quick and streamlined manner.

Learning Health

National Academies Press

https://nam.edu/programs/value-science-driven-health-care/learning-health-system-series/

Leadership Consortium for a Value & Science-Driven Health System has marshaled the insights of the nation's leading experts to explore in detail the prospects, and the necessity, for transformational change in the fundamental elements of health and healthcare. The assessments are reported in the 15 volumes of the Learning Health System Series, published by the National Academies Press.

The Agency for Healthcare Research and Quality (AHRQ)

www.ahrq.gov/learning-health-systems/

The Agency for Healthcare Research and Quality's (AHRQ) mission is to produce evidence to make healthcare safer, higher quality, more accessible, equitable, and affordable and to work within the U.S. Department of Health and Human Services and with other partners to make sure that the evidence is understood and used. AHRQ priorities are described.

Learning Health Community

www.learninghealth.org
The Learning Healthcare Project
www.learninghealthcareproject.org/
Clinical Lead for Data at NHS Digital, the organization that collects, analyses and distributes data for the English National Health System.

Information Usability, Visualization, and Presentation

Tableau.com
Tableau® is a leader in data visualization space and offers free trials, training, and support at www.tableau.com. Make sure to view the Tableau public gallery view for the new visualizations shared by the Tableau community. Dashboards may be deployed through secure servers, where the usability is fairly intuitive. However, dashboard developers must invest time and education to unlock the power and beauty of Tableau. Ben Fry and Stephen Few offer books, websites, and videos that explain the principles and practice of dashboard design.

General Topics

Healthcare Analytics Resource List
http://healthcareanalytics.info/healthcare-analytics-for-quality-and-performance-improvement-web-resources
Trevor Strome created this page with links to the many resources that are discussed in *Healthcare Analytics for Quality and Performance Improvement*.

Index